LOCAL AREA NETWORK ARCHITECTURES

INTERNATIONAL COMPUTER SCIENCE SERIES

Consulting editors   **A D McGettrick**   University of Strathclyde
J van Leeuwen   University of Utrecht

SELECTED TITLES IN THE SERIES:

LOCAL AREA NETWORK ARCHITECTURES

David Hutchison

University of Lancaster

ADDISON-WESLEY
PUBLISHING
COMPANY

Wokingham, England · Reading, Massachusetts · Menlo Park, California
New York · Don Mills, Ontario · Amsterdam · Bonn
Sydney · Singapore · Tokyo · Madrid · San Juan

Cover designed by Crayon Design of Henley-On-Thames and printed by The Riverside Printing Co. (Reading) Ltd.
Typeset by Quorum Technical Services Ltd, Cheltenham, UK.
Printed in Great Britain by Mackays of Chatham PLC, Chatham, Kent

First printed 1988. Reprinted 1989

British Library Cataloguing in Publication Data
Hutchison, David, *1949–*
   Local area network architectures. —
   (International computer science series).
   1. Computer systems. Local networks. Design
   I. Title   II. Series
   004.6′8

   ISBN 0–201–14216–3

Library of Congress Cataloging in Publication Data
Hutchison, David, M. Tech
   Local area network architectures/David Hutchison.
      p.   cm. — (International computer science series)
   Bibliography: p.
   Includes index.
   ISBN 0–201–14216–3
   1. Local area networks (Computer networks) 2. Computer network architectures.   I. Title.   II. Series.
TK5105.5.H88 1988
004.6′8—dc19   88-10421
                                                                        CIP

To Ruth, Claire, Paul and Emma

Preface

Local Area Networks (LANs) have figured prominently in research and development for the past ten years or so and commercial exploitation has been increasingly active in the 1980s. Connected with both of these is substantial national and international work on standards for LANs. Although they were originally investigated simply as a means of interconnecting computers in a loosely coupled way, there has recently been a great deal of interest in more tightly coupled systems and in network operating systems to be used on LANs. Furthermore, many potential applications of local networks are envisaged with varied degrees of coupling between the system components, including office automation systems, flexible manufacturing systems in factories, and management information systems in for example hospitals and industry in general.

In contrast to LANs, there is another well-established class of networks, wide area networks (WANs), interconnected using public telephone or data communications networks which span countries and even continents. For WANs, which have been in use for some 20 years, there is a significant amount of published material and a number of well-developed and emerging standards. However, very many aspects of WANs and LANs differ, including their communications technologies, their topologies, protocol requirements and applications. Until recently LANs have been included in a small way in texts on communications and networks, but now the subject of local networks needs to be treated in its own right.

This book aims to give such a treatment and to appeal to a variety of readers by covering the subject at an architectural level. The design of local networks is described in both hardware and software terms but too much detail is avoided. Furthermore, the description is based on the layering approach being adopted by the various standards bodies. The three main types of standard LAN architectures are covered in the core of the book, namely Ethernet, token ring/bus and Cambridge Ring. These represent the bulk of research and development work which has been carried out, as well as some of the most important commercial systems being implemented.

Other topics covered include comparisons of LAN architectures, higher level software protocols, internetworking, LAN applications, proprietary LANs, standards activities in the USA, Europe and the UK, and future developments in LAN technology. The text should be suitable for university and college students doing courses in communications and networking, for hardware and software engineers working in communications-related areas, and for those working in industry who need to learn about technical aspects of local area networks.

This book attempts to be reasonably self-contained, and does not assume previous knowledge of communications and networking. However, it is impossible to satisfy the demands of every reader. Therefore the references, bibliography and appendix material are chosen so as to point the interested reader towards the most suitable further reading and background material available.

The structure of this book reflects the architectural model of local area networks shown in the diagram below.

Chapter 1 forms an introduction to the history and characteristics of local area networks, and sets the scene for the remainder of the book.

Chapter 2 discusses the important open systems interconnection (OSI) reference model developed by the International Standards Organisation (ISO) and outlines the various other standards bodies active in this field, and how they relate to each other. It also describes work currently being undertaken at government level to promote the use of standards and discusses the problems of end users who have to implement systems and develop strategies in the midst of the sometimes conflicting efforts of the standards bodies and the computer manufacturers. The local network architectural model developed by the standards bodies is introduced and its logical link control layer described.

Chapter 3 describes and discusses the classifications of LANs in a number of different ways and introduces the three main architectures which form the core of the book.

Network management	(Distributed computing system) application		
	Higher protocol layers		
	Internetworking		
	Logical link control		
	CSMA/CD (Ethernet)	Token passing (ring, bus)	Slotted ring (Cambridge Ring)

Chapter 4 deals with the architecture often referred to as Ethernet after its origins, namely the CSMA/CD scheme.

Chapter 5 deals with the second type, namely the token passing systems, including the token ring scheme which is the basis of a LAN system offered by the IBM corporation.

Chapter 6 deals with the third type, namely the slotted ring or, as its main example is often called, the Cambridge Ring, again in reference to its historical origins.

Chapter 7 goes on to describe how local networks can exchange information with other networks by means of gateways and bridges, and discusses the internetworking of local networks in terms of the network and transport layers of the OSI reference model.

Chapter 8 looks at the use of higher level protocols – file transfer, virtual terminals, and job transfer in particular – over local networks, and discusses how the OSI session, presentation and application layers support these protocols.

Chapter 9 is devoted to the subject of network management, an increasingly important area as local networks become larger in scope and interconnected to wide area networks to form complex internetworks.

Chapter 10 looks at the subject of distributed computing systems applications in which the local area network is the communications subsystem. Remote procedure call (RPC) protocols are discussed as a building block of such distributed computing systems.

There follows a set of Exercises for all ten chapters, an appendix containing details of the various standards organizations worldwide, a bibliography for further reading and a glossary.

Several friends and colleagues have assisted, materially and spiritually, in the completion of this book: I owe them much. My brother Bill, originally to be coauthor, shaped the early part of the book, including the work on standardization. I acknowledge also the specific help of my colleagues Doug Shepherd, David Coffield and Jon Walpole with the material on the Cambridge Ring and internetworking, network management, and distributed transactions. Finally, my wife Ruth has been, as ever, a great strength, and Ian Campbell always a source of encouragement.

David Hutchison

Lancaster, December 1987

Acknowledgement

The author gratefully acknowledges the permission of Springer-Verlag to adapt material from Chapters 3 and 12 of *Local Area Networks: an Advanced Course* (D. Hutchison, J. Mariani and D. Shepherd, eds.), Lecture Notes in Computer Science, number 184 (1985).

Contents

Chapter 1
Local area networks: an introduction

This chapter introduces the topic of local area networks (LANs) and their architecture. By the end of this chapter the reader should have a firm understanding of what a local area network is, how it differs from a wide area network, and what constitutes the 'architecture' of a network.

1.1 Overview

The subject of local area networks has generated an astonishing amount of interest during the past several years. Articles have been published, seminars have been given, products have been released and standards have been produced. Yet it cannot be said that everyone even knows what a local area network (LAN) is – many of the articles published still attempt to educate the general readership in the basic area of definitions.

Progress is not as fast as was predicted at the time when the first commercial products arrived on the scene, around 1979. To date only a small number of LANs have been installed, compared with the enormous number of computer systems of all types which have been implemented during this period. Thus the market is still relatively uneducated. Some manufacturers may claim that in fact a large number of LANs have been installed, but this is merely symptomatic of the lack of agreement on definition. In this book we take a wide-ranging look at LANs and in this chapter we describe the characteristics of the LAN in a way which may exclude some of the products available today. Later, we classify LANs into various types to show how some order can be brought to the subject.

Why has there been such an interest in LANs? There is no simple answer. If we may speculate, however, this may be the result of a number of converging factors.

Firstly, although voice (telephone) technology is well established, the techniques used to transmit and switch the voice information are not widely understood. This is the province of the telephone engineer. The technology has always been controlled by someone other than the user, namely the telephone companies or the national PTT (post, telegraph and telephone) authority. LANs bring the technology inhouse, under the user's control.

Secondly, computing has now become available to the end user, to the non-technical department. The data processing department need no longer control the processing on the user's desk, in this age of the personal computer. Allied to the interest in office automation, the LAN highlights the end user's interest in computing and the transfer of information in electronic form.

Thirdly, LANs have become available at a time when data processing is becoming a commodity. There is no longer freshness in the subject, nor challenge in commercial computing: standard packages can do many jobs efficiently, despite the continuing need for tailored systems. Communications is the new area of interest, and local area networks have captured a great deal of that interest.

The subject is still very new, however, and so far the commercial exploitation of this new technology has lagged behind the amount of attention received.

The communication of information is a vital part of modern life. Information is increasingly being captured in electronic form and needs to be communicated to and from computers of different types.

Until fairly recently interest has been directed largely towards communication over long distances. Large volumes of information can be transmitted in short periods of time, a facility which has enabled business users to develop new applications areas and to change the ways in which business is conducted. More recently, studies have shown that the majority of information is exchanged within organizations and in particular within offices. There has, therefore, been a move towards the development of business systems aimed at increasing office efficiency through local area communications.

1.2   Historical perspective

What used to be called, a decade or so ago, simply 'networks' are now called wide area networks (WANs). We will now outline briefly how these networks evolved.

In the second half of the nineteenth century the telegraph and the telephone came into general use in the USA and UK, and the potential of each technology to bridge large distances quickly was realized. Widespread commercial use was limited, however, by a number of factors. The introduction of telegraph and telephone systems in the 1920s and 1930s accelerated the spread of these communications tools. In the case of telegraph, the public telex network was the result of a low-speed but reliable hard copy mechanism. In the case of the telephone, the public-switched telephone network (PSTN) was the result. The networks in question, first private then monopolized by the governments of various countries and given over to postal, telegraph and telephone authorities, consisted of a series of exchanges and trunk lines to permit flexible switching among a large number of points, a high rate of success when attempting to connect with a distant subscriber, and reasonable cost. Progress slowed down once the techniques used to set up and control such networks had been developed.

It was the development of the digital computer in the 1950s which paved the way for further advances. These have led to:

(1)   computer-controlled telephone exchanges including inhouse private automatic branch exchanges (PABXs), with software switching matrices. These offer much faster call set-up times than do the conventional electromechanical switching systems, and also improved reliability and flexibility.

(2)   the automation of telex using message switches which are computers programmed to dial and re-try automatically, log the progress of messages sent and received, and 'store-and-forward' messages till a distant subscriber can be contacted.

In both of these cases we see a number of techniques which are of relevance in the field of LANs, as well as the automation of a number of functions previously carried out manually.

In the 1960s the cost of computing began to fall, and technology enhancements led us away from the enormous room-sized computers with dedicated staff who programmed them for specific tasks, to general purpose business machines with the capability to process a number of tasks at once. At the same time, teletypes were used to interact with machines as online communication began to replace older forms of input. Applications were developed where jobs were submitted remotely from terminals, using punched cards, and the results received in printed form. These remote batch terminals, or remote job entry (RJE) stations, were among the first devices for which communications line protocols were written. Device emulation, best known in the IBM 2770 and 2780 (later 3780) protocols, was a practical application of a general set of rules for ensuring integrity of the data communicated between a specific machine and a central computer.

In passing, it should be noted that standards as such were not developed in the data processing communications sector. Looking back at telephone and telex systems, because an international service was developed between monopolized authorities, standards emerged quite naturally, particularly for voice. Of course, the technologies were relatively simple and we have omitted some of the details, but the essential point remains that because computers were developed in a commercial environment, and in specific countries, no such standards agreements came about. Fortunately, or possibly for some other suppliers unfortunately, IBM dominated the market to such an extent that many of its early developments have become *de facto* the standards in data communications. Many other suppliers have subsequently been forced to provide conforming systems in order to satisfy market demand. Nevertheless there is still a substantial number of suppliers and of different communication conventions, and it is only relatively recently that a concerted effort has been made to develop standards on an international basis. This is led by the International Standards Organisation (ISO) seven-layer reference model for Open Systems Interconnection (OSI) which we shall discuss later in more depth (Zimmermann, 1980), (ISO, 1983), (DesJardins, 1983).

Timesharing in the late 1960s and early 1970s, together with the development of the general-purpose minicomputer, opened the door for more advanced applications involving interactive communications from visual display units (VDUs) to one or more host computers. Methods of sharing lines and reducing the high costs of remote communications were developed. Increasing the efficiency of communications protocols also became the subject of further work.

Because no other networks existed specifically for data transfer, and since it would not have been economic to develop one, the public switched telephone network was used to carry data, and devices were developed to convert the digital signals used in computers into analogue form suitable for this network. Leased telephone lines (private circuits) were also used as the basis of 'private networks'. These lines were designed to carry speech, and the characteristics of the network had been designed such that the effective bandwidth, or transmission capacity, was quite low. This has proved a limitation in wide area networks. The analogue–digital conversion devices were called modems (*mo*dulator/*dem*odulator units). Fortunately, a set of 'standards' was developed in Europe in the form of recommendations by the CCITT (International Consultative Committee for Telephony and Telegraphy). These standards are known as the 'V' series (V for voice). In the USA there is a similar, although incompatible, set of standards referred to as the 'Bell' standards. These were developed by the Electrical Industries Association (EIA) in cooperation with Bell Laboratories (part of the vast AT&T company), whose modems have always been regarded as industry standards. The best known example of a CCITT V-standard is V.24, whose Bell or EIA equivalent is RS-232C.

Although modem technology is now mature, with very compact devices now available at low cost, the basic incompatibility of analogue telephone lines and digital computers remains. Much effort in WANs has been devoted to circumventing the problems caused by the low speeds, high costs and high error rates inherent in the analogue networks used.

In the early 1970s and continuing to the present day, computer networks have been undergoing development, in contrast to the terminal networks more commonly encountered. The Arpanet, used to link many academic and research establishments throughout North America and elsewhere in the world, was at the forefront of development. New techniques were established in routing, messaging, and other distributed computing areas. At the same time, packet switching was introduced, probably led by work at the National Physical Laboratory (NPL) in the UK. This new form of communication was based on the principle of splitting up data into small units called packets which could essentially be routed and carried separately through a network to be reassembled at the far end, resulting in a more efficient utilization of network capacity. This was also of importance in the (later) development of LANs. Subsequently, public data networks (PDNs), many based on packet techniques, have been established as alternatives to the old analogue systems still in use. Germany, Scandinavia and the UK are among the leaders in the provision of PDNs. Lower error rates, but not in all cases lower costs, are characteristic of such networks. In addition, circuit-switched data networks have been established in Germany and the Nordic countries. Although the transmission technology is not digital in all of these networks the trend now is towards digital trunks and increasingly, digital local circuits.

Table 1.1 Wide area networks headings.

Major headings
Telex
Teletext
PSTN
PSDN (PDN) – packet switched – circuit switched
Telefax
X-Stream – Kilostream – Megastream – Satstream
ISDN

In the UK at the time of writing, trials have begun to link subscriber premises using integrated digital access (IDA) to digital exchanges and circuits. Much of the trunk network in the UK already uses digital technology, some based on optical fibres. The exchanges in question are based on the System X programme of providing digital switches to control all forms of information communication, in particular voice and data, using the same circuits. The aim of this work is to provide an integrated services digital network (ISDN) which at current rates of progress may be available in the UK in the late 1980s.

All of these developments have occurred within the last 20 years and most within the last five or six, indicating the accelerating pace of technological progress. Advanced WANs are now provided in the private sector as well as the public, although the essential difference is that public service networks are carriers with little or no end user applications designed into their specifications, whereas in the private sector there is more concern with end user applications than with intra-network functions.

Clearly, WANs cover now a very wide range and various classification schemes could be adopted to distinguish between the main types. In Table 1.1 we list a number of major headings under which public WANs can be accommodated.

Various organizations use these public facilities, sometimes by leasing lines, to implement network systems for their own applications: for example, banks may use a mixture of leased circuits and public switched services to implement electronic funds transfer (EFT) banking networks. Some organizations provide so-called value added network services (VANS) on top of the basic public facilities and sell these services to their own customers.

Despite the progress made, computer networks are still in development. In particular the protocols and services associated with the OSI reference model are under intensive study and in various stages of user trials. The next section will discuss the emergence of LANs against this background.

1.3 Emergence of local area networks

We may risk the displeasure of a number of organizations and equipment suppliers by our interpretation of the historical development of LANs. The difficulty of establishing when and where the first LANs emerged is linked to the difficulty of definition.

We believe that the first LANs were really inhouse terminal networks of which there have been many going back over a period of probably some 25 years. They were not known as LANs, needless to say. The first references to the term LAN or LACN (local area computer network) began to appear in academic research literature in the early 1970s (Fletcher, 1973; Pierce, 1972; Rosen and Steele, 1973; Scantlebury and Wilkinson, 1974), and interested readers may consult the bibliography at the end of this book. Work in the field of LANs began, as indicated in the previous section, in parallel with research into computer networks in general (Clark *et al.*, 1978). See in particular the early taxonomy of local networks by Thurber and Freeman (Thurber and Freeman, 1979), the revised version by the same authors (Freeman and Thurber, 1980), and the annotated bibliography prepared by John Shoch at the Xerox Palo Alto Research Center (PARC) (Shoch, 1979).

The first commercial product may well have been the Datapoint Corporation's ARC (Attached Resource Computer), in 1977, although it was described as a distributed data processing system. Only later, in line with the terminology of the day, was it described as a 'LAN', and not always by Datapoint. The Hasler AG SILK (System für Integrierte Lokale Kommunikation), which is a register insertion system (see Chapter 6 for more details), must have been a close contender, appearing as early as 1974 in an academic paper. Later, in about 1978, it was available as a commercial product.

Two particular systems must be mentioned as having had a catalytic effect on the LAN marketplace. These are the DIX Ethernet and the Cambridge Ring.

1.3.1 DIX Ethernet

This is probably the best-known LAN in the marketplace because of wide publicity at the time of its transition from a Xerox Research product into a commercially backed *de facto* standard. This system was based on the principles of the earlier ALOHA radio network and developed at the Palo Alto Research Center under Metcalfe and Boggs (Metcalfe and Boggs, 1976). In 1980, Digital, Intel and Xerox (DIX) joined forces to put their respective strengths behind a new specification of Ethernet which was licensed and distributed as widely as possible to encourage standardization. Their aim was not entirely altruistic, since in the absence of established standards early market penetration was likely to popularize, and by default standardize, their offering. This approach has met with some commercial success and Ethernet is the basis of one of the international standards now being developed by the ISO.

1.3.2 Cambridge Ring

This began life in the Computer Laboratory at Cambridge University, England in the mid 1970s as the subject of research into connecting locally distributed computers for research purposes (Wilkes, 1975). The system is based on the principle of the so-called 'slotted ring' (for more details see Chapter 6). The basic developments were carried out and reported by Wilkes and Wheeler (Wilkes and Wheeler, 1979). The system was refined over a number of years and has been carried over into commercial products in the UK, in particular the Logica Polynet (Logica, 1981). It has also recently been endorsed as one of the potential local network international standards being specified by the ISO.

1.4 Definitions

We have already had occasion to refer to difficulties of definition in the field of local area networks. We must, therefore, set out our understanding of the terms used in the title of this book.

Approaching this problem in logical order, we begin with a definition of a network. A network can be regarded as a series of geographically separate points and the links which serve to interconnect these points.

One of our concerns here is with computers and terminals and the mechanisms used to facilitate information transfer between them. A terminal network consists of a number of terminals which communicate with one or more computers. The computers in such a network generally assume a position of importance and as such tend to dictate not only the topology of the network but also the rules governing communications. A network is a communication subsystem. In terms of the OSI reference model, the subsystem consists of the lowermost layers 1–3 (McClelland, 1983; Conard, 1983; Ware, 1983), that is:

- *layer 1: (physical)* which governs the interface to the transmission medium and the rules for controlling the streams of information sent and received,

- *layer 2: (data link)* which specifies the exchange of information between two points and ensures the accuracy of the information transferred (often referred to as a line protocol),

- *layer 3: (network)* which controls the routing and switching of information across a network of a particular type.

In addition to these so-called lower network layers, the upper four layers of the model, referred to as the application layers, complete the description of a communications system. It is the middle layer (4), the transport layer (Knightson, 1983), which decouples the application from the physical aspects of the network used to transport the information concerned, and therefore ensures that the user need not be aware of the details of the network itself. A computer network is concerned with the interactions of intelligent devices, such that the programs which run in them communicate, rather than the human operators who ultimately control them. In such a network there may be a number of equally important nodes and there is, therefore, a potentially great variety of suitable topology and protocol options.

Terminal and computer networks overlap, and it is not easy precisely to define their boundaries. For example, a set of dumb VDUs and printers connected to a central mainframe computer via cluster controllers would be a terminal network, while a set of intelligent banking terminals which control a number of functions, including cashpoints and bank office tasks, and are connected to the bank's central computer could also be considered a terminal network. At the other end of the scale, a set of linked mainframe computers carrying out cooperative processes and communicating automatically would be classed as a computer network. Such networks are likely to become commonplace in the future as the demand for automation increases and as network technology is enhanced. A number of problems remain to be overcome.

- Standards will have to be established, in particular for communication between different suppliers' equipment.

- Techniques for specifying, verifying and testing network communications protocols need to be fully developed to aid the network design and implementation process.

- Reliability and security will have to be increased to the extent that users will be completely confident of the integrity of the information processed.

For the foreseeable future we will assume that computer networks will involve a mix of manual, semi-automatic and fully automatic information exchanges among a mix of terminals and computers of varying intelligence.

A local area network is assumed to be just such a network, but closely delimited in its geographical coverage. It is a special case of a communications subsystem, that is layers 1–3 of the OSI reference model can be used to describe it. Its topology, however, is simple in contrast to wide area networks: there is only one route from any source to any destination in a single local network. The topologies commonly used are the bus, ring and (to a limited extent) star as opposed to the wide area network mesh.

A definition of local area network, therefore, states that it is a network with a limited geographical coverage and a simple topology. A further characteristic of local networks is that they tend to be privately owned in contrast to wide area networks in which the communications subsystem is based on the national telephone or data network. The consequence of this is that the organization which owns the local network has complete control over the hardware and software which comprise its communications subsystem.

Local networks can best be explained in comparative terms, as Chapter 3 will indicate in more detail. For example, a classification based on distance may be used to describe the notional boundaries as follows:

0–10 m	computer peripherals
10 m–10 km	local area networks
10 km+	wide area networks

In other words, LANs occupy the middle ground between tightly coupled components of individual computer systems, and the traditional loosely coupled communications networks already widely in use. We have decided to exclude from our definition the extreme case of a terminal network which is a simple 'star' consisting of a number of point-to-point links with no element of switching. On the other hand we wish to include the so-called 'third generation' PABXs which have the capability to route and switch data.

Normally, a local area network is understood to operate within an office block or across a factory or university campus, or other institution. The essential point is that a local area network does not come under the jurisdiction of the PTT or other national communications carrier. It is, therefore, normally a privately owned network, including the media over which the information is transferred. Other distinguishing features of local area networks are discussed in the next section.

Architecture is perhaps the most difficult of our terms to define. In computer literature there is no clear consensus. It is a term which has emerged to cover the broad area of the design principles on which systems are based. Previous definitions have ranged from Tanenbaum's 'set of layers and protocols' (in terms of the ISO reference model) (Tanenbaum, 1981) to what we consider hitherto the closest definition, contained in the Digital Equipment handbook (DEC, 1980): 'a standard approach to network design that defines the relationships and interactions between network services and functions via common interfaces and protocols'. In this book we are largely concerned with the architecture of local area networks and, therefore, according to our definitions, with the first three layers of the OSI reference model and the sets of services and protocols corresponding to these layers. In Chapter 8, however, we go on to consider higher layer issues since this is relevant to the applications areas in which LANs are and are likely to be used.

1.5 Characteristics of local area networks

The characteristics of the ideal local area network can be summarized as follows:

- high speed
- low cost
- high reliability/integrity
- installation flexibility
- expandability
- ease of access
- application adaptability
- interface standardization.

With all these features the ideal local area network will also operate satisfactorily over the distances implied by the previous definition.

1.5.1 High speed

As indicated earlier, the PSTN is limited by its basic design and cannot at present offer speeds of more than 2400 bits/sec (single dial-up), while leased analogue circuits cannot offer more than 9600 bits/sec (wideband circuits offer more). This makes the transmission of large volumes of data difficult, while compression techniques have to be developed in order to transmit high resolution document scanner output and video signals. The opportunity is there in LAN design to provide suitable communications paths for all types of information, particularly if digital technology is utilized. Baseband transmission on Ethernet systems, for example, operates at a standard speed of 10 Mbits/sec, while broadband systems can have bandwidths of more than 300 MHz, allowing multiple video channels as well as data and voice. Of course, if a single cable is used, as is common in many local area network implementations, high speed is essential in order to accommodate all the potential users of the system, each with his own contribution to the bandwidth requirement.

1.5.2 Low cost

Possibly the single most important factor in users' reluctance to invest in LAN-based systems is the current high cost of attaching to general purpose local area networks. There are low-cost networks available, based largely on microcomputers of a particular type, but this does not meet the needs of most business users. The current typical cost of an Ethernet interface to a computer is in the region of $3000. VLSI technology, increased manufacturing volumes, and accumulated development experience have led to cost reductions, and further substantial cost reductions are expected in the next few years. Cheap terminals cost less than $500 and microcomputers can now be purchased for $1000, therefore single-workstation network attachments are frequently unattractive. Suppliers have avoided this problem by offering network interface units (NIUs, or terminal interface units, TIUs) which permit a number, typically up to eight, of simple devices to attach via V.24 interfaces to a network, the interface unit acting as a protocol converter. However, this eliminates some of the advantages of using a LAN in the first place. It is expected that when interfacing costs are of the order of $200 or less, more significant interest will be shown by users.

Wiring costs

These can also contribute significantly to installation costs, and, although it is not possible to give a typical figure, a number of organizations have been sufficiently alarmed at the potential labour costs involved in laying cables in existing premises that LAN projects have not been pursued. Nevertheless, allowance has been made for LAN cabling in some new buildings and it is to be hoped that this trend will continue.

1.5.3 High reliability/integrity

Local area networks are likely to be employed in office automation and factory systems. The reliability of systems based on manual processes is taken for granted, and a lower level of reliability will not be tolerated in the automated successor. As an example, we have come so much to rely on the telephone in office life that any breakdown of the inhouse telephone exchange causes an enormous amount of user dissatisfaction. Computer systems are often less reliable than telephone systems – in some organizations a central mainframe computer will be 'off the air' once or twice a month – but an increasing dependence on these systems, particularly where online communication is concerned, is forcing systems designers and suppliers to provide systems with higher degrees of fault tolerance. If computer systems are to be connected using a LAN, then it is essential that the LAN provide adequate reliability.

Error rates

Public networks, often based on analogue technology, generally exhibit higher error rates than do local networks. However, techniques have been developed to detect and correct errors, so applications with high integrity requirements may be developed using public networks. Office and factory applications based on LANs will almost certainly require a very high degree of information integrity, which in these cases can be achieved using low-level error detection and retransmission techniques, leaving correction of (fairly infrequent) remaining errors to higher levels, possibly to the application itself.

1.5.4 Installation flexibility

LANs have to be installed in a variety of conditions. Locations may include a single floor of an office block, a shop floor, an industrial estate or a complex of buildings with different structural features. In many cases cabling has to be inserted into ceiling spaces and existing electrical cable ducts, and routes must be taken which necessitate penetration of walls or partitions. There may be electrical hazards, as well as other environmental obstacles to overcome. Systems may have to fit in with modern office furniture and any environmental standards dictated by the need to conform to ergonomic as well as safety standards. Installation is an aspect which some suppliers of LANs ignore at their peril. Some suppliers do not perform cable installation as part of their service, leaving this task to outside contractors, and there may be subsequent disputes concerning responsibility for system imperfections.

1.5.5 Expandability

In some cases it is not possible, or at least financially attractive, to install the basis of a LAN with future expansion already catered for, although some organizations have the foresight or the good fortune to be able to make provision for future growth at the outset. In many cases a pilot system is installed or a system is implemented to handle a particular application, and it is only the success of these early applications which leads to the later decision to expand. At this stage, the LAN must be capable of extension either to cover a wider geographical area, or to permit attachment of an increased number of devices or users, or both. Expansion may be performed in small increments or large; addition of further users in a gradual fashion may well require that the system is not taken out of service for this purpose, therefore the LAN must provide facilities for reconfiguration of a running system. Large upgrades may involve addition of entirely new user groups and applications with different traffic throughput requirements. Thus, expandability in terms of communications bandwidth requirements may become a necessity during the lifetime of the system.

1.5.6   Ease of access

In view of the environmental conditions in which LANs may be installed, ease of access is not always guaranteed. For the office user in particular, physical access must be gained easily, because the LAN may have to fit in with existing office accommodation and practice. If terminals, for example, are to be moved about, connected and disconnected, and new users added, the LAN access points must be so sited as to minimize any disruption to the office environment.

Logical access

This must also be easy, and is particularly important in the initial stages of a LAN-based system, in order to gain user acceptance. As far as possible, the user should be unaware of the particular details of the network which he is using to gain access to an application.

1.5.7   Application adaptability

There are, and there will continue to be, LANs developed for particular applications. However it may be argued that the most popular form of LAN will be the general purpose network capable of satisfying many application requirements and handling different information types and volumes. It is inconvenient to have to use different public service networks because of the need to remember logging on codes, passwords and procedures. It may also be more expensive to use separate networks in the long run. Potential users of LANs will be particularly cost-sensitive and will therefore be attracted to a product which can perform multiple functions. Indeed, some LANs may be regarded as merely transport mechanisms or information carriers, where only the devices capturing, processing and outputting the information need vary from application to application.

1.5.8 Interface standardization

The purpose of a LAN is to interconnect various terminals and computers. In many organizations these devices may be of different types and manufacturers – it can seldom be guaranteed that a user will standardize on equipment of a particular type. The LAN is of course a common factor and it is, therefore, essential that standard interfaces are provided across the range of equipment required to connect to it. The subject of standards is treated in further detail in Chapter 2.

References

Clark, D.D., Pogran, K.T. and Reed, D.P., (1978). 'An introduction to local area networks' *Proc. IEEE*, **66**,(11), November, 1497–1517

Conard, J.W., (1983). 'Services and protocols of the data link layer' *Proc. IEEE*, **71**,(12), December, 1378–1383

DesJardins, R., (1983). 'Afterword: Evolving towards OSI' *Proc. IEEE*, **71**,(12), December, 1446–1448

Digital Equipment Co. Ltd, (1980). *Peripherals handbook*

Fletcher, J.G., (1973). 'Octopus communications structure' *IEEE Compcon'73*, February, 21–23

Freeman, H.A. and Thurber, K.J., (1980). 'Updated bibliography on local computer networks' *Computer Communication Review*, **10**,(3), July, 10–18

ISO, (1983). 'Data processing – Open Systems Interconnection – basic reference model' ISO 7498, reprinted in an earlier form in (1981) *Computer Networks*, **5**,(2), April, 81–118

Knightson, K.G., (1983). 'The transport layer standardization' *Proc. IEEE*, **71**,(12), December, 1394–1396

Logica VTS Ltd, (1981). *Polynet product description*

McClelland, F.M., (1983). 'Services and protocols of the physical layer' *Proc. IEEE*, **71**,(12), December, 1372–1377

Metcalfe, R.M. and Boggs, D.R., (1976). 'Ethernet: distributed packet switching for local computer networks' *CACM* **19**,(7), July, 395–404

Pierce, J.R., (1972). 'How far can data loops go?' *IEEE Trans. Comms.* **COM-20**,(3), June, 527–530

Rosen, S. and Steele, J.M., (1973). 'A local computer network' *COMPCON'73*, San Francisco, February, 129–132

Scantlebury, R.A. and Wilkinson, P.T., (1974). 'The National Physical Laboratory data communication network' *ICCC '74*, Stockholm, August, 223–228

Shoch, J.F., (1979). *An annotated bibliography on local computer networks* Xerox PARC Technical Report SSL-79-5, 3rd edition, Xerox PARC, Palo Alto, California, USA, April

Tanenbaum, A.S., (1981). *Computer Networks*. Prentice-Hall

Thurber, K.J. and Freeman, H.A., (1979). 'A bibliography of local computer network architectures' *ACM Computer Communication Review* **9**,(2), April

Ware, C., (1983). 'The OSI network layer: standards to cope with the real world' *Proc. IEEE*, **71**,(12), December, 1384–1387

Wilkes, M.V., (1975). 'Communication using a digital ring' *Proc. PACNET Conference*, Sendai, Japan, August, 47–55 (plus a one-page Addendum dated December 1976)

Wilkes, M.V. and Wheeler, D.J., (1979). 'The Cambridge digital communication ring' *Proc. Local Area Communications Network Symposium*, Mitre Corp., Boston, May, 47–60

Zimmermann, H., (1980). 'OSI Reference Model – the ISO model of architecture for Open Systems Interconnection' *IEEE Transactions on Communications*, **COM-28**,(4), April, 425–432

Chapter 2
Local area network standards

In this chapter local area network standards are introduced and explained. The structures of the standards bodies and their interrelationships are described, and the ISO open systems interconnection reference model is discussed as the basis on which networks are designed. Much of the terminology to be found in later chapters is introduced here.

2.1 The importance of standards

Local area network standards are following the same path as their wide area network counterparts. Increased activity in the area of standards has resulted from a recognition that computer communications is a field so complex that without rationalization progress will be severely impeded. There are many computer equipment and system suppliers offering a plethora of communications protocols and conventions, and agreement among them on standardization would clearly be impossible without the existence of central standards bodies, both national and international. We will discuss the standards organizations which are of greatest relevance to local area networks in the next section.

Users typically have a variety of computing equipment including personal computers, word processors, minicomputers and mainframe data processing systems. Only in rare cases is it possible to interconnect these pieces of equipment without using protocol conversion devices, and even then compatibility is not fully guaranteed. Consumer networks inevitably face difficulties, unless there is prior agreement on limiting the choice of equipment to be used. The corporate network can often rely on a strategy to reduce the number of options which may occur and hence the cost of circumventing inconsistencies.

In this context local area networks are particularly at risk, given their intended role in interconnecting a variety of devices in many cases. Justification for purchasing a LAN or developing a new application using a LAN may depend on smooth integration with existing systems and on the ease with which new systems can be added. Particularly within a small geographical area, information can be transported physically and unless a cheap and efficient replacement for such services can be demonstrated, organizations are unlikely to change their practices. A particular example of this difficulty would be the case of two computers located in the same premises where information is exchanged using tape transfer by messenger or operator. In this case only a link offering high speed and integrity would be contemplated as an alternative. A second example concerns the use of standalone word processors. Typically, documents would be transferred between these machines by means of diskette exchange, so here again an electronic link would have to offer the advantages of improved speed and reliability before a capital outlay would be authorized.

At a time when it has become accepted that voice communication is a commodity and, in fact, an essential element of business life, on which large capital sums are frequently expended, it is unfortunate that the same cannot be said of electronic data and text communications. Even the physical connection of a simple microcomputer to the public telephone network can be a task requiring a great deal of effort. Even once the correct interface details have been ascertained, it is not unusual to find that the software used is incompatible with that used in the remote system.

In view of such difficulties there has been an enormous increase in the interest shown by both users and manufacturers in the importance of standards in the last few years.

2.2 The standards bodies

The organizations which contribute to the standards-making process are usually referred to as the standards bodies. This is an area where until recently even industry observers were confused by both the numbers of 'standards' organizations, and the mechanisms used to formulate and agree standards. It is instructive to review first of all the relationships of the most important of these organizations to each other and to the subject of local area networks. Table 2.1 lists a number of acronyms which may be familiar to readers of computer and trade journals.

Table 2.1 Main standards bodies.

ISO	International Standards Organisation

National standards bodies (members of ISO)

ANSI	American National Standards Institute
BSI	British Standards Institution
DIN	Deutsches Institut für Normung eV (West German Standards Institute)
AFNOR	Association Française de Normalisation (French Standards Institute)
UNI	Ente Nazionale Italiano di Unificazione (Italian Standards Institute)
JISC	Japanese Industrial Standards Committee
SCC	Standards Council of Canada

Telecommunications standards

ITU	International Telecommunication Union
CCITT	International Telegraph and Telephone Consultative Committee (Comité Consultatif Internationale Télégraphique et Téléphonique)

Other standards-making bodies

ECMA	European Computer Manufacturers Association
IEEE	Institute of Electrical and Electronics Engineers (USA)
NBS	National Bureau of Standards (USA)
IEC	International Electrotechnical Commission
IFIP	International Federation for Information Processing

Table 2.2   Some UK participating organizations.

FOCUS	UK Committee set up to identify areas of work needed on information technology standards and to promote action
BABT	British Approvals Board for Telecommunication
NCC	National Computing Centre
ITSU	Information Technology Standards Unit
BCS	British Computer Society
BETA	Business Equipment Trade Association
CSA	Computing Services Association

Within individual countries there are yet other organizations involved in setting standards. As an example, Table 2.2 lists some of the organizations in Britain which participate in the formation of standards.

Most of the organizations listed do not deal solely with communications issues, the exception being CCITT. This is the forum of PTT authorities and is the primary organization responsible for international telecommunications standards. However, the ISO is assuming an increasingly important role, and is becoming the focal point of local area networking standards. Both of these bodies are based in Geneva, Switzerland. (The Appendix gives details of their addresses.)

Membership of the ISO consists of the national standards bodies representing the major developed countries – 89 at the time of writing. Only one organization is allowed to represent each country, for example BSI from the UK and ANSI from the USA. ISO's work is carried out by a large number of technical committees (TCs) each responsible for an area of technology or industry – for example, TC68 (Banking) and TC97 (Information Systems). The latter is the one which concerns us in this book. Within TC97 as in other subject areas there are subcommittees (SCs) with specific responsibilities and within these there are working groups (WGs) which collaborate on the production of standards proposals between official meetings of the subcommittees. The structures of the ISO and of this TC are extremely complex and Figures 2.1 and 2.2 attempt to elucidate them.

Each proposed standard goes through a number of drafting stages and voting procedures before the stage of draft proposal (DP) is reached. This can take a number of years since there are not only technical but also commercial and political issues to be resolved. Recently, surprise has been expressed at the speed with which much of the OSI work has appeared. This is due in part to the widespread agreement on the need for such standards, but also to the realization that technical progress could easily outstrip the traditional processes by which standards are developed.

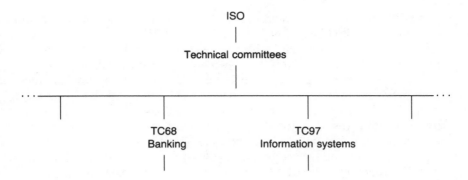

Figure 2.1   Details of the structure of the ISO.

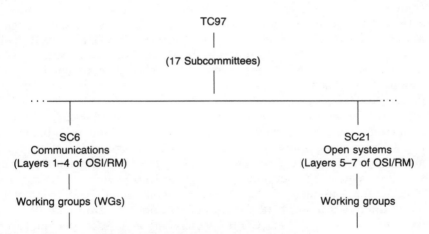

Scope of TC97: 'Standardization, including terminology and definitions, in the area of information systems, including computers and office equipment'

Figure 2.2   Structure of TC97 (information systems).

Once these DPs have been accepted they are registered with the central Secretariat as draft international standards (DIS). From DIS to full international standard (IS) status is usually relatively quick (of the order of months) assuming that no dissenting voice is heard in the latter stages. The OSI basic reference model (ISO, 1983) became an IS in late 1983. Work is continuing on the service and protocol standards associated with the model and these will be discussed in Section 2.3.

The organization which has had the most significant influence on local area network standards has been the American IEEE. In 1980 it began its 'Project 802 – local network standards'. The IEEE has done most of its work in interfaces, some of which have been adopted as *de facto* standards in the world of industry. Most of the participants in IEEE 802 are representatives of major US semiconductor and computer companies, so that its output usually carries considerable weight. ANSI recognizes IEEE as an important source of standards work and it channels the results to ISO when appropriate. In the case of Project 802, a number of important standards have emerged and are currently well on the way to acceptance within ISO.

Local area network standards were somewhat independently investigated by ECMA, which began work some time later than IEEE. Its technical committees TC24 and TC25, which already existed to study communications protocols and data networks respectively, extended the scope of their activities to include LAN standards beginning with the DIX/Ethernet 'blue book' specification (DIX, 1980). This specification was in fact also adopted by IEEE Project 802 since it was the first available and demonstrable. Since that time the two organizations have fortunately permitted the two versions to converge as presented to ISO.

As far as the UK is concerned, apart from the BSI, where a number of participants have been active in the essentially administrative task of pushing the standards through the system, a more pragmatic approach has been adopted. In 1981, the FOCUS committee was set up to recommend specific actions to the Department of Industry for aligning the activities of the various national bodies concerned with information technology standards. Apart from the DoI and BSI, its members are from CCTA (Central Computing and Telecommunications Authority), NCC, British Telecom and representatives of both suppliers and users. The Secretary of State for Industry commissioned the important *local area networks* (FOCUS, 1982) report of August 1982 on the recommendation of this committee. FOCUS has also produced a document entitled *The User View of Communications Standards* (FOCUS, 1983) which discusses the approach private sector users should adopt in the matter of standards selection during the present period of uncertainty.

As part of Information Technology Year (1982) the UK Department of Industry – later the Department of Trade and Industry (DTI) – created a group whose task it was to identify and specify standards for use by UK companies. Called the Information Technology Standards Unit (ITSU), this group then produced and promoted its 'Intercept' strategy, which aims to interpret the international standards scene and select those standards which are likely to become fully ratified and thus represent a secure basis for users and suppliers to adopt. In intercepting the standards on their way to international recognition, ITSU also aims to identify so-called 'interim' standards to fill in any gaps left by the absence of specifications suitable for international consumption.

Also in the UK, the NCC has set up a conformance testing service which will become a necessary part of a communications environment where suppliers develop products to internationally agreed specifications but lack the necessary testing facilities. The task of conformance testing is particularly difficult and is likely to be shared among a number of organizations, each perhaps dealing with specific protocols or subsets of the ISO reference model.

The common basis for describing communications systems, not only in local area networks but also in wide area networks, is the OSI basic reference model. The protocols and services which are discussed later in this book are part of this model and the IEEE 802 conventions can also be mapped onto the model. These topics are discussed in the next two sections.

2.3 The open systems interconnection reference model

In 1977 work began within the ISO on the subject now known as OSI, under the TC97.

In March 1978 the first meeting of SC16 took place in Washington DC with the title 'Open systems interconnection'. Its task was to develop an architectural model to describe the basic intercommunication between information processing systems. It is arguable that IBM's Systems Network Architecture (SNA) provided the initial impetus for this work. SNA, which first appeared in a crude form in around 1974, began life as a three-layer model. The concept was gradually adopted and refined as time went on. This subject caught the interest of a number of major computer manufacturers and academics. In 1980 Zimmermann published the principles of layering, which established the reasons for splitting the communications process into a number of discrete entities so that a simple interface existed between them (Zimmermann, 1980). By October 1982 the basic reference model became available as a draft international standard with the number 7498. This received full international standard status in May 1983 (ISO, 1983). The full title is: 'Data processing – open systems interconnection – basic reference model'. Meanwhile, CCITT produced an equivalent (though not identical) document with the number X.200, which has converged with 7498, except for the introductory parts which reflect the different natures of the organizations. The roles of SC16 and SC6, which had already existed to examine basic data transmission standards, became better defined as the layering principles became better understood. SC16 dealt with (until late 1984) the upper layers of the reference model (4–7), while SC6 was considered to deal with layers 1–3. It is important to note that even among experts there is some disagreement on the precise functions carried out by each layer of the model, particularly in the higher layers. In fact, as protocol specifications have been developed, each layer has seemed to develop a life of its own, with an internal structure, and sometimes the inviolable nature of a layer is in danger, with talk of functions being carried out in the upper or lower parts of the layer. Clearly, further substructuring would render the model undesirably complicated, possibly resulting in the loss of its attraction as a mirror of the communications process.

Since the basic structure of the model was first agreed, a great deal of work has been devoted to the specification of protocol and service standards relevant to each layer of the model. As a result of the progress of these standards and the increased understanding of the layer functions, the subcommittees were reorganized in late 1984. A new committee, SC21, was established as being responsible for layers 5–7, together with management, database access, graphics terminal and other standards. SC6 was additionally given responsibility for layer 4, and SC16 was dissolved. SC5, which was an older subcommittee responsible for 'programming languages', but which was extending into graphics and database areas, was subsumed into SC21. This was as a result of a higher level grouping of ISO subcommittees into

- applications elements (SC1, SC7, SC14)
- equipment and media (SC10, SC11, SC13, SC15, SC17, SC19, SC23)
- systems (SC2, SC6, SC18, SC20, SC21, SC22).

Further reorganization is likely to continue as information technology develops and extends.

The OSI model has been the subject of much interest in technical literature and the basic concepts have been widely written about (for example Zimmermann, 1980; Wood, 1982; Linington, 1983; DesJardins, 1983). Briefly, we will examine the model to put into perspective the position of local area networks within the layering principles established. Figure 2.3 shows a classical representation of the communication between two systems at A and B connected by a relay.

Relays are required in wide area networks which use a store-and-forward system, where the route between end systems (A and B in this case) passes through intermediate switching nodes; each switching node corresponds to a relay. In local networks, relays are not required within a single network. However, they are required between networks, and are

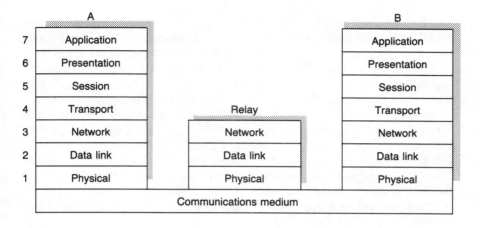

Figure 2.3   OSI model architecture.

called gateways or bridges in this case. Chapter 7 deals further with the subject of internetworking.

In Figure 2.3, each end system is represented by seven layers as shown, with well-defined interfaces between the layers. This is analogous to the modular approach taken in designing a computer software system, particularly in the field of operating systems. The design and implementation problems are made more manageable by splitting up the task into several smaller ones. Maintenance and enhancements become more efficient since each layer can in theory be replaced without alteration to the interfaces at the upper and lower layers. The model has, however, attracted some criticism from users because it may be unnecessarily complicated in a simple point-to-point communications system. Users fear, with some justification, that the software required to perform the various layering functions may be both extensive, taking up large amounts of memory, and slow in operation, involving a number of possibly redundant steps.

The seven layers can be summarized as follows.

2.3.1   Physical layer

This layer is concerned with the electrical and mechanical means of transmitting and receiving information using a particular communications medium. It specifies the details of connecting cables and processing digital signals. The level of detail provided is more than sufficient to enable manufacturers to build equipment conforming to the standard. Since basic data communication is a well-understood subject there are already a number of industry standards available. Hence this layer is normally assumed to be a simple one in terms of agreeing a standard, but in fact this is not the case. It is important to realize from the outset that there is not necessarily any one specific standard within each layer; there may well be a number of suitable standards developed, from which a selection can be made depending on the requirements. X.21 (CCITT) is the best example of a standard in this layer, as it is designed for digital network interfaces. However, as we shall see later, local area network interfaces can involve different standards. The ubiquitous (but not standard!) V.24 or RS-232 interface recommendation is still the most common form of interface used in practice, and this is recognized since the new digital X.21 interface recommendation designated X.21 bis has V.24 as an interim solution.

2.3.2 Data link layer

This layer is responsible for maintaining the integrity of information sent between two points. In other words, it provides a reliable channel for data transmitted over a physical medium which is usually in practice 'noisy' and therefore a mechanism is required to enable errors to be detected and corrected. Many such communications protocols have been developed over the years, the best known of which are IBM's binary synchronous communications (BSC) and synchronous data link control (SDLC) together with ISO's HDLC. (CCITT's version of HDLC is called LAPB or X.25 level 2.)

2.3.3 Network layer

Communication takes place frequently within a network, either public or private, where links have to be traced between source and destination by means of addressing and routing mechanisms. This layer has the responsibility of ensuring that information is transferred correctly across a network. It involves setting up and maintaining the links necessary. X.25 level 3 is the best example of this, though each of the proprietary architectures including IBM's SNA and DEC's DNA has equivalent layers to this. Between networks the network layer has the responsibility for internetwork routing.

2.3.4 Transport layer

In practice, information has to be transferred, depending on the application, across more than one network, or a choice of networks may be available. In order to maintain the principle that changing one layer does not affect adjacent layers, this layer was introduced with the aim of shielding upper layers from the details of specific networks across which information is to be transmitted. It should provide a network-independent service to the so-called application layers, which are found immediately above it.

2.3.5 Session layer

The purpose of this layer is to provide a means of establishing a communications session between two applications processes with facilities to police the session and to terminate it in an orderly fashion. It provides support for synchronization and checkpoints to which a return can be made in case of failure.

2.3.6 Presentation layer

Information can be represented in a number of different ways – for example the basic character representation can be either ASCII or EBCDIC. This layer resolves the differences between the applications entities by providing translation facilities. Information may also be formatted in different ways and again it is the task of this layer to ensure compatibility between the cooperating processes.

2.3.7 Application layer

This is the most difficult layer of all, as can readily be appreciated by considering the numbers of different applications which exist. In this layer particularly, a number of standards are certain to emerge and already a classification of applications types has been made as follows:

- terminal handling
- file handling
- text interchange
- job transfer and manipulation.

These are known as specific application service elements (SASEs) and will increase in number as new applications develop.

Progress towards terminal handling standards is likely to be somewhat slow in view of the fact that five classes of terminals have been identified, namely:

- basic class
- forms
- graphics
- image
- mixed.

As we shall see in Chapter 8, there is a common application service element (CASE) in the application layer, intended to provide the facilities required in common over all the specific protocols mentioned above.

The uppermost three layers are normally referred to as being application layers, while layers 1–3 are referred to as the network layers. The transport layer provides the bridge between user-specific and network-dependent processes. Referring to Figure 2.3, the entities in each layer communicate with their counterparts by means of protocols which operate through exchange of protocol data units. Connection is established using the next lower layers and service data units are used in these exchanges. Information may not be transmittable directly from one system to another, in which case a transit or relay system is involved, as shown in Figure 2.3. Message switching systems normally involve at least a two-part transmission. The transit system may only involve the network layers of the model, in particular to resolve the differences in the addressing structures employed by the two networks and the differences in the physical media employed.

There is no reason to assume that local area networks differ in principle from wide area networks as far as the model is concerned. Therefore a treatment under the network layers should be sufficient.

In fact most of the work done so far by IEEE and ECMA concerns layers 1 and 2, or at least their equivalent in terms of the IEEE 802 project.

2.4 The IEEE/ECMA LAN reference model (LAN/RM)

Corresponding to the OSI reference model (or OSI/RM) is the local area network reference model (which we shall call the LAN/RM). The work in developing the LAN/RM was done largely by the IEEE Project 802 committee in the USA, but valuable work was also undertaken in parallel by ECMA in Europe. Basically the LAN/RM has only three layers: these correspond to the lowermost two layers of the OSI/RM (data link and physical). Figure 2.4 shows the relationship between the two reference models.

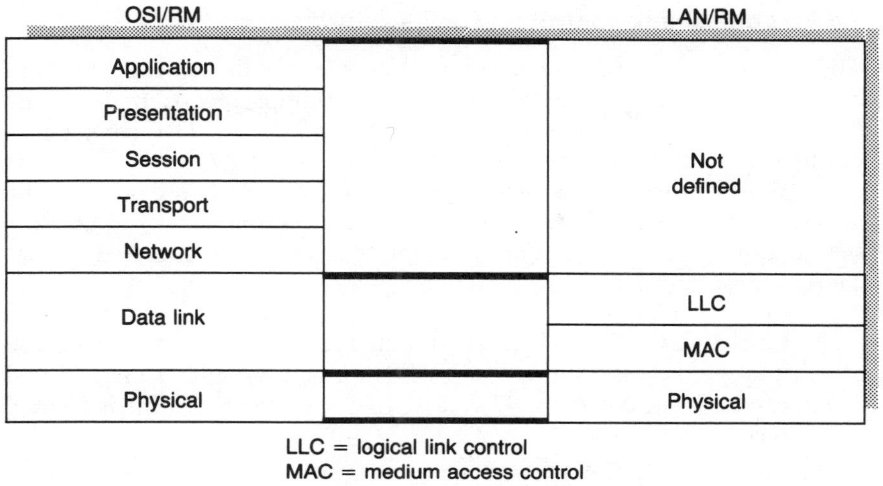

OSI/RM		LAN/RM
Application		
Presentation		
Session		Not defined
Transport		
Network		
Data link		LLC
		MAC
Physical		Physical

LLC = logical link control
MAC = medium access control

Figure 2.4 Correspondence between OSI/RM and LAN/RM.

The three LAN/RM layers are briefly as follows.

2.4.1 Physical

For each of the four specific technologies (to be described shortly) this defines the operation, interfacing to, and transfer of information on a particular physical medium with particular characteristics including speed.

2.4.2 Medium access control (MAC)

As the name suggests, this layer provides a means of sharing a common medium among a number of different devices. Clearly such control is necessary to allow for efficient utilization of the available bandwidth and to avoid deadlock when competing for a single bandwidth. MAC is medium-dependent.

2.4.3   Logical link control (LLC)

This provides a medium-independent protocol for both connectionless and connection-oriented communication among multiple peers. It forms the top sublayer of the equivalent ISO data link layer. The connection-oriented protocol is similar to LAPB or HDLC.

IEEE Project 802 has involved a necessary compromise between the views of different computer and communications suppliers. The result is the support given to the four different technologies mentioned above. These are as follows:

- *CSMA/CD (802.3)*   The bus-oriented technique called carrier sense multiple access with collision detection is a broadcast method and results from the initial DIX Ethernet specification. This is treated further in Chapter 4.

- *Token bus (802.4)*   The token passing bus scheme is here defined for a broadcast medium and involves the use of a particular piece of data called a token which regulates the transmission of information by permitting only one station, namely that which is in possession of the token, to transmit at any one time.

- *Token ring (ECMA-RR, subsequently also 802.5)*   The token passing ring scheme involves a loop or ring medium where, again, the token controls transmission, normally sequentially around the ring. This is treated further in Chapter 5, together with the token bus scheme. Token ring is the technology favoured by IBM for its new generation of LAN products.

- *Metropolitan area network (MAN, 802.6)*   This access technology is still under study but it involves areas of geographical coverage significantly greater than those addressed by local area networks thus far. For example, a large area of a city may be 'wired' to provide high speed services for a large number of subscribers. The MAN is not sufficiently well developed for us to talk about in this book.

In addition, another well developed scheme will be covered in Chapter 6, namely the Cambridge Ring, or slotted ring as it is generically named. This scheme was developed in the UK (Wilkes and Wheeler, 1979) and is in use in a number of commercial products, but has only recently been put forward as an international standard. As a result of the ITSU initiative, the CR82 specifications have been modified to conform to BSI format and to enable them to stand alongside the IEEE technologies. The Cambridge Ring is now a British Standard and is being incorporated into the ISO framework.

At present there are no standards for personal computer (PC) networks. A number of proprietary PC networks are already on the market and installed, principally to link together a number of devices of the same type (typically up to 32, but sometimes up to 256) in order to permit hard disk storage to be shared. It is increasingly likely however that PC networks will be designed according to at least subsets of available international standards.

An area of technology also not covered by standards at present is that of PABX-based local area networks. This is discussed further in Chapter 3. Despite the fact that new generation PABXs have been designed with data transmission in mind, they are still principally oriented to the switching of voice traffic, and the interface speeds used (64 Kbits/sec to 256 Kbits/sec) are not typical of either data devices or LAN transmission rates. The topology of a PABX-based system is normally a star; therefore it is likely that different techniques will be required to those employed in bus and ring networks.

Two areas currently under intensive study in the wider context of the OSI/RM are management and security.

There is a growing realization of the need for management of communications resources and the subject of management is being studied as part of the applications layers of the OSI/RM. Similarly, in a local area network, the use of the distributed computing resources which the LAN typically connects should be optimized. This subject will be considered further in Chapter 9.

Work is being carried out in conjunction with SC20 (data encryption) on the placement of security features within the OSI/RM. An addendum to IS7498 is being put forward as a DP and will outline which of the layers will host the security mechanisms. At the lowest level this will involve encryption of the information placed on the transmission medium and decryption at the point of exit, using a standard algorithm, while at the highest level issues such as key management have to be addressed.

2.5 LAN standards

In this section we will examine briefly those standards which are largely complete, and being prepared for international standard status at ISO.

The IEEE standards in question are the series 802.1 to 802.6 and these are shown in Figure 2.5, in a form which indicates their relationship to each other.

These are considered in turn.

2.5.1 Internetworking (802.1)

This document gives an overview of the other standards and explains the relationship to the OSI/RM in some detail, and considers higher-layer protocols, internetworking, and management.

802.1 Internetworking			
802.2 Logical link control			
802.3 Medium access	802.4 Medium access	802.5 Medium access	802.6 Medium access
802.3 Physical	802.4 Physical	802.5 Physical	802.6 Physical

Figure 2.5   IEEE LAN standards.

2.5.2   Logical link control (802.2)

This describes, for any of the media access protocols below, the control procedures used in both connection-oriented and connectionless operation. Thus, two basic classes of LLC operation are defined, namely class 1 (connectionless) and class 2 (both types).

2.5.3   CSMA/CD (802.3)

This defines the MAC interfaces upwards and downwards and the operation of the sublayer itself. It defines the physical layer for baseband coaxial operation speeds of 1, 5, 10 and 20 Mbits/sec, and it also specifies the electrical and physical details required for operation.

2.5.4   Token bus (802.4)

This defines the MAC and physical sublayers for the following broadcast media

- baseband coaxial at 1 Mbits/sec
- baseband coaxial at 5, 10 Mbits/sec
- broadband coaxial at 1, 5 and 10 Mbits/sec.

Four classes of priority are defined for access.

2.5.5   Token ring (802.5)

This defines MAC and physical sublayers for the use of a token on a sequential medium, namely: twisted pair at 1, 4 Mbits/sec.

There are eight classes of priority access specified.

2.5.6   Metropolitan area networks (under study) (802.6)

This would involve operation at speeds of over 1 Mbits/sec on media yet to be agreed, but over distances of up to 50 km.

2.5.7   Higher layers

The issue of network service provision is now being studied, whether connection-oriented or connectionless. Progress is being made on network addressing. Because LANs involve connectionless communications, the general approach until recently has been to implement connection-oriented transport services on top of the connectionless lower layers. This is usually considered best for supporting the traditional applications of file transfer and remote log in. However, connectionless transport services (to be built on top of connectionless network layer services) are under consideration. (An addendum to the transport service definition for this purpose is being studied.)

It may be argued that the standards specified for the higher layers will operate without modification on local area networks – in other words, there should be no difference in the services offered above the network service boundary. This cannot be guaranteed, however, until more practical experience has been gained. Questions of quality of service and bandwidth exploitation have still to be answered.

The issue of internetworking between LANs and WANs is something which the ISO is well placed to study, given that its subcommittees have interests in both of these areas. The IEEE is currently working on a number of further issues in the field of local area networks, particularly internetworking between different types of medium-access technology. As a point of interest, proposals for a low-cost CSMA/CD scheme at around 1 Mbits/sec are being studied in response to the clear need to provide commercially, as well as technically, feasible solutions to users' problems.

2.6   Layering

The international activities described so far led to the publication as an international standard, in 1983, of the reference model for OSI (ISO, 1983). Often referred to in brief as the OSI/RM, the reference model has been successful as the basis for network architectures produced during its development and, since publication, by manufacturers and commercial organizations.

There are those who argue that the OSI/RM should not be a standard in the sense that it is no more than an architectural definition, literally a model used for reference. Nevertheless it now stands alongside the other international standards in communications and networks, most of which are specifications from which implementations can be directly derived. The OSI/RM should properly be regarded as an overview document to set the scene for the various layer specifications which are associated with it.

In this section and the following ones we present the ideas and terminology which are prerequisites for understanding the documents describing the new standard LAN architectures: CSMA/CD (Ethernet), token ring and bus, and slotted (Cambridge) ring.

A fundamental idea is that of layering. Layer n in a given network node has neighbouring layers $n - 1$ and $n + 1$ below and above respectively. Layer n uses the services offered by layer $n - 1$ and in turn offers services to layer $n + 1$. Each layer contains protocols which process data being passed between layers.

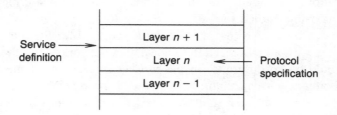

The upper interface of a layer is defined in a **service definition**, while the processing within a layer is defined in a **protocol specification**.

It is important to realize that when nodes in a network intercommunicate, it is the corresponding layers in the nodes which talk to each other. For proper communications to take place each node must contain identical protocol layers. **Peer protocol** layers exchange messages which have a commonly understood format: these messages are known as **protocol data units** (PDUs) (more about these in Section 2.11). The protocol in a

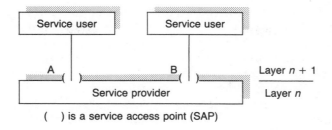

Figure 2.6 OSI/RM service user and provider.

particular layer has to know only about the service definitions at its boundaries and nothing at all about protocols in other layers or services at other layer interfaces.

The OSI/RM introduces the notions of service user and service provider as shown in Figure 2.6.

Every layer n is a service provider for the user layer $n + 1$ above (the term 'user' does not mean the human user at the application level). In Figure 2.6, A and B are service access points (SAPs), an important abstraction used in the OSI/RM documentation. User access to a provider is by means of SAPs; each SAP has its own address at a particular layer boundary. Service access points to each underlying layer are labelled with a prefix identifying the layer, so for example:

- TSAP – transport layer SAP
- NSAP – network layer SAP
- LSAP – data link layer SAP.

The function of a layer is often defined as being to provide the functional and procedural means for communications between SAPs (of the corresponding type) at different nodes.

2.7 Service and protocol specifications

In the ISO and IEEE documents protocols and services are specified by mixtures of English text, diagrams and tables.

Each protocol layer should be regarded as a **state machine** which has a set of allowable states, and a set of transitions which cause the machine to move from one state to another. A state machine – or finite state machine (FSM) – is the theoretical equivalent of a digital computer, or alternatively of a sequential digital logic circuit. It can be seen by the outside world as a black box having sets of inputs and outputs: outputs appear as a result of changing input conditions. The internal states and transitions are the things which govern the operation of the black box. These correspond to the protocols inside a layer in the OSI/RM, while the black box inputs and outputs correspond roughly to the elements of the services seen at layer interfaces.

The user of a particular layer need know only about the services offered but of course the network implementer must know the protocol specification in order to build the state machine mechanisms.

Characterizing each layer's services is its set of **service primitives**. These are concise statements containing the service name and its associated information to be passed through the service access point. They look rather like function or procedure calls in a programming language (and indeed could be implemented exactly as such, though there is no intention in the specification to influence the implementation to be used).

For example, a network layer request to the underlying data link layer to send data to another network layer entity is specified by the following primitive:

L_DATA_REQUEST(destination address,data)

while the arrival of that data at the destination is handled by another primitive:

L_DATA_INDICATION(source address,data)

In each case the 'L' stands for data link layer, and REQUEST and INDICATION are examples of service primitive **types**. This transfer of data can be illustrated in a diagram (see Figure 2.7) which also shows how the transfer uses service access points in the provider layer.

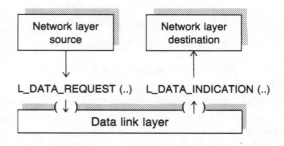

Figure 2.7 Service primitives example.

2.8 Service primitive types

In the OSI/RM four primitive types are identified, while in the original LAN/RM there are basically only three, as shown below:

Primitive types

OSI/RM	LAN/RM
REQUEST	REQUEST
INDICATION	INDICATION
RESPONSE	—
CONFIRMATION	CONFIRMATION

To explain these types, and the difference between the models, it is best to introduce the **time sequence diagram** as used in the OSI and IEEE documents. Figure 2.8 is an outline of such a diagram, in which the service user layers are now left and right of the provider. The local user is the one on the left, where activities are assumed to be initiated, and the right hand one is a remote user, that is somewhere else on the network.

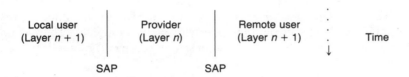

Figure 2.8 Time sequence diagram format.

The vertical lines represent service access points (SAPs) while the passage of time is from top to bottom of the diagram. As will be shown shortly in an example, primitives are represented by arrowed lines but there is no time relationship between primitives in local and remote user layers unless specifically marked by means of a dotted line.

Figure 2.9 (a) and (b) illustrates the primitive types for the OSI/RM and LAN/RM on time sequence diagrams.

In both the OSI and LAN/RMs REQUEST and INDICATION have similar meanings. The REQUEST primitive is used to request an operation of the underlying provider layer or the remote peer protocol layer.

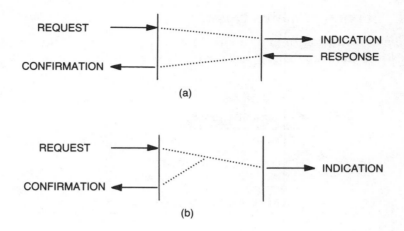

Figure 2.9   Illustration of service primitive types: (a) OSI/RM; (b) LAN/RM.

INDICATION is the way in which the provider can notify the user that there is an incoming message for its attention, or that an another event of significance has occurred (for example a REQUEST has been unsuccessful in the sense that the provider could not carry it out).

CONFIRMATION usually has a different meaning in the OSI and LAN models. In OSI it gives an end-to-end confirmation that a remote operation has been successful, i.e. that the remote user has successfully processed the requested operation. In the LAN/RM it simply gives confirmation of delivery from the underlying service provider. There is no confirmation in the LAN that the request was processed by the intended remote user.

RESPONSE is provided in the OSI/RM and is the means by which a destination can send off an end-to-end acknowledgment of a successful (or otherwise) operation. This illustrates the original difference between two models: the OSI/RM is connection-oriented while the LAN/RM is connectionless. More recently, however, the two models have adopted both properties.

The original LAN/RM primitive types are thus a subset of those in the OSI/RM. If it is required to provide end-to-end acknowledgments within LANs using the LAN/RM this can be done by employing two sets of REQUEST operations to give the effect of the OSI/RM four-primitive set, as shown in Figure 2.10. Alternatively acknowledgments can be provided at a higher layer by sending data explicitly for this purpose – this has been a commonly used strategy in local networks, because the underlying transmission system is so reliable that messages sent almost always reach their destination successfully. On the other hand, there is even then no

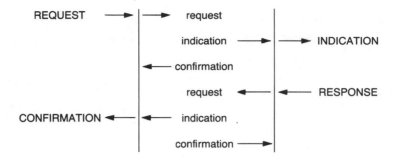

Figure 2.10 LAN/RM primitives as a subset of those in OSI/RM.

guarantee that the intended destination host is ready to receive messages (as it may be out of action due to some failure).

For simplicity in Figure 2.10 the service provider identity and type of operation requested are not included along with the primitive labels.

2.9 Examples of use

Examples of the use of service primitives, using time sequence diagrams, are shown in Figures 2.11 (a) and (b). An unsuccessful attempt to REQUEST a connection with a remote entity results in the service provider responding with an INDICATION (rather than a CONFIRMATION).

The successful attempt at connection illustrates the use of all four service primitive types in the case of the OSI/RM.

Note that the time relationships are indicated by use of the dotted lines, in the direction of the arrows on the initiating lines. In this example a network (N) layer service provider is used for illustration. The exact inter-relationship between primitive operations is dependent on the layer providing the service.

2.10 Summary on service primitives

We have introduced the basic service primitive types for the two network models, OSI and LAN. From the examples so far it should be evident that the primitives in use are qualified both by the associated operation and by the provider layer identity. So for example:

L_DATA_REQUEST

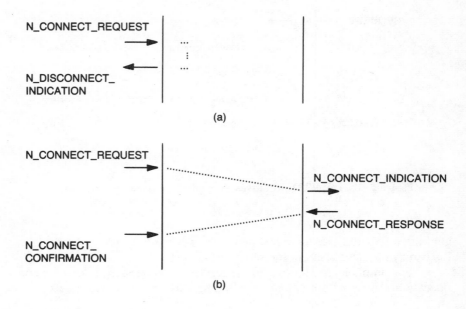

Figure 2.11   Examples of the use of (OSI/RM) service primitives: (a) example of unsuccessful connection request; (b) successful connection request sequence.

asks for data to be transmitted by the data link layer, the qualifiers being DATA and L respectively.

Taking another example,

N_CONNECT_INDICATION

is an indication of an attempt by a remote user to set up a connection through the network layer service provider. The qualifiers in this case are CONNECT and N.

2.11   Protocol data units

As stated in Section 2.6, peer protocol layers in different nodes communicate by exchanging protocol data units (PDUs). These are nested by virtue of the layering at each node, so that at the (lowest) physical layer the exchange of data is in terms of bit streams whose encoding both the transmitting and receiving nodes understand.

At the data link layer above, these bits are dealt with as a frame or group of bits with addressing and control information surrounding the data at this layer of protocol. The data is what the network layer has passed down at the transmitting end and which in turn will be passed up to the network layer at the receiver. The combined address and control information is referred to as the data link header: this is added by the transmitting data link layer and removed by the corresponding layer at the receiving end.

Nested PDUs are illustrated below:

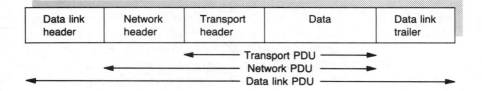

Note that in local area networks there is normally also a data link trailer consisting of error detection bits and, in the case of some ring networks, a response field to indicate if the transmitted PDU was accepted at its intended destination.

Sometimes it may be necessary for a protocol layer to break up the data it is given by a higher layer into smaller units for transmission. This will depend on the characteristics of the underlying network which the layer above has no need to know about. The data passed through a SAP from a higher to a lower layer needs therefore to be distinguished from what is exchanged with its peers by the lower protocol layer (the PDU) and is termed the **service data unit** (SDU). This is illustrated below:

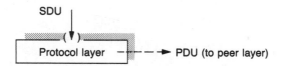

The exchange of PDUs is shown conceptually by a horizontal dashed line to a peer protocol layer, although of course the PDU, or sequence of PDUs if the SDU is broken up, is actually packaged with the appropriate header and passed down in turn as a SDU to the layer beneath.

The transport layer in general has the task of breaking TSDUs into smaller TPDUs should the underlying network require it. Particular local networks may carry out data segmenting at the network and data link layers, but at the physical layer this is not relevant.

2.12 Local network LLC layer

Referring to Figure 2.4, the primary layers specified in the LAN/RM are the LLC (logical link control), MAC (medium access control) and physical layers. Internetworking is left as an area for further work but corresponds to the combination of network and transport layers in the OSI/RM.

Descriptions of the specific LAN technologies – Ethernet (CSMA/CD), token bus and ring, and Cambridge Ring – follow in Chapters 4, 5 and 6. In the present chapter we now give a description of the common LLC layer (IEEE, 1985) using terminology introduced in the earlier sections.

Together, the LLC and MAC have equivalent functionality to the OSI/RM data link layer (Conard, 1983). Each MAC provides access to the shared communications medium for its attached node by means of its own characteristic medium access protocol. It also does a limited amount of address resolution.

2.12.1 HDLC frame and protocol

The details of the LLC and MAC have largely been derived and adapted from the well-known high level data link control (HDLC) protocol which is the basis of the data link layer of X.25 used in accessing wide area networks. HDLC is an international standard published by the ISO.

At this level of protocol, frames of data are exchanged between a source and destination. The frame contains user data and addressing information, plus fields specifically required by the protocol operation. The data link builds directly on top of the physical layer (which deals only with individual bits), so the frame is a structure which groups bits and gives them collective meaning. The frame carries the user data packet within it on behalf of the layer of protocol above.

There are various forms of data link protocol, differing in detail but not greatly different from the HDLC protocol in principle or operation. Detailed discussion of data link protocols can be found in, for example, the books by Tanenbaum and Halsall – see the Bibliography.

The standard format of the HDLC frame recommended by the ISO is shown in Figure 2.12.

The flag character which prefixes and terminates each frame is a unique combination of bits, namely 01111110. Address and control are 8-bit fields indicating respectively the intended destination for the frame

| 8 | 8 | 8 | ≥0 | 16 | 8 bits |

| Flag | Address | Control | Data | CRC | Flag |

Figure 2.12 Standard HDLC frame format.

and the type of frame (whether an information frame, or a supervisory or unnumbered frame used by the protocol for controlling the data link).

Only a destination address is used in this frame (in contrast, both destination and source addresses are in local network link level frames). This is because of the original use of HDLC (and similar protocols) in communication systems where there is one 'primary' and a larger number of 'secondary' stations. The primary controls all the communications, and all transmit and receive actions pass via the primary. In transmission, the primary identifies the appropriate secondary by means of its address. This is also the case when the primary 'polls' each secondary asking it to send data. When the primary receives from a secondary, the information is labelled with the address of the secondary (in this case, actually, the address is that of the source of the information).

In local networks all stations are considered equal, so there is no concept of primary or secondary. Messages may be sent from any source to any destination. Therefore both source and destination addresses are required.

The data field contains any number of bits and is immediately followed by a 2-byte CRC (cyclic redundancy check) value which is calculated by the transmitting node, and allows the destination to tell whether the data block has been transmitted correctly. The efficiency of the CRC falls off as the data field becomes longer: a typical maximum data size is 1–4 Kbits.

Within the frame, the uniqueness of the flag character must be ensured: six 1s must never occur consecutively, other than as a flag sequence. Wherever six 1s would occur in the data stream the transmitting node must employ a technique called bit-stuffing or zero-bit insertion after the fifth 1. At the receiving end an inverse operation must be performed to remove any zero which occurs after five consecutive 1s.

The protocol itself – called the 'rules of procedure' by the ISO – uses the control field to communicate information between the two ends of the data link. In addition to identifying the frame type, the control field contains sequence number information. This is used for two purposes: firstly, to implement flow control so that one end cannot flood the other with a sequence of frames too quickly to be processed; and secondly, to enable retransmission of frames which have not arrived successfully (in particular frames whose CRC field indicated an error and were discarded).

In implementing flow control each end maintains a window of frames with consecutive sequence numbers which it is willing to send or receive. Typically the sequence number is modulo-8, that is it increases from zero up to seven, then recycles to zero. In this case the window size is at most eight frames. The sender retains frames within its window until such time as they are successfully acknowledged by the receiver. The receiver's window size determines how many frames it can accept and buffer pending processing: acknowledgment of any frame means that frame has been processed, and another can now be accommodated within the receiving window.

In this protocol, all frames are validated and acknowledged and (though not necessarily received in order of sequence number) passed to the higher level at the receiver in the correct order. HDLC is a **connection-oriented** (CO) or **virtual circuit** protocol, in which the data link must be established (each end initialized with respect to sequence numbers and window buffers) before frames can be exchanged. The connection must be properly terminated at both ends after the data exchange.

2.12.2 LLC frame structure

The basic framing in the standard local networks scheme is done by the MAC sublayer. MAC frames carry the LLC protocol data units (PDUs), which have the following structure:

1	1	1	≥0	octets
DSAP	SSAP	Control	Data	

where an 'octet' is an 8-bit group (as used by the standards bodies). DSAP and SSAP are the destination and source service access points respectively, in other words addresses within the LLC sublayer. The layer above uses the concatenation of DSAP and MAC (LAN-specific) addresses for transmission: the DSAP goes into the LLC PDU, while the LAN destination address is set up in the MAC frame in which the PDU is transported. On reception, the full source address (SSAP and LAN source address) is passed up to the higher layer.

The control field serves the same purpose as in HDLC, but its contents are different depending on the type of LLC service being used.

2.12.3 Service options in LLC

Provided by the LLC layer is a choice of types of service as follows:

type1	Connectionless (datagram)
type2 (optional)	Connection-oriented (virtual circuit)
type3 (optional)	Acknowledged connectionless
type4 (optional)	Polled response

The type2 service is very like the HDLC protocol outlined in the previous section. In this case, the control field contains sequence number and frame type information for controlling the operation of the connection-oriented link. Type1 is considerably simpler, and provides only a basic datagram service. In other words each frame is sent on a 'best effort' basis, with no acknowledgement, retransmission or flow control. Each frame will have been checked using a form of CRC by the MAC sublayer, but frames found to be in error are simply discarded: it is then up to higher protocol layers to make a decision about the missing frame data.

In LLC other facilities are provided including loop-back test (for diagnostic purposes), exchange of identity with other LLCs, and (optionally) downline loading for higher level protocol software.

Confusingly, **classes** of LLC are also identified. These allow for different combinations of optional types together with the mandatory connectionless type1. Only two classes are recognized meantime:

Class I	type1 only
Class II	type1 and type2

Other classes are likely to be added, namely class III which would consist of types 1,2 and 3, and class IV consisting of types 1,3 and 4. The purpose of the classes is to ensure that implementers (and users) know which are the allowable combinations of LLC types so that nodes with closely defined functional properties can be built (and selected for use).

Although the basic choice at the LLC level is between connectionless (CL) service, i.e. datagram, and connection-oriented (CO) service, i.e. virtual circuit, the choice of which to use will not be made in isolation but rather in conjunction with requirements at higher levels in the protocol hierarchy. For example, if a datagram internetworking facility is being used but CO operation is required as a base for a file transfer capability, then LLC type1 will be selected, together with a CL network service; CO operation can then be ensured at the transport layer.

Conversely, if virtual circuit internetworking is to be used, CO operation can be provided either by selecting LLC type2 and enhancing it or by putting a CO network service on top of LLC type1.

The primitives for type1 and type2 are as follows:

Type	Primitive	Meaning
type1	L_DATA	Send data
type2	L_CONNECT	Set up connection
	L_DATA_CONNECT	Send data
	L_DISCONNECT	Clear connection
	L_RESET	Async clear
	L_CONNECTION_FLOWCTL	Limit data rate

where for each primitive (where appropriate) the usual operation types apply:

L_PRIMITIVE.request
L_PRIMITIVE.indicate
L_PRIMITIVE.confirm

A brief description of the four LLC types now follows.

Connectionless (type1)

In this type of operation a frame of data is sent off into the local network with full addressing information, i.e. where it is going and where it has come from. No state information about the data frame is retained by the sending LLC layer. It is a 'best effort to deliver' system, rather like sending a letter by the postal system. In local networks (like the postal system) the reliability of the communications medium is very high, so there is a correspondingly high probability that the data frame will be delivered correctly at the destination. Of course there is a chance that the recipient node may not (be able to) accept the frame, and in this case the effect to the sender is the same as the frame not arriving; the sender is quite unaware of either event.

Connectionless operation, therefore, relies on high reliability of delivery and high probability of acceptance, and typically also acknowledgements arranged by a higher level protocol. There may indeed be some local network applications in which no acknowledgements are demanded even at a higher level. An example is a process monitoring system where values are transmitted on a fixed interval basis from an instrument to a management computer which processes the collected data. In this case, the very occasional missing value will make no difference to the operation of the process being monitored – as long as 'very occasional' stays within a known limit calculated by the system's designers to be acceptable. Type1 is also known as a datagram service.

In local networks there is in addition the facility of multicast and broadcast (multiple destinations and all destinations in the network respectively) in contrast to the usual specification of a single destination address in the LLC frame. This facility is provided by the MAC sublayer addressing, where broadcast is identified by an address field of all ones, and multicast (or selective broadcast) by other addresses having the most significant bit in the address field set to one. In the former case, all stations on the network will read the broadcast message, but in the case of multicast a group of stations can be set up with a particular (logical or physical) address and will all respond to messages containing that destination address.

Connection-oriented (type2)

This is much more complex than type1 and requires a connection (or virtual circuit) to be established before data is sent. Its operation is very similar to that of HDLC. In the case of LLC, a set of particular message primitives has been defined within the LAN/RM; to set up a connection, an L_CONNECT.request message is sent to the destination; the destination LLC layer sees an L_CONNECT.indication message, acts on it and returns an L_CONNECT.confirmation message saying whether the virtual circuit has been set up thus giving an end-to-end notification.

Data frames are sent using L_DATA_CONNECT.request messages. The remote peer LLC layer sees an L_DATA_CONNECT.indication message, and acknowledges using the L_DATA_CONNECT.confirmation.

Closing down the connection is achieved under normal circumstances using the L_DISCONNECT operation in its request, indication and confirmation forms. Clearing the link under abnormal conditions requires the use of L_RESET.

Acknowledged connectionless (type3) and polled response (type4)

These types were originated by request from the PROWAY (process control data highway) user group. PROWAY is discussed further in Chapter 5 as an application which has specified the use of the token passing bus LAN for its MAC and physical layers.

Type3 offer services between type1 and type2. It is a request–reply protocol, or a half-duplex protocol where the transmitter waits for an acknowledgment that the previous frame has arrived before sending the next.

Type4 may be used in cases where a low-cost master–slave arrangement is adequate for the purposes of the application. This occurs when slow input devices are attached to the network, as in some monitoring systems in process plants or factories. It is likely that this type will be used on top of the token passing bus or ring LAN. The idea is that a designated master station polls slave stations to ask them to send data to the master within a certain time period. Should the occasional reply message go missing this would not cause problems for the application. Thus a datagram basis is acceptable for this type.

In both cases the control field in the LLC PDU will be redefined to suit the needs of the protocol operation.

Finally, a likely option is that both acknowledged connectionless and polled response could be defined within a single new type3 of LLC.

References

Conard, J.W., (1983). 'Services and protocols of the data link layer' *Proc. IEEE*, **71**,(12), December, 1378–1383

DesJardins, R., (1983). 'Afterword: evolving towards OSI' *Proc. IEEE*, **71**,(12), December, 1446–1448

Digital, Intel and Xerox Corporations, (1980). 'Ethernet: a local area network – data link layer and physical layer specifications', version 1.0, September

FOCUS Committee, (1982). *Local area networks – report to the FOCUS committee* UK Dept of Trade and Industry, August

FOCUS Committee, (1983). *The user view of communications standards* UK Dept of Trade and Industry, May

IEEE, (1985). *Logical link control* Draft Standard 802.2, July

ISO, (1983). 'Data processing – Open Systems Interconnection – basic reference model' ISO 7498 reprinted in an earlier form in *Computer Networks* **5**,(2), April 1981, 81–118

Linington, P.F., (1983). 'Fundamentals of the layer service definitions and protocol specifications' *Proc. IEEE*, **71**,(12), December, 1341–1345

Wilkes, M.V. and Wheeler, D.J., (1979). 'The Cambridge digital communication ring' *Proc. Local Area Communications Network Symposium*, Mitre Corp., Boston, May, 47–60

Wood, B., (1982). 'International and national standards activity for open systems interconnection', Infotech State of the Art Report Series **10**,(1), *Network Architectures* Solomonides, C., editor

Zimmermann, H., (1980). 'OSI Reference Model – the ISO model of architecture for Open Systems Interconnection' *IEEE Transactions on Communications*, **COM-28**,(4), April, 425–432

Chapter 3
Types of LAN

As a preliminary to the detailed descriptions of local networks that follow in the next three chapters, this chapter compares and classifies the different types of local area network, and introduces the CSMA/CD (Ethernet), token ring and bus, and slotted (Cambridge) ring. A brief comparison of these specific local networks is given. Finally, technology trends in local networking are reviewed, including FDDI and integrated services local networks (ISLNs).

3.1 Introduction

So far we have described LANs as communications subsystems in the context of standards developments, and introduced specific local network technologies which are actively under standards consideration in the UK, USA and Europe. These are:

- CSMA/CD (Ethernet)
- token ring and bus
- slotted ring (Cambridge Ring).

Much of the research and development in LANs over the years is reflected in these three, and for this reason these technologies will be explored in greater detail in Chapters 4, 5 and 6. Many of the other interesting local network issues which have emerged during their development will be described along the way.

The fact that these networks are included in the LAN reference model (LAN/RM) is an indication of their 'openness' in the sense of open systems interconnection. They are intended to be interconnected with other LANs through bridges or gateways and so their protocols and addressing schemes are specified with internetworking strongly in mind.

In addition to the standard LAN technologies there are many other 'non-standard' LANs. Some have been developed as research vehicles (for example, Hutchison and Shepherd, 1981; Georganas and Mwikalo, 1982; Hutchison *et al.*, 1984), some as solutions to specific problems in various environments, and others as proprietary commercial products. Mostly they are 'closed' in the sense that they never require access by devices other than those currently attached on the one hand, or connection to external networks on the other hand. Often non-standard LANs interconnect only one manufacturer's computers or are used for only a very specific application (such as control of a chemical process plant). It is frequently found that privately developed protocols have been produced, tailored to the needs of the specific LAN.

Such LANs will continue to exist, although probably the emergence of new products will slow down as standards become more widely available. A reason why tailored LANs are likely to remain popular is that they can be designed from the 'top down', starting with the application requirements. The underlying software or hardware can be implemented to meet these needs in the most efficient way.

Standard LANs, on the other hand, attempt to provide a general purpose base on which applications software can be implemented. The criticism here is that the layers may impose unacceptably high performance overheads and thus may prove to be inefficient in operation. Time will tell whether the standard bases already available will suffice for a variety of applications. As experience with using LANs increases it may well be that new 'standard' architectures are developed to meet application needs. The LAN/RM is set up to accommodate new architectures.

In the case of the standard CSMA/CD, token ring and bus, and slotted ring, when we refer to 'technology' we mean their physical and MAC layers within the LAN/RM.

Architecture, as explained in Chapters 1 and 2, is a much wider term, covering all layers up to and including application software. Through a detailed study of the standard LAN technologies and associated developments, we shall learn about LAN architectures. There are, however, other issues in local area networking which can be missed by concentrating only on LAN/RM architectures; these come to the fore when we consider how LANs can be classified.

3.2 Classification of LANs

Perhaps the most common classification is that based on topology; this defines the way in which stations are connected to each other, and gives the logical shape of the network (rather than its physical layout).

3.2.1 Topologies

The basic topologies are shown in Figure 3.1. The star, bus and ring together are sufficient to cover all LANs if we consider these topologies as basic building blocks. The star has a central switch S which is responsible for making connections between sending and receiving nodes: this is regarded as an uninteresting LAN topology. The chief example of this type of LAN is the PABX, used to implement localized telephone systems for many years and now extended in capability to carry both voice and data.

Ethernet is usually said to have a bus topology, but in reality it is a tree consisting of a number of connected bus segments. Another, less convenient, way of looking at this is that a bus is a special case of a tree, being a tree which has no branches.

Topology, however, tells us only about the logical shape of the communications medium as it interconnects stations on the network, and is thus a rather restrictive means of classification. It does not even detail the topography of the LAN – this is the actual path which the communications medium takes. For example, as we shall see in Chapter 5 (on the token ring), it is common practice to arrange the topography of a topological ring in the shape of a star – this improves fault tracing and system availability. Topographical layout is usually determined by engineering considerations or simply geographical constraints and is itself hardly worthy of inclusion as a classification criterion.

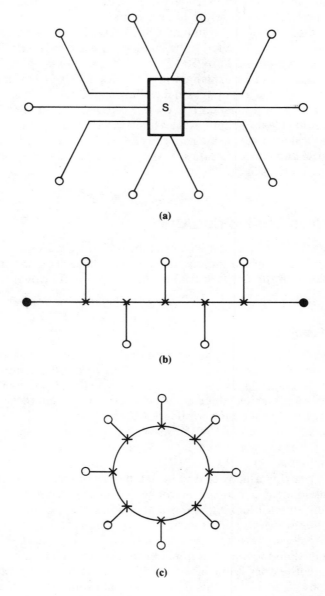

Figure 3.1   Basic LAN topologies: (a) star, (b) bus, (c) ring.

Nevertheless, topology has been found to be a useful means of distinguishing LANs because it is simple to understand. Figure 3.2 shows the sort of classification which can result.

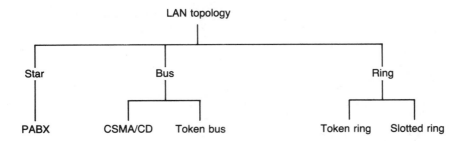

Figure 3.2   LAN classification by topology.

3.2.2   Other classification criteria

Other classification criteria include:

- network access protocol
- communications data rate
- LAN functionality
- application domain.

The first two of these, along with topology, depend solely on the LAN technology and not on any LAN/RM layer higher than the MAC. Access protocol is the chief characteristic of the MAC layer, while data rate is determined within the physical layer beneath. Table 3.1 gives a classification matrix using the three features of topology, access protocol and data rate. Together these are normally used to categorize LAN technologies.

The features in this diagram give no clues about the use of the corresponding standard LANs. Whereas in the first years of LANs' evolution the majority interest lay in precisely these technological features, nowadays there is much more emphasis on applications or what capabilities a LAN has in terms of the sort of traffic it can handle.

Although in this book we concentrate on the standard LANs, it must be reemphasized that in addition there are very many proprietary networks which collectively use a variety of access protocols (and operate at a wide variety of data rates). Following Hammond (1986) we may classify network access protocols into the following categories:

- fixed assignment
- random assignment
- demand assignment
- adaptive assignment.

Table 3.1 A LAN classification matrix.

	Feature		
	topology	*access protocol*	*data rate*
Standard LAN			
Ethernet	bus (tree)	CSMA/CD	10 Mbits/sec
token bus	bus	token passing	1, 5 or 10 Mbits/sec
token ring	ring	token passing	1 or 4 Mbits/sec
Cambridge Ring	ring	empty slot	10 Mbits/sec
Non-standard LAN			
PABX	star	(not applicable)	(various)
micronet	bus or ring	(various)	typically < 1 Mbits/sec

Fixed assignment

The first of these categories assigns a fixed proportion of the available bandwidth to each station (whether it is transmitting or not). The two main examples of this are FDM (frequency division multiplexing) and TDM (time division multiplexing). In the first case each station is allocated a particular frequency sub-band and in the second each is allocated a regular time slot which repeats in a cyclic fashion. Despite the simplicity of fixed assignment, its obvious disadvantage is the preallocation of bandwidth to stations which may not always need their portion.

Random assignment

Random techniques include the CSMA/CD method used in Ethernet, but cover a range of protocols each having slightly different characteristics. The 'most random' of all is that of pure ALOHA (the inspiration for Ethernet, to be outlined in Chapter 4), in which a station wishing to send a message simply does so, onto the common broadcast medium. Messages are acknowledged by the receiving station. This works well for a rarely used medium, but collisions between competing transmissions occur so increasingly frequently as traffic increases that the maximum utilization of an ALOHA system is only some 18% of its possible bandwidth. In this and the following schemes, collisions are deduced by a lack of acknowledgment, after a certain timeout period, from the station to which the message was sent.

Pure ALOHA can be improved on by introducing a slotted scheme in which transmission time is split into time slots, and transmission is allowed to begin only at the beginning of a slot. This simple measure doubles the maximum utilization of the pure (non-slotted) ALOHA method.

However, it was discovered that 'listening before talking' or CSMA (carrier sense multiple access) is a very effective technique, in which a station wishing to transmit first senses the medium to see whether it is quiet and thus available for use. This avoids unnecessary collisions and greatly improves the network utilization, but requires a strategy when a station discovers that the medium is being used by another station. These strategies vary according to the **persistence** of the station in retrying to access the medium.

A **non-persistent** protocol will wait for a random time before re-sensing the medium. This wastes bandwidth should no other station be ready to transmit once the medium becomes quiet. A **1-persistent** protocol continuously monitors the medium until it becomes quiet and then transmits. Of course two or more concurrently waiting stations are bound to find their messages collide (determined by a lack of acknowledgment). Between these extremes is the **p-persistent** scheme which attempts to make a compromise between using bandwidth to best effect and reducing the number of collisions. If the medium is busy, the station monitors it until it becomes quiet. Once quiet, the station transmits with probability p, or else waits with probability $(1 - p)$ for one time slot equal to the maximum propagation delay of the network. The key choice in the p-persistent scheme is what value p should have. The larger the value the more likely that collisions will occur; if smaller, collisions will be reduced in number but stations will have to wait longer on average before they may transmit. A vital factor is that the product $n \times p$ must be less than 1, where n is the expected peak number of stations waiting to transmit simultaneously – otherwise at peak times there will be successions of multiple collisions, the network will break down and will give no service at all.

Another refinement is that of 'listen while talking' or CSMA/CD (carrier sense multiple access with collision detection), the well-known Ethernet access protocol, which attempts to ensure that bandwidth is not wasted throughout the transmission of colliding frames. This protocol will be taken up and described in detail in Chapter 4.

Demand and adaptive assignment

These protocols allocate bandwidth as and when required by stations wishing to transmit messages, avoiding idle stations as best they can. Demand schemes use either central control, as in polling systems, or distributed control, as is found in many ring networks (including token passing and slotted rings).

Adaptive protocols are little used in practice, being rather complex in operation. These attempt to adapt to varying network conditions and may require each station to have knowledge of the current network loading. In the schemes that have been implemented, it is common for the protocol to adapt at high loads to polling or TDM, but at low loads to be some form of random access.

3.2.3 LAN functionality

In 1982 the UK report to the FOCUS committee entitled *Local Area Networks* (FOCUS, 1982) stated that potential LAN users were primarily interested in the functionality of LANs. This is not quite the same as application domain as we shall see shortly. The report lists four categories of functionality which users require:

(1) micronets
(2) non-integrated networks
(3) integrated networks
(4) videonets.

The first two were by and large already well satisfied by available commercial products, the others however being future developments. Non-standard LANs are not excluded from the list – in fact all examples of category (1) are non-standard at present. Under each heading the report includes the essential and some typical characteristics of the class.

3.2.4 Micronets

Micronets usually exist to provide shared disk storage for a number of microcomputers of the same type. In order to make them commercially attractive they must have low-cost connections to attach devices to the network, where low cost means roughly a few hundred dollars (as opposed to a few thousand to connect devices to Ethernet). Typically, says the report, this type of LAN will have up to 64 or so attached devices, and its use is primarily to give access to shared resources such as printers or file servers. The implication is also that this would be a closed type of network, although the report points out that there may be a need to provide a gateway to external facilities in some cases. Although no data rates are specified, to achieve the target low costs it is unlikely that micronets will have data rates exceeding 1 Mbits/sec and more usually the figure would be nearer 100 Kbits/sec. Commercial examples of micronets are:

- Omninet
- PC-net
- Point 32

- Econet
- Clearway.

Research examples include Strathnet (Hutchison and Shepherd, 1981) and Platon (Georganas and Mwikalo, 1982). The LAN/RM will include examples of micronets in the future, and such an example may be Cheapernet which is presently being groomed for standardization. This works in the same way as Ethernet but achieves, as the name suggests, the same functionality at considerably lower cost. In the terminology of the LAN/RM, Cheapernet has the same MAC layer protocols as CSMA/CD but differs at the physical layer by employing cheaper (CATV technology) coaxial cable and connection techniques. Cheapness is also made possible by using an Ethernet chip set, which (when volume sales bring down costs to the expected tens of dollars – or pounds) cuts down the complexity of controller board implementation. Intended costs are half that of 'full' Ethernet versions, which brings Cheapernet in firmly at the upper end of conceivable micronet price and performance ranges.

3.2.5 Non-integrated networks

Non-integrated networks are further sub-classified into four types:

- probabilistic datanets
- deterministic datanets
- voicenets
- broadband datanets.

These are non-integrated in that data and voice are carried on separate communications media and incidentally require separate network management facilities. Most of the current standards interest centres round this type of LAN, and the subclasses reflect the current technologies of the LAN/RM.

The notion of network management (NM) has only recently arisen in respect of local networks (Coffield and Hutchison, 1985). In its widest sense NM means providing facilities for ensuring the proper day-to-day operation of the network so that users are given as high an availability as possible. This involves monitoring for faults, checking network performance, ensuring smooth handling of maintenance operations and, if necessary, accounting for usage.

Although for example results have been published showing that Ethernet is capable of supporting voice and data on a shared cable (Shoch, 1980; Swinehart et al., 1984), and digital PABXs can support data transmission in addition to voice, shared LAN interfaces for voice and data are at an early stage of development and this is why separate cabling (and NM) are said to be needed in the non-integrated class of LAN.

The subclass capabilities directly reflect current LAN technologies. Probabilistic datanets are CSMA/CD systems primarily, deterministic are exemplified by token passing systems and the slotted ring, voicenets are digital PABXs, and broadband datanets include non-standard LANs such as Wangnet and Sytek's LocalNet.

3.2.6 Integrated networks

The integrated LANs are also subclassified, into

- broadband
- high speed baseband.

The intention is that the first of these will include real-time voice as a channel within the broadband datanet subclass of the non-integrated network. The second will combine deterministic datanet and voicenet capabilities within the single baseband channel. Typical characteristics indicate that these LANs would provide at least 100 Mbits/sec raw data rates.

In the wide area network networking domain the integrated services digital network (ISDN) is being developed so that true integration of voice and data is provided using a common standard interface and common cabling (Wiley and Hutchison, 1985; Rutkowski, 1985). The local network equivalent, the ISLN, has been the subject of more recent work, and an important development towards a standard technology is the FDDI (fibre distributed data interface) which has emerged from the ANSI X3T9.5 working group (Flatman and Caves, 1986).

ISDN

In the early 1980s the CCITT began to develop detailed recommendations on an integrated services digital network, with the goal of eventually producing a network capable of using the same switching and communications equipment for the whole range of traffic, in particular voice, data, facsimile, and video.

In fact, the idea (and the term ISDN) already existed within the CCITT in 1972, even though the technology did not exist at the time to carry the idea to completion. It was recognized that several steps would be required to achieve the full development of ISDN, from a 'narrow-band' integrated digital access (IDA) at a basic rate of 64 Kbits/sec with segregated networks behind the scenes (the PSTN and PDN, leased lines etc.), to a broadband system operating at many Mbits/sec over a truly integrated network.

In the late 1980s, **basic rate** systems are already available in several countries, and so-called **primary rate** (at 2 Mbits/sec) is fast being introduced. However, the most important part as far as the user is concerned is the access or user interface to the ISDN (whether there are segregated networks or a single one transporting the information should in any case be invisible to the user). This has been recognized by the CCITT, which has been developing the I-series protocols which define the user interface to the ISDN, and it is towards these standards that national ISDNs are being progressed.

Several important factors in determining the route to complete network integration are technology capabilities, technology costs, and regulatory issues, of which the last may well prove to be the most challenging. It may be that these factors dictate the long term existence of separate networks in some cases, with integration being provided only at the user interface.

The two standardized user interfaces at present, the basic rate and primary rate, are covered by the I.420 and I.421 recommendations respectively. In the same way as the X.25 access protocol for packet switching networks has three components corresponding to the lowermost three layers of the OSI model, the ISDN access protocol details are further covered by I.430 (basic) and I.431 (primary) for layer 1, by I.440/441 for layer 2, and by I.450/451 for layer 3.

There are two types of channel in the ISDN, called B channels (for voice or data) and D channels (for signalling and system use). The main purpose of the D channel is to allow so-called **out-band** signalling; in other words network systems functions such as call setup and error indications to be passed using a separate channel from the data/voice channels. The D channel can also be used to convey user data if required. Contrast this with the present (analogue) telephone system, in which call setup and voice transmission use the same channel, at different times.

The configurations offered at the basic and primary rate user interfaces are as follows:

    basic: 2B + D
    primary: 30B + D (UK and Europe)
               23B + D (USA and South East Asia)

Basic rate interfaces are intended for domestic and similar individual network users, and offer two data/voice channels each capable of 64 Kbits/sec operation, plus a signalling channel of 16 Kbits/sec. This will be offered at a wall socket in much the same way as the present telephone service. The provision of ISDN into domestic premises will, fortunately, not require the replacement of all the existing local 2-wire loops which run from the telephone to the local exchange. These local loops (average length of a few kilometres) are sufficient to allow the basic rate transmission of 192 Kbits/sec (2B + D as above, plus system timing equivalent to 48 Kbits/sec). What basic rate in the home does imply, of course, is the replacement of the existing telephone by suitable network terminating equipment which will incorporate the ISDN equivalent of OSI layers 1–3, plus adaptors for the various end user equipment to be attached to the ISDN. This will include a digital telephone incorporating a codec chip for digitizing voice.

Primary rate will be used by businesses, typically those having a PABX and requiring a multiplicity of 64 Kbits/sec lines. Some applications may require a bandwidth greater than 64 Kbits/sec, for example slow-scan video may need 256 Kbits/sec, and interprocess communication in distributed computing a similar (if not greater) bandwidth. This is termed **wideband** ISDN.

It is intended that wideband ISDN can be provided by concatenation of 64 Kbits/sec channels, so long as the setup procedure ensures equal delays along the multiple 64 Kbits/sec paths. This is currently a matter for research; whether the underlying network is circuit or packet based there are (separate) problems in ensuring successful concatenation.

The above represent **narrowband** ISDN developments, which will not be commercially available in most European countries or in widespread use in the USA until the late 1980s. Even before this comes about, significant development work is taking place on **broadband** ISDN, in which video (bandwidth requirement at least 5 Mbits/sec) and other high bandwidth applications will be carried. For example, in Europe, the RACE R&D programme aims to develop an IBC (integrated broadband communications) network by the mid 1990s having information channels of aggregate bandwidth well into the Gbits/sec range (i.e. thousands of Mbits/sec capacity).

FDDI

The fibre distributed data interface is intended as a standard for a 100 Mbits/sec fibre optic ring. Based on the IEEE/ISO 802.5 token ring, it was originally intended as a fast interconnection medium for CPUs and peripheral devices – a serial replacement for a backplane bus. The first edition, FDDI-I, was indeed a 100 Mbits/sec version of 802.5.

However, this is likely to be superseded by FDDI-II which combines the 'packet switching' features of the first version with a 'circuit switching' capability. This combination of capabilities makes FDDI-II a strong candidate for standardization as an ISLN, because ISLNs will have to interwork with PTT networks, offering end-to-end guaranteed bandwidth based on multiples of 64 Kbits/sec as well as a packet switching alternative.

Basically, the bandwidth is split up into 16 channels each of 6.144 Mbits/sec plus a residual 1.696 Mbits/sec. The residual bandwidth is intended for control and system timing in much the same way as the D channel is used in the ISDN.

The 6.144 Mbits/sec channel is adequate for carrying video images, currently one of the highest bandwidth applications envisaged for ISLNs or ISDNs. Each 6.144 Mbits/sec channel is composed of 96 individual 64 Kbits/sec subchannels, and can be reserved for either circuit or packet switching. It is also possible to use around 1 Mbits/sec of the residual 1.696 Mbits/sec bandwidth for packet switching data purposes, if required.

3.2.7 Videonets

The fourth class of LAN is the videonet, which certainly seems to be a more futuristic system. The aim here is to have a very high speed baseband transmission giving full video capabilities; this would require bandwidths of the order of several hundred megabits per second and furthermore individual station interface transfer capabilities of 100 Mbits/sec.

3.3 Applications

Functionality and application domains are not the same thing. Given, for example, a deterministic datanet with a raw data rate of 4 Mbits/sec, its applications could be as different as an office automation system or a factory shop floor management and control system or a shipborne real-time control network. Building a LAN for use in a specific application implies the provision of higher level software to tailor the LAN for that use. We are not here concerned with the higher level software but in the demands made by the application on the communications subsystem. The questions which users are interested in asking are these:

- Is the underlying LAN suitable for my application?
- Is the technology up to the job?
- Is this LAN the most cost-effective one for my application?

This is much the same as questioning whether a given operating system is suitable for a particular application. LAN technologies bear the same sort of relationship to their application domains as do operating systems to theirs. Thus in much the same way as no one operating system has been universally acclaimed as an ideal basis, so the same is true of LANs.

A good initial grouping of LAN application domains is into the following two broad areas:

- office
- industrial.

The terms used here are broadly indicative of two different types of requirements, on which very little has been published, but which are clearly very important for LAN users. The majority of LANs at present are used in 'office' applications, including the so-called automated office (Naffah, 1981).

Typically a number of word processing stations and simple VDU terminals – or, increasingly, personal computers – are linked together for the dual purposes of interpersonnel communication through electronic mail/messaging and sharing of resources such as filestore or quality printers. Similarly, in university computer centres there are now LANs used basically for these same purposes.

These are both examples of 'office' applications because they share the following requirements of the underlying LAN:

- high speed communications, so that each station gets significantly more bandwidth than the 9600 bits/sec normally available with a V.24 serial line. Probabilistic access to the network may suffice for each station.

- no real-time requirements other than to satisfy a user's wish for subsecond response times. (In a few cases LANs are used to swap disk pages and in this sense the critical time of the disk unit imposes a real-time constraint. An example is the use of the Cambridge Ring for swapping in the Cambridge Distributed Computing System (Needham and Herbert, 1982).)

- the environment is not hostile, i.e. there are no significant electromagnetic noise sources. Nor is there likely to be physical damage from the environment.

- there is normally no problem in reconfiguring the system; units can be added or removed by asking or insisting that users log off. Users in any case expect 'down time' in the normal course of events.

On the other hand, 'industrial' LAN applications have very different requirements (Le Lann, 1983). Take the case of a network used as the basis of a distributed monitoring and control system within an aircraft:

- Communications may need to be not only high speed but also deterministic. It may be essential for proper operation of the application system to guarantee a minimum bandwidth for each station.

- There are thus stringent real-time requirements to be met by the LAN. Furthermore, there may be a need to cater for emergency messages which have higher priority than normal transmissions.

- This type of LAN would normally be situated in a hostile environment, where the chance of significant noise or radiation may occur and the system must be protected against these. This involves the use of fibre optic communications media, radiation-hardened chips, 'military specification' standards and specially rigorous predelivery hardware (and software) testing.

- In this type of application reliability and availability are critical; loss of life and heavy financial losses may occur should the LAN go faulty.

- Automatic fault detection, reporting and use of replicated standby units is necessary.

It seems certain that LANs classification in the future will take strong account of applications. It remains to be seen which LAN bases will be suitable for the broad classes of office and industrial applications, and within these which LANs best fit the exact requirements. Much more user experience with LANs is necessary before this can be done.

The remainder of this chapter introduces the basics of the standard LANs as a concise description of the different types of technologies. We then look ahead a few years to the types of LAN which will be developing.

3.4 Technologies

Putting aside the circuit switched PABX LAN technology, the majority of LAN advances have been based on bus and ring topologies and on their associated protocols. Because the communications medium is shared amongst all the attached network devices, an arbitration scheme must be provided to resolve competition between devices wishing to transmit data.

Rather than having a single master device which acts as arbiter, LANs use distributed control, i.e. they let the devices, which all have equal status, sort out cable contention themselves. This avoids having to rely on the master never failing. These distributed control schemes are called medium access control (MAC) protocols in the LAN standards documents and it is primarily these protocols which serve to distinguish one type of LAN from another.

The most prominent MAC protocols:

- CSMA/CD (Ethernet bus),
- token passing (bus or ring),
- empty slot (Cambridge Ring),

are briefly explained as follows.

CSMA/CD, as we have previously seen, means carrier sense multiple access with collision detection. In this scheme a station's network access unit (NAU) wishing to transmit data first senses the bus to see whether any traffic is already passing along it. If so, the NAU tries again a little later. If not, the NAU begins to transmit. It is possible for two or more NAUs to begin transmitting at exactly the same instant, however, both or all having seen the bus free. A collision would then occur, in which the data streams from transmitting NAUs would corrupt one another. Each NAU therefore watches the bus, as it transmits, and if it observes a collision its own transmission is stopped. Each NAU involved in the collision backs off for a random time interval before beginning the bus sensing procedure again. In this way further collisions between the original participants are extremely unlikely.

Two characteristics of CSMA/CD are worth mention. Firstly, when the demand on the bus becomes very high (many stations trying to transmit around the same time) the probability of collisions goes up rapidly and the number of successful transmissions tends to zero. Secondly, an upper bound cannot be given on the access time for a given station trying to access the bus for transmission: the CSMA/CD scheme is said to be **probabilistic** because of this. Section 3.4.1 discusses performance issues further.

The token bus and ring operate in a similar way to each other, except that in the bus topology (which uses coaxial cable) the stations form a logical ring in which each station knows the address of both its logical predecessor and successor. A free token which carries the right to use the transmission medium circulates continuously round the physical ring (in the case of the ring topology) or the logical one (in the case of the bus). A station wishing to transmit data waits for the free token to arrive, marks it as busy and sends a data packet. At the end of transmission the token is marked as free and sent on to the next station in the ring. This scheme is fair because the right to use the medium passes in a round-robin fashion from one station to the next.

A maximum length is defined for data packets being transmitted, so an upper bound can be placed on the time a given station must wait before it can use the bus or ring. This can be calculated knowing how many stations are in the ring (physical or logical) and is the case when all stations send a maximum length packet during one complete traversal of the ring by the free token. Thus token passing LANs are said to be **deterministic** and it is for this reason that potential LAN users in the industrial real-time area side with token passing rather than CSMA/CD. There is a problem which affects guaranteed upper bounds on token network access times, and that occurs when the token becomes corrupted following noise or some failure on the network. The LAN standards define complicated token recovery procedures which it is yet to be demonstrated will satisfy the rather strict timeliness requirements of real-time LAN users.

At increasingly high loads token passing systems do not degrade as CSMA/CD does, but lightly loaded token LANs have the overhead of a fixed access latency (the free token traversal time round a quiet ring) whereas stations in CSMA/CD LANs do not need to wait before transmitting data. Section 3.4.1 gives more details on comparative performances.

The Cambridge Ring, developed at Cambridge University Computer Laboratory, but now commercially available from several UK companies, uses the empty slot principle. In this system a fixed length minipacket continuously circulates the ring. In the header there is a bit indicating whether the minipacket is full or empty. A station wishing to transmit data can use an empty minipacket as it passes by marking the header bit full and filling the data part of the minipacket. The minipacket cannot be reused by the same station twice or more in succession without being sent downstream on the ring with the header bit marked empty. This ensures fairness amongst stations.

The minipacket is so called because it tends to be very short (40 bits in current implementations, and only 16 bits of this for data) in order to fit it into the closed ring. Depending on the number of stations in a given configuration, there may be room for a few minipackets head to tail round the ring. The medium used tends to be twisted pair wires, but some rings have segments of fibre optic cable which allow the distance between stations to be increased without using intermediate repeaters and give the prospect of higher speed Cambridge Rings (100 Mbits/sec implementations are currently being developed).

3.4.1 Comparison of technologies

A vitally important aspect of LAN technologies is their comparative performance. For the end user the importance is in the end-to-end performance of the network at the application level, for example how fast does a particular network transfer a file of a certain size, or what is the response time when logging in or editing a file on a computer located remotely over a network. If we assume the OSI model and imagine the same set of upper layer protocols whatever the underlying network technology, then our comparison reduces to distinguishing between the specific layer 2 and 1 protocols on the different LANs, or using the IEEE 802 terminology, between the combination of MAC and physical layer protocols for each LAN.

In this section we summarize the known results of comparisons between the standard LANs. We are mainly concerned with CSMA/CD (Ethernet), the token passing LANs and the slotted ring. For a fuller account of their comparative performance analysis, see Hammond (1986).

But what exactly is meant by 'performance'? Two measures are normally used: delay and throughput.

Delay refers to the time that a station having a frame ready to send must wait before it is allowed to access the medium. The lower the delay, the better. Although the average delay for a particular type of LAN may be acceptably low, in some applications (where real-time response is a critical issue) the maximum delay a station may experience is more important. In measuring performance it is usual to evaluate delay as a function of the total traffic load being offered to the network by the attached stations.

As already mentioned, the CSMA/CD access protocol is probabilistic and cannot guarantee an upper bound on a station's access time. Unless the probability of the access delay being within some critical figure is high, say 99.5% – which could be obtained by ensuring that the maximum loading on the network is low (say 50% of maximum capacity) – then the CSMA/CD protocol is likely to be unacceptable for real-time users.

On the other hand, the token passing protocols and the slotted ring are deterministic and yield upper bounds for a station's access delay, in the absence of failures, and are usually considered suitable for time-critical applications.

In a lightly loaded network, particularly one having a large number of attached stations, the average access delay is still significantly large because the token or minipacket still has to visit all the stations in turn. A station in a lightly loaded CSMA/CD (or other random access) LAN is likely to be able to access the medium with very low delay since there is a very low probability of a collision occurring. In such circumstances a CSMA/CD network would seem to be preferable.

The **throughput** of a LAN refers to the rate of information it can carry. This too is measured as a function of the total load being offered to the network.

Several factors contribute to the evaluation of a network's performance. Principally these are:

(1)   capacity

(2)   propagation delay

(3)   frame length

(4)   number of stations

(5)   offered load

(6)   access protocol

(7)   error rate of the medium.

The last of these can be dismissed for LANs because of their inherently low error rate (the same cannot be assumed for wide area networks operating over the PSTN or over leased lines). For a given LAN, all the other factors apart from (5) are determined by the network configuration and the layer 1 and 2 protocols.

Capacity is the maximum raw data rate (R) in bits per second of the medium, for example 10 Mbits/sec for the standard CSMA/CD LAN. Each station transmits its frames at this rate.

Propagation delay is the time taken for a frame to travel the length of the network. Because the propagation speed (S) of the various media used in LANs is much the same, approximately two thirds of the speed of light or 200 million metres per second, this delay is entirely determined by the length (L) of the network.

Frame length (F) is the number of bits in the transmitted frame. Apart from the slotted ring, LANs operate a range of frame lengths, typically from a few tens of bytes up to a few thousand bytes.

The maximum number of stations on any LAN is fixed by the layer 1 and 2 protocols. Obviously the more stations, the less bandwidth they can each use if they all wish to transmit frames. Assuming a fair access protocol, each of N stations attempting to transmit frames continuously gets $1/N$ of the network capacity on average.

The network loading depends on the aggregate traffic generated by all N stations attached to the network. It is possible for the offered load (O) to exceed by far the capacity of the medium, and in that case the ideal behaviour of the LAN protocol is to ensure $1/N$ bandwidth sharing. However, LANs operating under random access protocols (including CSMA/CD) do not exhibit this behaviour and the performance of these networks tends to break down under heavy loads.

The access protocol itself is therefore a key factor in determining the performance of the LAN, and much attention has been paid to comparing the different sorts of protocols under a variety of conditions. Both analytical and simulation studies have been employed (Hammond, 1986), the former to provide mathematical or 'paper' models of the key elements of a network, the latter to build a fairly realistic model of a network in operation.

The conditions under which the comparisons are made depend on the values chosen for factors (1)–(5) above. Typically, F and L are varied using a fixed R and a fixed number of stations. For each combination of F and L the offered loading is varied.

In order to minimize the number of combinations, F is perhaps allowed to take only two different values, say the minimum and maximum frame lengths allowed by the (layer 2) protocol. L is perhaps given only two or three different values, say 10 m, 100 m or 1000 m, again within the range allowed by the (layer 1) protocol.

From such studies emerges a very important measure, namely the ratio of propagation delay to frame transmission time (Stallings, 1986). As we shall see below, this measure is important in determining the throughput of a network. The ratio is given by:

A = propagation delay divided by transmission time

= L/S divided by F/R

= LR/SF

But LR/S represents the length of the LAN in bits, so the ratio can alternatively be expressed as:

A = bit length of LAN divided by frame length

The standard CSMA/CD LAN, with a 500 m segment length and transmission rate of 10 Mbits/sec, has a 'bit length' of 25 bits. This represents the number of bits in transit along the length of the medium during transmission. By contrast, a wide area or long haul network may have thousands of bits in transit, while a typical multiprocessor system operating over a very short distance may have only a few bits (or bytes) in transit on its communications bus (which may be a parallel rather than serial bus). The bit length of a network has an impact on the nature of the communications protocols which may, or should, be implemented. For example, on a long haul network a stop-and-wait protocol, whereby each packet has to be separately acknowledged by the receiver before the transmitter sends the next, may be highly inefficient in its use of bandwidth if the average packet length is significantly shorter than the bit length of the medium.

Another point of interest arising from the formula derived is that keeping the product LR constant ensures constant behaviour of a network, for example a network with L=500 m and R=10 Mbits/sec is equivalent to one with L=1000 m and R=5 Mbits/sec. This is because both networks have the same bit length.

Returning to throughput as one of the important measures of performance, this may be quoted as a percentage of its capacity R, in which case the figure is interpreted as the utilization (U) of the network. Ideally, as O increases, the utilization (and throughput) should steadily increase, until the offered load matches the capacity of the network to carry traffic. It should be possible to keep increasing the offered load beyond the maximum capacity without the network performance degrading. Figure 3.3 shows the ideal utilization of a LAN. Notice that the offered load O is also 'normalized', i.e. quoted as a ratio against capacity R.

Unfortunately, real LANs do not conform to this ideal. Importantly, the access protocol itself limits the utilization which can be achieved. In all cases the protocol imposes overheads due to the control information

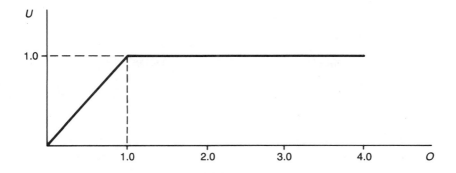

Figure 3.3   Ideal utilization of a LAN.

carried in each frame. Furthermore, in CSMA/CD LANs collisions consume bandwidth; in the token passing LANs token rotation consumes bandwidth; and in the slotted ring a fixed (and considerable) percentage of the raw bandwidth is taken up by the continuously circulating minipackets.

Let us consider how the ratio A affects throughput in a local network. We make the assumption that each transmission begins when the previous one has just been received at the farthest station on the network. The utilization U is the ratio of frame transmission time to the sum of frame transmission time plus propagation time along the length of the medium. That is:

$$U = (F/R) \, / \, (F/R + L/S)$$
$$= 1 \, / \, (1 + LR/SF)$$
$$= 1 \, / \, (1 + A)$$

This is a protocol-independent result and shows that U varies inversely with the value of A, i.e. for good utilization A must be kept as small as possible. This implies long frames and as short a network length as possible. Figure 3.4 shows the variation of U against A.

Taking the value of A into account, Figure 3.5 is a revised version of Figure 3.3 showing how U varies with offered load for different values of A. Thus A places an upper bound on the utilization which can be achieved for a particular network. Over and above the limitations on utilization implicit in A, each access protocol imposes its own overheads depending particularly on the offered load on the network.

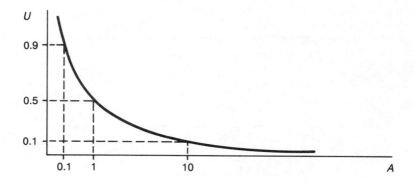

Figure 3.4   The effect of A on utilization.

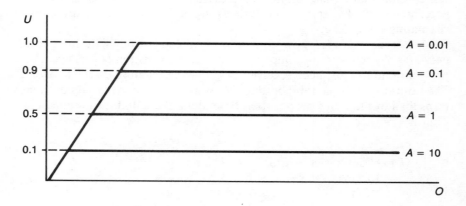

Figure 3.5 U against O for different values of A.

A comparative study of the different access protocols would investigate both delay and throughput. In fact access delay may be plotted as a function of throughput for several combinations of factors including A and offered load. The results for the common LAN access protocols are well documented (Hammond, 1986).

If ring LANs are compared, it is found that the token ring gives best performance under a variety of conditions, whereas the slotted ring performs best when the number of stations is large and the ring propagation delay is long.

When CSMA/CD is compared with the token bus, it is found that the token bus makes more effective use of bandwidth than CSMA/CD. Under most conditions, the token bus gives a maximum utilization close to 1, whereas CSMA/CD is sensitive to the value of A. For example, for a standard 10 Mbits/sec CSMA/CD with a bus length of 2.5 km, A is 0.23 for minimum length frames of 64 bytes – and this gives a maximum value for U of only 0.46. For maximum frames of 1518 bytes A is 0.01, giving a maximum U of 0.93. In general, CSMA/CD gives smaller access delays at low offered loads, whereas the token bus gives a greater maximum throughput of data.

In terms of performance, there is no 'best' LAN for all possible circumstances. When it comes to choosing a LAN for a particular application, there may indeed be other factors which are more fundamental in determining which LAN to use. These include the availability of network access units for the customer's host computers and the cost of the hardware offered by the various vendors. In this respect, as mentioned in Section 3.2.2, an area of some research interest is the development of hybrid access protocols which attempt to combine the best features of existing protocols, for example taking the characteristics of CSMA/CD at low loads but adapting to, say, a token passing scheme at higher levels of loading.

3.5 Looking ahead

Once ISO accept the draft LAN standards proposed by IEEE 802 and ECMA (and also BSI) there will be a firm foundation for LANs of the near future. Technology developments and new MAC protocols will fit in with the LAN/RM structure and give a well organized growth path in which LAN manufacturers and software developers in particular can feel comfortable because of the existence of, and presumably adherence to, standards.

Many new developments in LANs are going to happen over the next few years, some of these are already under way. There will be a very large increase in the number and variety of LAN applications, particularly in the industrial real-time areas where volume sales will be greatest. New VLSI chips specially developed for LAN interfaces, and embodying the MAC plus higher layer protocols, will reduce implementation costs. Already available are CSMA/CD, token ring, token bus and Cambridge Ring chip sets.

The semiconductor companies will be keeping a close watch on progress in the PROWAY/miniMAP working group which is defining standards for process control 'data highways' or LANs. This group operates under the IEC (International Electrotechnical Commission) and is working in close cooperation with IEEE 802 and ISO so that the standards when produced fit in with the LAN/RM. The PROWAY group have chosen a modified token bus as a basis for their technology (see Chapter 5 for further details of PROWAY).

A related, and growing, activity is that of Fieldbus, which is a developing specification for a low cost, moderately low performance network for use in monitoring and control applications in industrial environments such as manufacturing and process control. There are several contenders aspiring to be the basis for the standardized Fieldbus. These include the 1553B avionics multiplexed bus, the Intel Bitbus, the IEEE P1118 bus, and a French offering called FIP.

Other research and development work worldwide is investigating technologies and protocols suitable for real-time applications, in which issues such as reliability, correctness, promptness and reconfigurability are vital. The General Motors MAP (manufacturing automation protocol) initiative has generated much interest and activity in the related issues of networking in factory manufacturing applications. The communications technology chosen is token passing bus, for reasons to be outlined in Chapter 5. Its working groups in the USA and Europe are closely connected with the OSI standardization process, and are now mainly concerned with the relevance of higher layer protocols (session layer and above) to manufacturing applications, particularly the manufacturing message service (MMS) which is one of the OSI layer 7 SASE protocols.

Many other future directions for LANs can be seen. Some of these are as follows.

- Higher data rates will be used for existing communications media, principally using broadband techniques. It is expected that the cost of transmit and receive equipment will come down, mainly as a result of using CATV technology.

- Fibre optic media will become much more widely used, once it costs less. Extremely high bandwidth is available, and other advantages over copper media include freedom from electromagnetic noise problems, lightness and very small diameter.

- There will be an increased range of LAN types which will become identifiable with classes of applications, offering the customer different price/performance characteristics. The cost of stations, with associated firmware or software, will be reduced from those of today by a factor of ten within five years or so.

- LANs will be used as a basis for closely-coupled systems. In these systems, the high speed and reliability characteristics of LAN technologies enables remote procedure call (RPC) protocols to link remote processes together as if they are within the same physical processor. Distributed operating systems and their associated resource management protocols will be developed for closely coupled LAN configurations. There are many possible application domains for such systems, including integrated project support environments (IPSEs) for large scale software development, and real-time process control.

- Automotive and domestic applications will become more prominent, using fibre optic or CATV technology and specially developed VLSI chips. Home management systems including central heating control and security are likely to be based on LANs – but these depend heavily on LAN costs dropping dramatically. The replacement of thick wire bundles in cars and other vehicles by fibre optic highways is already under consideration and indeed development by manufacturers, but once again lower costs of components are crucial. In the car of the future we shall see monitoring and control of engine and other parts by means of distributed microprocessors interconnected by a LAN. This sort of technique is now being used in some of the newest aircraft and is referred to as 'fly-by-wire'. Shipborne applications of this nature are also under development. Of course reliability is at least as important as cost in these sorts of LAN.

- In office applications, principally, the ISLN (integrated services local network) is going to become very important. This is the localized counterpart of the ISDN (D for digital) beginning to be offered as a service by British Telecom and other national PTTs. The ISLN will be capable of carrying voice, data, facsimile and video using the one integrated communications medium. Very high bandwidth is required for video, so at present separate LANs are likely to be used for this purpose. Contenders for reduced capability ISLNs today are the PABX and the standard LANs described earlier, one of the strongest being the recent FDDI developed by ANSI. However, whereas the PABX is good for carrying voice, it is less flexible for data applications, and the other LANs which were developed for data traffic are less obviously capable of transmitting voice. Though PABXs will capture much of the market in the short term, high speed baseband and eventually broadband LANs look set to be the basis for the ISLN of the more distant future.

3.6 Ongoing issues

Independently of advances in technology there are two important issues about which there is ongoing debate amongst researchers and those involved in standards work. First, whether connection-oriented (CO) or connectionless (CL) operation is better for particular applications, and whether and how these can be made available as alternatives throughout the layers of the OSI and LAN reference models (Chapin, 1983).

Not unrelated to this is the second issue, that of whether the OSI upper layers (principally layers 5 to 7) are suitable for building a variety of distributed computing applications.

3.6.1 CO *vs* CL operation

CO operation involves setting up a virtual circuit between two hosts which wish to transfer data from one to the other. Once the connection is established, packets are passed between the two ends with the benefits of flow control and checks for missing packets. A disconnection procedure is necessary once the data transfer sequence is complete.

While the connection oriented service can be likened to the telephone system, the connectionless service has a parallel in the postal system. Packets of data – individual datagrams – are sent independently of each other and with no guarantee of delivery (although with a very high probability of success). With the datagram service the responsibility for checking correct arrivals rests not on the delivering agency but on the sender and receiver themselves at a higher level.

There is a divergence of opinion amongst LAN implementers concerning which type of service is better – virtual circuit or datagram. Both, however, can be provided given the existence of the basic packet level on top of the underlying communication mechanism. As far as the majority of LAN users are concerned it will not matter whether the underlying mechanism is a Cambridge Ring or an Ethernet or a token passing system. All types of LAN can be made to look functionally identical above the transport service as defined in OSI. This transport layer is built on top of either a virtual circuit or datagram service and provides a network-independent set of data transfer facilities for the network user (typically a software process running in an attached host).

Initially, the standards work in OSI was targeted at CO protocols. This was undoubtedly because of the background of wide area networks and network applications from which most standards bodies participants had gained their experience. It is usual for WAN services, as in the X.25 protocol, to be virtual circuit in nature. This is partly in order to build a reliable service on top of the relatively unreliable WAN communications subsystem. However, it is also necessary for the traditional sorts of application for which the network is used, namely log in to remote hosts, file transfer, and (batch) job transfer. All of these require a reliable transport service which can only be satisfied by a CO service.

The LAN standards work begun by IEEE 802 changed the assumption that the communications subsystem was unreliable, and introduced the fact that the underlying protocols in LANs are CL in nature. Thus the

ISO introduced working groups to study CL protocol alternatives at the network, transport and higher layers of OSI. These alternatives are being made available by vertically sublayering the layers of OSI protocol.

Remaining as a subject for further study is how the various alternatives of CO and CL protocols might fit together in a harmonious hierarchy.

3.6.2 Higher layers in OSI

The introduction of CL protocol alternatives into OSI has been essentially because of a bottom-up requirement; LANs bring connectionless protocols into the arena, so there is a need to study how to incorporate them into the OSI model.

However, LAN researchers have also questioned the validity of the assumption that remote log in, file transfer and job transfer are the only classes of application which networks will be required to support (Cheriton, 1986). Importantly, the use of high bandwidth networks (whether LAN or upcoming fast WAN technology) to support closely coupled distributed computing systems is likely to gain momentum. Such applications are characterized by short transactions which require to be fast, though not necessarily having the properties that transactions underlying file transfer might be expected to have. Chapter 10 discusses this subject further.

References

Chapin, A.L., (1983). 'Connections and connectionless data transmission' *Proc. IEEE*, **71**,(12), December, 1365–1371

Cheriton, D.R., (1986). 'VMTP: a transport protocol for the next generation of communication systems' *ACM Computer Communication Review*, **16**,(3), August, 406–415

Coffield, D. and Hutchison, D., (1985). 'Managing local area networks' *Computer Communications*, **8**,(5), October, 240–246

Flatman, A.V. and Caves, K., (1986). 'Progress with FDDI' *Proc. EFOC/LAN86*, Amsterdam, June, 298–303

FOCUS committee, (1982). *Local area networks – report to the FOCUS committee*, UK Dept of Trade and Industry, August

Georganas, N. and Mwikalo, R., (1982). 'Platon: a university local area network' *Computer Communications*, **5**,(6), December, 308–312

Hammond, J.L. and O'Reilly, P.J.P., (1986). *Performance analysis of local computer networks*. Addison-Wesley

Hutchison, D. and Shepherd, W.D., (1981). 'Strathnet: a local area network' *Software & Microsystems*, **1**,(1), October, 21–27

Hutchison, D., Balfour, J. and Mariani, J., (1984). 'A dual interface to Cambridge Ring and Ethernet-type local networks' *Microprocessing and Micropro-gramming*, **13**, 97–104

Le Lann, G., (1983). 'On real-time distributed computing' *Information Processing 83*, (Mason, R.E.A. editor), Elsevier Science Publishers

Naffah, N., (1981). 'Distributed office systems in practice' *Online Conference on local networks and distributed office systems*, London, May

Needham, R.M. and Herbert, A.J., (1982). *The Cambridge Distributed Computing System*. Addison-Wesley

Rutkowski, A.M., (1985). *Integrated Services Digital Networks*. Artech House

Shoch, J.F., (1980). 'Carrying voice traffic through an Ethernet local network – a general overview' *IFIP WG 6.4 International Workshop on Local Area Computer Networks*, Zurich, August

Stallings, W., (1986). 'The importance of a' *Data Communications*, October

Swinehart, D.C., Stewart, L.C. and Ornstein, S.M., (1984). *Adding voice to an office computer network* Xerox PARC Technical report **CSL-83-8**, Palo Alto, CA 94304, USA, February

Wiley, A.J. and Hutchison, D., (1985). 'An ISDN for the UK' *Computer Communications* **8**,(5), October, 235–239

Chapter 4
Ethernet

The subject of this chapter is the CSMA/CD LAN, popularly known as Ethernet after its first working example. The aim is to show how Ethernet was developed and how its technology and protocols have evolved into the standard IEEE 802/ISO CSMA/CD form.

4.1   Background – the ALOHA system

One of the papers reprinted in the 25th Anniversary issue of the *Communications of the ACM* was the famous paper by Robert Metcalfe and David Boggs, entitled 'Ethernet: distributed packet switching for local computer networks', first published in July 1976.

Despite the fact that for several years beforehand there had been a certain amount of research into localized communications networks, no one system had captured the imagination of computer scientists in the way the one presented in this paper did. Mostly, the previous research centred on ring topologies, using either token access or the empty slot or register insertion techniques (on which more is written in Chapters 5 and 6). Perhaps the novelty of the Ethernet bus was one factor in the attention immediately paid to it. However, the apparent simplicity of its shared access scheme, using a passive communications medium, undoubtedly attracted the greatest attention. As with so many designs in computing, engineering and other fields, simplicity is seen as elegance and is instantly appealing.

The Ethernet was devised at the Xerox Corporation's Palo Alto Research Center (PARC) and developed over a few years in the early 1970s. By the time Metcalfe and Boggs' paper appeared the Experimental Ethernet, as it became called, had been in active use for some time.

It is perhaps important to remember that Ethernet was developed with a particular application domain primarily in mind. In the terminology of Chapter 3, this was an office application, more specifically a program development environment consisting of a number of 'computing stations' (a term used in Metcalfe and Boggs' paper). This environment contained personal workstations such as the Alto, larger multiuser computers, printing servers, and disk and tape file servers. Specifically, Ethernet was not intended for use in industrial applications and its designers have made no claims in this direction.

The idea for Ethernet grew out of the packet radio broadcast system known as ALOHA reported a few years previously (Abramson, 1970; Abramson, 1973), and briefly introduced in Chapter 3. This system, at the University of Hawaii, used a distributed radio transmission network as illustrated in Figure 4.1. (For more details of ALOHA read, for example, Chapter 6 in Tanenbaum, 1981).

The need for radio arose from the distributed nature of the University of Hawaii, with its seven different sites spread across several islands. Radio was estimated to be less expensive to install and operate, and more reliable, than underwater telephone cabling. Two different transmission frequency bands (each of 100 KHz) were allocated, one for the computer centre's outbound transmissions and one for the other sites collectively. (Allocation of radio frequencies is a matter for the

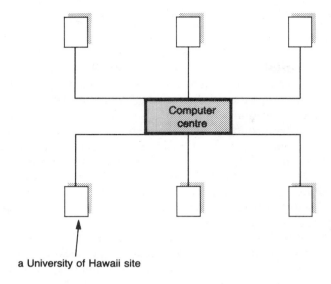

a University of Hawaii site

Figure 4.1   ALOHA packet radio broadcast system.

International Frequency Registration Board of the International Tele-communication Union and cannot be chosen arbitrarily by a user.) Every transmission, either by the computer centre or by an individual site, is of course a broadcast – all the other sites will 'hear' the message sent.

There is no direct site-to-site communication in ALOHA. The network operates as if it were a star configuration, in that all transmissions are either to or from the computer centre, which acts as the central node of the star. Where ALOHA differs from conventional radio broadcast systems is that it does not use frequency division multiplexing (FDM) as a way of giving each site its own share of the communications bandwidth. In FDM each site would have its own preallocated channel which would remain unused while that site was not transmitting messages. In ALOHA only one channel is available to all sites other than the computer centre.

On the assumption that the traffic tends to be bursty – a typical characteristic of intercomputer communications – and that in total, over all sites, the usage of the channel bandwidth will not approach 100%, it should be possible to share a single channel by competing for its use when required.

ALOHA thus uses a **contention** scheme in which a site simply transmits on the single channel when it needs to. If another site already happens to be transmitting, or begins to transmit while the first is doing so, a collision of packets occurs. The central site can detect collisions because all packets carry sum checks appended by the transmitter; a collision will produce, in all probability, an error.

In the normal course of events the central site sends an acknowledgment to the sending site. If no acknowledgment arrives at the sender within a reasonably large time period, the sender will retry the transmission after a random time interval.

In the ALOHA scheme bandwidth is wasted due to collisions. This has to be weighed against the bandwidth which would otherwise be wasted by static channel allocation as in FDM. Various refinements based on ALOHA have been proposed and analysed to see whether they can improve performance, as introduced in Chapter 3. In particular the **slotted** ALOHA (Abramson, 1973) was suggested, in which transmission time is split up into fixed size slots slightly larger than the time to send one packet. Sites are permitted to begin transmissions only at the beginning of a time slot. Synchronization of sites is achieved by the central station regularly broadcasting special synchronizing messages. The so-called vulnerable time for a packet, that is when it can suffer a collision, is reduced in the slotted scheme to the minimum, being equal to one packet transmission time. This contrasts with the pure ALOHA technique in which the vulnerable time is twice as long. In slotted ALOHA there is therefore twice as much capacity or effective bandwidth for transmissions.

Further schemes include the **reservation** ALOHA in which individual sites are dynamically allocated time slots. The results produced can increase packet throughput significantly, but at the expense of additional complexity in the transmitting stations.

4.2 The Xerox PARC experimental Ethernet

At Xerox PARC the ALOHA technique was broadly applied to a coaxial cable medium instead of using radio, retaining the basic ideas of the protocol. The name 'Ethernet' is a reference to the early days in physics when it was thought that electromagnetic waves travelled through a substance in the air with special properties called the luminiferous ether. The implication here is that the Ethernet technique is equally applicable to other broadcast media, including radio. The 3 Mbits/sec experimental Ethernet described in Metcalfe and Boggs' 1976 paper was experimental in the sense that it was not intended as a commercial product. Rather it was used 'inhouse' at Xerox PARC as the basis for a number of local computer networks. Early on it became evident that each local network, located in a particular building or laboratory, could profitably be interlinked with the others to give users access to even more remote computers and to communicate information between separate groups working on their own local networks, in the form of file transfers or electronic mail.

With its Ethernet-based internetwork, Xerox PARC was experimenting in the mid to late 1970s with software development tools residing on personal workstations. A distributed computing system was created in which users on workstations ('clients') communicated with 'servers' of various kinds including file and printing servers.

An important aspect of this work was the development of network protocols to support client–server interactions not only across single Ethernets but over the entire internet. PARC produced its own internet protocol hierarchy, based on the PUP (PARC universal packet). This was a datagram-based internetwork packet format which could encapsulate each of the higher level protocol formats and which itself could be accommodated in the data portion of a network frame, whether Ethernet or another technology. This PUP internet will be described further in Section 4.4.

4.2.1 Ethernet description

The original Ethernet, still in active use at Xerox PARC, uses a coaxial cable bus terminated at both ends for communications at data rates of just below 3 Mbits/sec, and belongs to the class of LANs known as CSMA/CD (carrier sense multiple access with collision detection) systems. Figure 4.2 illustrates the structure of an Ethernet, which consists of one or more segments interconnected by means of repeaters.

Each segment is terminated at both ends by an impedance characteristic of the coaxial cable communications medium. Thus, although each segment is physically a bus topology, the overall Ethernet topology is that of a non-rooted tree. A message transmitted from any station on one of the segments is broadcast to all stations on all segments. The purpose of a repeater is simply to copy the electrical signals from one segment to the next.

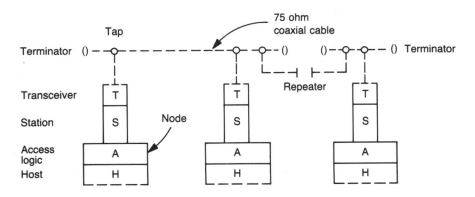

Figure 4.2 Ethernet topology.

Each node, which may incorporate a computer, a user terminal or some other peripheral, is connected to the network cable by means of a transceiver and a tap. The tap and transceiver make a physical and electrical connection onto the cable conductor and the latter contains logic to transmit and receive serial data to and from the cable. The station implements the Ethernet CSMA/CD protocols (see Section 4.2.2) and has suitable access logic to interface to the attached host. In Ethernet terminology the combination of station and access logic is called a 'controller'. Each station has a unique physical address on the network, usually implemented by means of a hardwired address plug or a row of switches.

4.2.2 CSMA/CD protocol

CSMA/CD operates as follows. When a station wishes to send data to another on the LAN it first senses the communication medium to discover whether any data is presently being carried. If there is, the station defers to the passing traffic until such time as it detects silence on the network. Thus the Ethernet protocol is 1-persistent as introduced in Chapter 3. As soon as silence occurs, the station waits for a mandatory period to allow the network to settle, and then begins to transmit its data. As it does so, it must again listen to the network, this time to look for a collision.

Collisions are possible because of the multiplicity of devices sharing the communication cable, and happen when two or more stations decide simultaneously that the cable is quiet and that they can safely transmit data. If this 'simultaneous' transmission occurs, the bits of data from each source will collide and cause all transmitted packets to become corrupted. So a transmitter listens to the cable and compares the data bits transmitted with those present on the cable. Any difference indicates a collision, upon which transmission must stop. The technique adopted is for the transmitting device to 'jam' the network for a short time by sending out a specific data pattern then to 'back off' for a random time interval before restarting the transmit data sequence.

Each transmitting station involved in the collision will therefore wait for a different time interval and the chances of a subsequent collision are low. A special algorithm is used for the generation of a random time interval. Called a 'binary exponential backoff', it is designed to resolve contention amongst the stations attached to the Ethernet. See Metcalfe and Boggs (1976) for details of the backoff algorithm.

The idea of stations transmitting 'simultaneously' needs some explanation. When a station transmits, its signals propagate onto the coaxial cable and take a small but finite time to reach the extremities of the Ethernet. In the limit, two potential transmitters may be at opposite ends of the cable, so it is possible after one begins a transmission for the other to begin within the propagation delay of the whole length of the Ethernet. Simultaneous in this context, then, means within the propagation time of the whole cable length.

Propagation times must also be taken into account when considering collisions, specifically the 'round trip propagation delay' of a bit on the cable, that is the time for a bit to travel from one end of the cable to the other plus the time for a bit to travel all the way back. As we shall see in Section 4.3, this approximates to the 'slot time', a parameter used to characterize Ethernet collision handling.

Consider again two stations at opposite extremities of the Ethernet. From the time one of the stations begins to transmit it cannot be sure that the other has detected its traffic and is deferring to it until the round trip delay time has passed. After this time (also called the 'collision window') the transmitting station is said to have acquired the medium. Thus, there is an upper bound on the size of collision fragments (partially transmitted packets) and this is also related to the round trip propagation delay.

4.2.3 Packet format

Data is transmitted in the form of packets which have the layout shown in Figure 4.3. There is a leading synchronization bit, followed by two 8-bit address fields, one for destination and the other for the source. A variable length data field (with a maximum of 500 bytes) and a 16-bit cyclic redundancy check (CRC) form the remainder of the packet.

Up to 256 stations can be accommodated on one Ethernet given the addressing capability of the destination and source fields. In practice address zero is reserved as a 'broadcast' address, meaning that all stations should listen to packets containing this destination value. Each station has a unique address within one Ethernet. Whenever a transmitting host forms a packet, it fills in the required destination and its own source value,

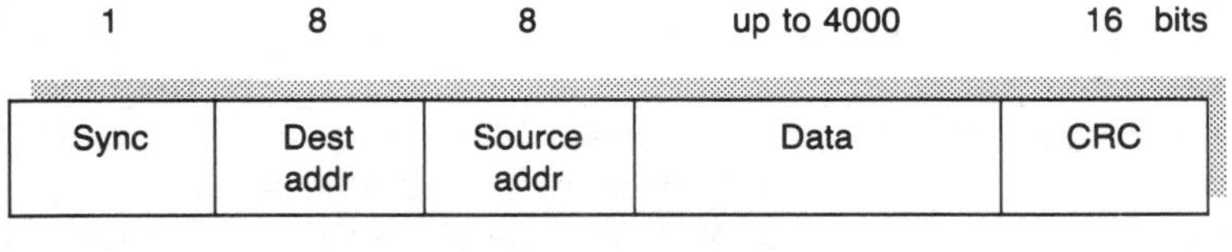

1	8	8	up to 4000	16 bits
Sync	Dest addr	Source addr	Data	CRC

Figure 4.3 Packet format for the experimental Ethernet.

appends the data to be sent and passes the packet to the controller. The CRC is calculated and attached to the end of the packet as it is being transmitted. Note that there are no low level acknowledgments of Ethernet packets. Sending is on a 'best effort only' basis, i.e. once a successful transmission has been achieved, all that can be assumed is that the packet has been accepted at its destination with a very high probability of success. Error rates in Ethernet systems are extremely low, and will usually be detected by the CRC in the packet.

Even though a transmitted packet has made its way along the Ethernet successfully and without bit errors, the next step is for the intended recipient to read the packet. In Ethernet systems, all stations hear all passing packets. There is a low level address filter which compares the packet's destination field with the address of the station and will accept the remainder of the packet if there is a match. Otherwise the rest of the packet is ignored. Broadcast packets are always accepted as indicated above.

Simulations and analytical models have been used to make detailed comparisons of the Ethernet CSMA/CD operation with that of other local network access protocols, including token passing and Cambridge Ring protocols. See, for example, the papers by Bux (1981) and Blair and Shepherd (1982).

4.2.4 Higher protocol levels

What has been described so far is the packet protocol level on top of CSMA/CD. Higher level software protocols will be implemented in the stations and will use the data portion of the Ethernet packets for fields appropriate to these protocols. For example, it is usual in the experimental Ethernet system for the first 16 bits of the data field to define a packet type. There are five types: data, acknowledgments, abort, end, and endreply. Together, these are used to implement a file transfer protocol, in which individual packets are given sequence numbers to ensure a check on the arrival of packets in the correct order. Other fields within the packet are used for sequence numbers, block length, and for the data itself. Since no acknowledgments are present at the lowest level in Ethernet, the higher protocol layers put them in as required. A point which needs to be made is that by the time the station is dealing with file transfer protocols as described, the data is no longer network-dependent and could just as easily have been transported across a ring or some other type of LAN. More details of higher protocol levels implemented on top of Ethernet basic transport mechanisms are given in Sections 4.4 to 4.7, which describe the important network architectures developed in research and standards work.

4.3 The DIX Ethernet

The experimental Ethernet described above has been superseded by the so-called 'commercial' Ethernet. This new version was introduced in the specification document published jointly by Digital, Intel and Xerox in the USA towards the end of 1980 (DIX, 1980). Sometimes the names 'DIX' (after the originators) or 'Blue Book' Ethernet are seen in print, the latter presumably on the assumption that everybody knows the colour of the DIX cover. The intention was to 'open' the Ethernet to manufacturers by encouraging the adoption of a *de facto* industry standard. A good paper on the progress made from the experimental Ethernet up to the DIX version is by Shoch *et al.* (1982).

Much was made in this new specification of the availability of a licence from Xerox enabling an independent manufacturer to build an Ethernet product. The licence could be obtained by a 'one-time payment of $1000', a nominal sum for a serious manufacturer. Many purchasers were forthcoming, at least in the USA. In the event, as we know from Chapter 2, the DIX specification was basically adopted by the IEEE 802 local area networks standards committee and has since been amended in some details. Standardization is a lengthy process and it took until 1984 to have a draft international standard ready. More will be said on the latest Ethernet standard in Section 4.7.

The DIX Ethernet consists of three architectural layers, namely:

- client layer
- data link layer
- physical layer.

The client layer is undefined but is intended to represent the collection of higher level protocols which use the underlying network. The DIX is usually defined by its lowermost two layers as follows:

- Physical layer:
  - data rate: 10 Mbits/sec
  - maximum station separation: 2.5 km
  - maximum no. of stations: 1024
  - medium: shielded (50 ohm) coaxial cable, baseband signalling
  - topology: branching non-rooted tree.
- Data link layer:
  - link control procedure: fully distributed peer protocol, with statistical contention resolution (CSMA/CD)
  - message protocol: variable size frames, with 'best effort' delivery.

In addition, the round trip (end-to-end and back again) propagation delay for a bit is specified as 45.0 μs maximum, and there is a minimum interpacket spacing of 9.6 μs to allow time for data link controllers and the physical channel to recover from handling the previous packet and be ready for the next. The round trip propagation time is important because it determines the maximum number of bits (namely 450) which can be transmitted by a station at one end of the network before a collision at the other end becomes evident. In fact, because transmitting stations involved in a collision send out a 'jamming' signal of up to 48 (arbitrary value) bits, a single parameter called the 'slot time' is used to characterize the Ethernet collision handling. This has the value 51.2 μs, or 512 bit times.

This definition is in terms of 'layers', the physical and data link being the lowermost two layers of the International Standards Organisation's open systems interconnection (OSI) reference model introduced in Chapter 2. In the context of the DIX LAN the model is regarded only as a basis for discussion and definition, since the details of the recommended seven layers were applicable more to WANs. In the case of the DIX specification the upper layers are simply referred to collectively as the client layer and are left for later definition.

Both the experimental and DIX Ethernets use a scheme called Manchester encoding for bits transmitted on the network cable. This is a self-clocking scheme whereby each bit cell is guaranteed to have a level transition in the middle. A positive transition implies that the bit cell contains a '1', whereas a negative transition implies a '0': in other words the first half of the cell contains the complement of the bit value, and the second half the bit value itself. An example of Manchester encoding is as follows:

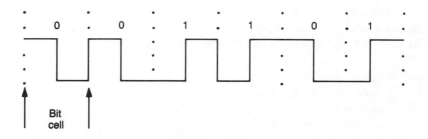

Lastly, Figure 4.4 shows the packet format for the DIX Ethernet. Basically the fields contain the same information, in the same order, as for the experimental version but each is extended. The synchronization bit is replaced by an 8-byte preamble which allows receiving stations time to synchronize onto the packet bit cells, and the new frame check sequence (FCS) is simply an extended cyclic redundancy check.

8	6	6	2	46–1500	4	bytes
Preamble	Dest addr	Source addr	Type	Data	FCS	

Figure 4.4 Packet format for DIX Ethernet.

The destination and source address fields are now very large. This is to allow for the use of global addresses, since it is assumed in the future that internetworking will be common and there will be many Ethernets (and indeed other types of LANs) all connected together by means of bridges or gateways. Individual Ethernets will not support more than the maximum 1024 stations. Each field is transmitted with the least significant bit first. The first bit of the 48-bit destination address field is called the 'physical/multicast' bit; if this bit is 0 the remaining 47 bits specify a unique station address. If the bit is 1, the remaining address bits refer to a so-called multicast address – the message may be accepted by a group of stations all sharing the same multicast address. If all 48 destination bits are 1 then the message is a 'broadcast' and is intended for all stations.

Notice that there is a minimum as well as a maximum size for the data part of the packet. This is to ensure that no packet can be confused with a collision fragment. Thus Ethernet is inefficient if stations wish to send data blocks smaller than the minimum data field size of 46 bytes. Efficiency increases towards the maximum packet size.

4.4 The Xerox Internet

Before we go on to describe the most up-to-date Ethernet developments let us go back to the protocol work at Xerox PARC since this produced a valuable contribution to LAN and internetwork architectures.

Going back furthest of all, to the 3 Mbits/sec experimental Ethernet, a protocol hierarchy (based on the PUP) was developed as mentioned in Section 4.2. The PUP was designed to make gateway (or bridge) operation as simple and as fast as possible. Only two actions had to be performed by the gateway, namely address mapping (checking the packet destination) and 'fragmentation'. The latter is necessary for an underlying network capable only of transporting short frames of data (such as packet radio); a packet received at the gateway may need to be broken up into smaller fragments before being sent out onto the network. Figure 4.5 outlines the PUP protocol hierarchy.

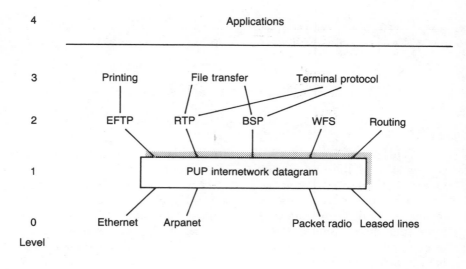

Figure 4.5   PUP protocol hierarchy.

This layered scheme is in many ways similar to the LAN/RM, certainly not in detail but in principle and partly in the functionality of its levels. As we shall see in Sections 4.5 and 4.6, and also in Chapter 6, there are several other protocol hierarchies along equally similar lines – the new Xerox XNS protocols, the DARPA Internet used in Berkeley 4.2 UNIX distributions, the Cambridge Distributed Computing System protocols, and also in proprietary networks such as IBM's SNA, DEC's DECnet, ICL's IPA, and the Burroughs and UNIVAC systems.

Level 0 in the PUP hierarchy roughly corresponds to levels 0 and 1 in the LAN/RM – the physical, MAC and LLC layers. Then comes the correspondence of level 1 in PUP with the LAN/RM networking layer. After that there is no easy correspondence to be made, except to note that PUP makes explicit such protocols as file transfer and terminal protocols, whereas in the LAN/RM these are left as 'higher-level' issues for further study.

The level 2 protocols are briefly described as follows.

- *EFTP* – easy file transfer protocol, is a simple protocol for transferring bulk data split into packets. Each packet must be acknowledged before another is sent. Retransmissions occur periodically should an acknowledgment not return within a reasonable time. The purpose of EFTP is to support printer server facilities at level 3, but it has also been used for bootstrap loading of computers on the network.

- *RTP* – rendezvous and termination protocol. This is used to set up and close down byte stream connections between processes in different computers.

- *BSP* – byte stream protocol, is used for reliable two-way transmission of data between processes. Together, RTP and BSP give a suitable basis for file transfer and virtual terminal protocols at level 3. They are equivalent to the single Arpanet protocol called TCP – transmission control protocol – and, in fact, were originally inspired by the earlier Arpanet work.

- *WFS* – Woodstock file server, is a protocol used for accessing fast, large volume disk filestore on the internet. The form of the protocol is request–reply transactions where commands, responses and data are carried in the transmitted packets. As we shall see in Chapter 6 this protocol is similar to the Cambridge SSP (single shot protocol).

Lastly, there is a routing protocol used for exchange of PUPs between hosts and gateways. This exchange keeps the routing tables in the gateways up to date, particularly necessary when there are any changes in the internet topology. The key aim is to minimize the number of gateways through which a PUP travels between its source and destination.

The PUP packet at level 1 is transported in the data section of the lower level frames. In turn, higher level (2 and above) protocols are encapsulated within a PUP. This nesting of protocols is a common feature of layered systems and is sometimes known as the 'onion-skin' effect as illustrated in Figure 4.6 which applies to the PUP internet.

Between the source and destination hosts there could be several gateways, at each of which the PUP at level 1 is decapsulated then again encapsulated before continuing its journey across a new network.

One of the most useful features about a structure like the PUP is that any higher level protocols can be transported in it. Across a gateway there could be many different types of protocol being carried from sources to destinations, but the gateway only requires to know about the structure of the PUP itself and not about the meaning or structure of the higher level protocol being carried in the data field.

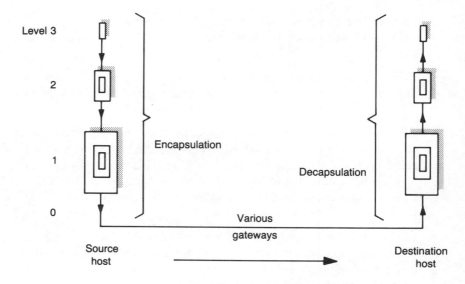

Figure 4.6 Onion-skin protocol layers in PUP.

The PUP itself was designed for simplicity. Its format is shown in Figure 4.7.

4.4.1 PUP format

The PUP has a maximum length of 532 bytes (for data) plus a standard 20-byte header plus a 2-byte software check sum, giving 554 bytes maximum in total. This length seems to have been chosen because there might often be disk pages of 512 bytes being transported around the internetwork, with another 20 bytes being allowed for higher level protocol type and control information.

The length and check sum functions are obvious. The control field contains a 4-bit hop count subfield which is zeroed by the source process. Each gateway through which the PUP passes increments the hop count by one (and also increments the check sum rather than recalculating it). Should the count reach its maximum value at a particular gateway, the PUP is discarded on the assumption that it could be in an infinite routing loop. Of course this means the PUP cannot validly traverse an internetwork path having more than 15 gateways, but this is a design decision where this event was considered unlikely to occur. The limitation of data structure fields is an ever-present problem in applications where growth may cause fields to exceed their capacity.

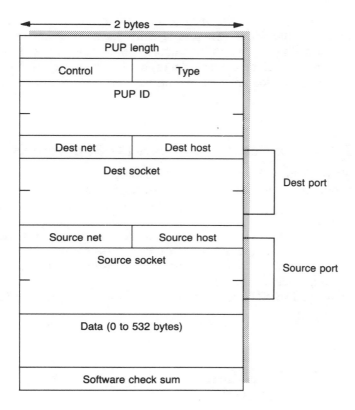

Figure 4.7 PUP format.

The PUP ID (identifier) is normally used by higher level protocols to hold a sequence number which can distinguish one PUP from another. As we shall see shortly this field has been removed in the latest version of the Xerox internet system.

The most important fields in the PUP are the destination and source ports. In the design of these a key issue was the lengths of their constituent parts. In the PUP internet, communication is considered to take place between sockets in the source and destination host computers. A socket is basically a bidirectional data transmission structure associated with a process. It has its origins in the Arpanet project's end-to-end host communication protocols. When a PUP is to be sent the source process constructs two triples – the network, host and socket numbers for both itself and the intended destination. If the destination is a server, its port details will be available from a name table (which itself may be in a name server on the network). Since the destination host will typically contain a good many processes performing different tasks, the socket number is a particularly important distinguishing feature to identify the eventual destination for the PUP. Servers usually have 'well-known' socket numbers which do not have to be created dynamically unlike the sockets used by other communicating processes. In the case of the PUP, network and host fields are 8-bit quantities, and sockets can be up to 32 bits long.

4.5 The Xerox Network Systems (XNS) protocols

The PUP work has led to an updated set of internetwork protocols and an amended internet packet format. Although the new packet is no longer the same, it is still referred to as the PUP. Its format is shown in Figure 4.8.

The protocols themselves are a more mature set developed by Xerox over the experimental years of PUP. They are used in various workstations produced by Xerox and will probably become included in UNIX communications software supported by other workstation manufacturers. The XNS protocol hierarchy is illustrated in Figure 4.9.

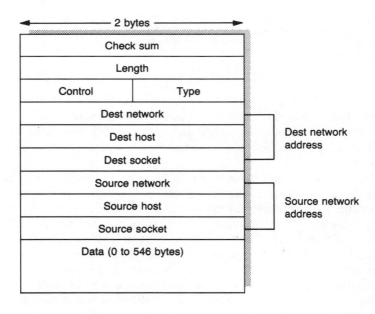

Figure 4.8 XNS internet packet format.

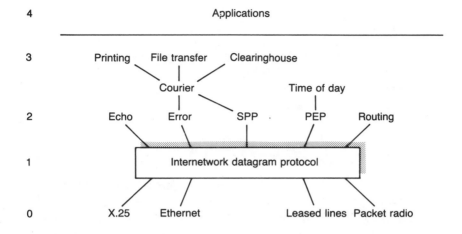

Figure 4.9   XNS protocol hierarchy.

These protocols are described in a set of Xerox documents called the *Xerox system integration standards*, where 'standard' can be taken to apply strictly to Xerox-supplied systems. These are the:

- Internet transport protocols (Xerox, 1981a) – describes levels 1 and 2

- Courier (Xerox, 1981b) – a remote procedure call protocol (see Section 10.4 for more details)

- Clearinghouse (Xerox, 1981c) – an internetwork name service.

Also important is the paper on '48-bit addressing' by Dalal and Printis (1981) which explains the major differences between the PUP and the new internet packet format, namely the longer network and host addresses.

The protocols at levels 2 and 3 are now different in the following respects.

An echo protocol is supplied to determine that other hosts are alive and well. A well-known socket in each host should be supplied for this purpose.

The error protocol provides a means for a destination to send an error indication to a source originating a faulty packet. Error indications returned may include check sum failure, or packet not accepted because of lack of destination resources, or non-existing socket number.

SPP, sequenced packet protocol, is like a combination of the former RTP and BSP and provides for the setting up and closing down of links and of reliable data transfer between processes.

PEP, packet exchange protocol, is a request–reply protocol intermediate in reliability between direct internet datagrams and the SPP, and hence intermediate in complexity. It is like the Cambridge SSP (single shot protocol).

4.6   DARPA Internet

The United States Department of Defense (DoD) has produced a set of 'standard protocols' called the Internet or TCP/IP protocols. These derive from the Arpanet initiative and have been developed within the DARPA programme (D for Defense). Their history goes back to 1973 when it was decided to design a set of protocols specifically for the multiple network environment. More recently these protocols have been regarded as a foundation for an evolving protocol architecture similar to the OSI model, but optimized for heterogeneous network systems. The two protocols which mainly characterize this set, IP (internet protocol), and TCP (transmission control protocol), are fully described in Postel (1980a and 1980b).

Briefly, IP is a simple datagram protocol which uses globally assigned addresses and is very similar to the Xerox PUP and XNS internet packet. The Internet gateways deal with routing, encapsulation/decapsulation, fragmentation, congestion control, type of service and accounting. The great advantage of datagram gateways is that little state information needs to be maintained as would be the case with a virtual circuit gateway. TCP is a connection-oriented protocol, providing reliable, flow controlled, bidirectional transmission of data, and is the basis for file transfer and terminal protocols at a higher level.

The structure of the TCP/IP protocol set is shown in Figure 4.10. It is very similar to PUP, and to its successor XNS, and was developed at about the same time as PUP, with much the same aims.

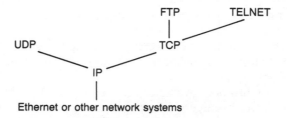

Figure 4.10   TCP/IP protocol structure.

In addition to TCP and IP themselves there are also:

- *UDP*: a simple, unreliable datagram protocol, on which can be based higher level protocols of the user's own design (U stands for user).
- *FTP*: a file transfer protocol using the connection-oriented features of TCP.
- *TELNET*: equivalent to a virtual terminal protocol, allowing users to log into remote computers, making the intermediate network(s) transparent. Also uses TCP as its basis.

This protocol set is becoming well known to the academic computing community throughout the USA, UK and Europe because it is included with the Berkeley System Distribution (BSD) 4.2 version of the UNIX operating system, a version which received funding from DARPA, the developers of TCP/IP. This was the first version of UNIX to provide network support and remote interprocess communication (Joy, 1983; Leffler *et al.*, 1983). Ethernet software drivers are also provided with 4.2 BSD UNIX, supporting some of the commercially available hardware controllers. The result is that many academic departments in universities and colleges are running their first Ethernet system using the TCP/IP protocol set. Furthermore, since these protocols were designed to support internetworking, local Ethernet systems can be readily linked to the wide area Arpanet in the USA (or the DARPA Catenet as it is now known). In the UK and Europe, wide area networks are mostly based on the X.25 protocol, but gateways have been developed to allow local UNIX-based Ethernet systems to be linked to X.25-based networks.

Interprocess communication within TCP/IP, and thus within 4.2 BSD UNIX, is based on sockets as in the Xerox PUP system. A socket is a bidirectional end point for communication and can be one of three different types: virtual circuit, datagram or raw. Basically, a socket has to be bound to an Internet address in order to be used. In 4.2 BSD UNIX there is another protocol provided called ARP (address resolution protocol) whose job is to translate between 32-bit DARPA Internet addresses and the 48-bit Ethernet addresses used in the local Ethernet domain.

4.7   The standard Ethernet

The PUP and XNS protocol hierarchies described above are two of the LAN architectures which have been developed on top of specific technologies. Much work has gone into the protocol software, but nevertheless these are not standard architectures in the true sense of the word.

Through the efforts of the IEEE in the USA and ECMA in Europe, as explained in Chapter 2, a standard LAN architecture has now been developed and is almost complete (ECMA, 1982; IEEE, 1982 are the early drafts). Draft international standards (DISs) are now ready for the final approval stage. These include IEEE 802.3, the document specifically on the CSMA/CD access method and its associated physical layer. Inspired by Ethernet, and using most of the details originated in the DIX specification, this LAN is still unofficially called Ethernet rather than using the cumbersome term CSMA/CD.

The IEEE 802.3 document is a refinement of the DIX specification which brings it into line with the other standard LAN technologies incorporated under the LAN/RM structure. There is a set of documents with the following relationship:

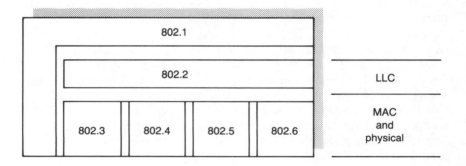

As explained in Chapter 2, 802.1 is an overview document which covers the general architectural principles on which the LAN/RM is based. It also deals with internetworking and with network management, the latter being applicable to all layers in a network. There will be further discussion of network management in Chapter 9.

The issue of internetworking is a complex one, to be discussed at greater length in Chapter 7. For the present let us assume that above the logical link control (LLC) layer is the network layer in which gateways to other networks, be they wide area networks or other LANs, are handled. The problem of internetwork addresses is not evident at the link layer, where network-specific addresses are used.

Of course, this diagram can be replaced by one containing ISO equivalent numbers for the IEEE 802 versions, thus for example:

802.2 becomes 8802/2
802.3 becomes 8802/3
and so on.

The following chapters on token passing and slotted ring LANs will individually explain the details of the corresponding IEEE/ISO standards. Although the slotted (Cambridge) ring does not appear in the LAN/RM diagram, it will be explained how this technology is being fitted into the LAN/RM architecture.

4.7.1 Frame structure

The details of the CSMA/CD standard frame are the same as those for the DIX frame previously shown in Figure 4.4. They are however illustrated in expanded form below to provide more detail.

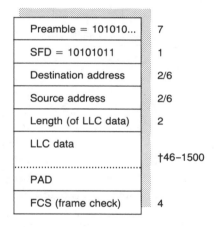

(† note that this assumes 6-byte addressing)

The octets (bytes) in the frame are transmitted from top to bottom and the bits in each octet transmitted from left to right, least significant bit first.

Addressing will be dealt with in Section 4.7.2.

SFD is the start of frame delimiter. It can be regarded as the last octet of the preamble in which only the last two bits differ from the repeating 10 pattern; the final 11 denotes the start of the frame proper.

The length field gives the number of LLC data octets placed in the data field. Since the frame size (excluding the preamble) must be 64 octets long or more, the PAD field is used to make the frame up to this length should the LLC length fall below 46 bytes in the case of 6-byte addressing or below 54 bytes for 2-byte addressing. It is likely that the 2-byte address option will be little used in practice since most existing implementations are using the 6-byte version, which in any case offers more flexibility (note that the DIX specification provided for only the 6-byte case).

4.7.2 Addressing

The destination and source address fields are split into subfields as shown below.

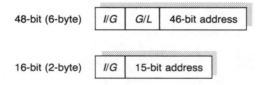

where

I/G = 0 for individual address
      = 1 for group (or multicast) address
G/L = 0 for globally administered address
      = 1 for locally administered address.

A group address is one associated by higher level convention with a group of logically related stations on the network. A specific case of this group address is where all the bits in the address field (for either 2- or 6-byte addressing) have the value 1; this is called the broadcast address meaning that the message is intended for all stations on the network.

The idea of having globally administered addresses is to enable blocks of addresses to be allocated to organizations in a centralized manner; with 48-bit addressing there is plenty of scope to give each organization a very large allocation. Equally well there is scope for utter chaos should addresses be randomly allocated. In the hope or expectation that one day there will be a single global internetwork linking all willing LAN and WAN users, it is a good idea to start with an organized scheme for assigning network addresses.

Lastly, the use of local/global addresses can allow selective filtering of addresses at gateways or bridges between networks. This could give benefits in improved security and in reducing traffic in a particular network.

4.7.3 Service and protocol specifications

Specifications in the CSMA/CD document, as in the other specific technology documents, are in terms of:

- English text
- formal definitions
- state diagrams.

The English text is used in both the MAC and physical layer descriptions, the formal definitions (in terms of Pascal program fragments) to give the primary specification of the MAC. State diagrams support the formal definitions – they are intended to be descriptive rather than definitive, though implementers may find that the diagrams are most helpful of all in designing and implementing the protocols.

The ISO has initiated work into formal specification techniques for communications protocols, and two main streams have produced specification languages called LOTOS (International Standards Organisation, 1985a) and Estelle (International Standards Organisation, 1985b). The first of these derives from work at Edinburgh University by Milner on a Calculus of Communicating Systems (CCS) (Milner, 1980). LOTOS uses a highly abstract notation which describes protocol processes in terms of black boxes and their interaction with the environment in terms of events.

Estelle is based on Pascal but has an extension to the language which allows the description of finite state machine mechanisms and is thus suitable for describing the operation of communications protocols.

The idea of these languages is that they can be used to give concise and complete specifications at each layer of the OSI/RM (and presumably LAN/RM) and that their formality allows verification of both service and protocol.

The present specification documents, however, are less formal and implementation is a matter of interpreting the mixture of English and diagrams and program fragments before proceeding to code in a conventional programming language such as C or Pascal. It should be noted that the specifications do not imply that implementations must be made in software; they can be in firmware or hardware, and will increasingly tend to be so towards the data link and physical layers.

We have already given a textual description of the CSMA/CD protocol at the beginning of the chapter. The protocol operation has not changed from the experimental through the DIX to the standard Ethernet, and will not be repeated here. It is useful to show how the standard service specifications are given, in the form common to all OSI/RM and LAN/RM layer boundaries, as this gives a very clear summary of the LLC to MAC and MAC to physical layer interfaces.

- *MA_DATA.request*: transfer data to peer LLC(s). The LLC data unit contains sufficient information for the MAC sublayer to construct destination address and length fields

- *MA_DATA.confirm*: signifies success or failure of the request operation within the MAC sublayer

- *MA_DATA.indicate*: arrival of valid frame which has a destination address corresponding to this MAC, or indicating a broadcast or multicast packet arrival

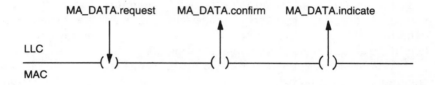

- *PH_DATA.request*: request transfer of single bit to peer MAC(s)

- *PH_DATA.confirm*: physical layer is ready to accept another bit for transfer

- *PH_DATA.indicate*: arrival of a bit from a peer

- *PH_CARRIER.indicate*: gives the status of the transmission medium

- *PH_SIGNAL.indicate*: signal error, including collision indication

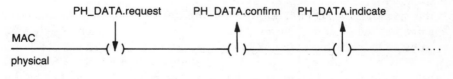

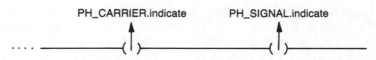

4.7.4 Station management

In order to maintain proper operation of the local network, the IEEE 802 working groups have specified sets of network management service primitives at the LLC/MAC and MAC/physical layer boundaries. There is a so-called station management entity at each layer of the protocol hierarchy which calls on the services provided by the management entity at the layer below. These primitives are dependent on the local network technology, i.e. are different for CSMA/CD and each of the token passing systems. Basically the primitives allow for monitoring and control of the protocol layers.

In the case of Ethernet, for example, the physical layer provides the SQE (signal quality error) test and the jabber function. See Section 4.7.5 below for details. The MAC layer provides collision statistics and information on improper frames, and can operate in promiscuous mode whereby all frames are received whether addressed to this station or not. There is also a loopback facility for checking out the station's own transmit–receive sequences.

Chapter 9 deals with the subject of network management, including IEEE layer management in local networks and the ISO work in this area.

4.7.5 Implementation issues

The physical realization of Ethernet stations is closely specified in the standards document at the physical layer. This deals with not only the coaxial cable communications medium but also the electrical and mechanical connections between the medium and the station itself. The paper by Crane (1982) gives good implementation detail in a *Designer's Guide* to the DIX Ethernet (see Section 4.3).

The physical components of an Ethernet station are illustrated below.

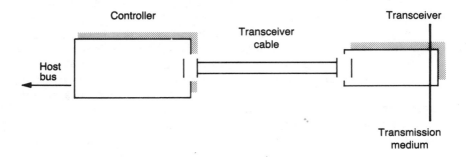

Usually the Ethernet station is interfaced to the backplane bus of the computer host, for example to the UNIBUS backplane of the Digital Equipment Corporation VAX or PDP–11 range, or to the Multibus backplane of several ranges of popular 16-bit microcomputers. In this case the controller consists typically of one or two printed circuit boards which locate in the host backplane and draw their electrical power from the host.

Logically the controller contains three parts:

- host bus interface logic
- data link layer functions
- part of the physical layer functions

and where the controller is implemented as two boards, it is usually split into a host bus-specific board and a network-specific (data link plus part physical) board.

The remainder of the physical layer functions are contained within the transceiver (or 'tap') which attaches the controller to the Ethernet transmission medium, a 50 ohm coaxial cable with characteristics specified in the standards documents. The transceiver and controller are connected by means of a transceiver cable containing four twisted-pair wires carrying the following signals:

- transmit
- receive
- collision detect
- electrical (dc) power.

The transmit and receive signals are in Manchester encoded form whereby the encoding and decoding are handled in the physical layer part of the controller, which also generates the carrier presence signal (using the receive signal) required by the data link layer functions. Collision detect is produced within the transceiver and passed via the controller to the data link layer. Power for the transceiver is taken from the controller, or rather the host in which the controller is situated.

The transceiver performs two additional important functions. First, it contains a jabber function which electrically isolates the transceiver from the Ethernet cable if it detects an overlong transmission (which could originate within either the transceiver itself or the controller). An overlong transmission is one which significantly exceeds the maximum allowable frame length of 1518 octets (excluding the preamble). The intention is to prevent a faulty station hogging the transmission medium.

Secondly, there is a heartbeat (or SQE, signal quality error) function which exercises the collision detect circuitry at the end of every transmission. A short signal burst is produced on the collision detect wire pair to demonstrate healthy operation. This SQE test is mandatory in the standard CSMA/CD specification but was not in the DIX document. Consequently mixing controller/transceiver equipment built to standard and DIX specifications can cause problems. A DIX controller with a standard transceiver will flag a collision when the SQE test is performed; conversely a standard controller attached to a DIX transceiver will call a network management function because it does not see the expected SQE test after transmission.

Connecting the transceiver onto the Ethernet cable is done in one of two ways:

(1)   The transceiver contains a channel with a fixed pin into which the unbroken cable is laid. A cover is attached over the cable, causing the pin to penetrate the coaxial cable until it makes mechanical and electrical contact with the centre conductor of the cable. This pin connects the conductor to the transmit/receive circuitry in the transceiver. The idea of this type of attachment is that stations can be connected and disconnected without disturbing the operation of the Ethernet.

In fact operational evidence shows that once a transceiver is connected to the Ethernet cable it is rarely moved. Should the host or controller go faulty or otherwise require maintenance then the controller is simply unplugged from the transceiver cable. Few sites seem to experience a need to move stations from one position on the Ethernet to another. Bearing this in mind, a second type of connection is available which is possibly more robust and certainly adequate for most sites.

(2)   The Ethernet cable is cut and connectors attached onto each end. The transceiver, with connectors of the opposite sex from those on the cable ends, has one of the cable ends plugged onto either side and becomes physically part of the Ethernet cable run. Should this type of transceiver need to be removed for any reason, a barrel connector can be attached in place of the transceiver. In fact this is the usual way of connecting segments of Ethernet cable together. Since an Ethernet cable is required to be earthed at one point only (the outer conductor of the coaxial cable attached to ground potential), care should be taken to cover such barrel connectors with a non-conducting sleeve in case it comes into contact with neighbouring metal objects.

Practical matters in the operation of an Ethernet are important to note. Unlikely though it may be to exceed the limits in most cases, these must be strictly observed or else the network may malfunction. An

Ethernet system can consist of a single or a number of segments, each segment being terminated at both ends with the characteristic impedance (50 ohms) of the coaxial cable medium. Each segment can be up to 500 m in length. Segments can be connected by means of repeaters, which are attached to each segment using normal transceivers and transceiver cables. The repeater simply copies the signals propagating on one segment to another.

There is however a limit on the number of repeaters which can be inter-connected. This is actually determined by the maximum end-to-end distance between any two stations on the segmented Ethernet, namely 2.5 km (equivalent to the slot time of 51.2 ms). So the maximum number depends on the topography of a particular network configuration. A limit of four repeaters in series is also imposed, as is a maximum of 101 segments.

On each segment a maximum of 100 stations can be connected. This is because each attached transceiver causes a small discontinuity on the transmission line and the accumulation of these discontinuities can cause malfunctioning. A total of 1024 stations on a segmented Ethernet is specified, but this is an administrative rather than a performance limit. Transceivers should be spaced out along an Ethernet segment at intervals no closer than 2.5 m – in fact standard Ethernet coaxial cable is marked with black rings at 2.5 m intervals.

Cheapernet

A low cost version of Ethernet called Cheapernet has been specified, which retains the 10 MHz data rate and the same functional characteristics, but employs cheaper physical layer components. These include thinner, and consequently cheaper, coaxial cable (RG58 – as used in television aerial attachments) and BNC coaxial connectors. No transceiver cables are used – the transceiver is integrated into the controller. In order to achieve the operational specification, limits of 200 m segments are imposed, together with a maximum of 30 transceivers per segment. The minimum inter-transceiver spacing is set at 0.5 m.

4.7.6 The DEUNA controller

As previously mentioned, the Ethernet controller has a host bus-specific part and so can be connected only to the appropriate type of computer. Many different Ethernet controllers specific to host computers are therefore available on the market, but all are similar in structure and operation.

In this section we take the example of the Digital Equipment Corporation (DEC) DEUNA controller for their VAX and PDP–11 range of computers. This example illustrates what is necessary to interface a typical computer to Ethernet, including how the controller is programmed from the host computer.

The DEUNA is illustrated in block diagram form below:

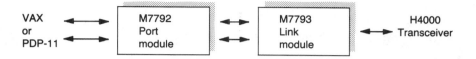

The DEUNA consists of two circuit boards, one (the port) for local memory buffering and interfacing to the VAX or PDP–11 UNIBUS backplane, the other (the link) to perform the data link and part of the physical layer functions. The port module is microprocessor-controlled and contains transmit and receive buffer memory areas for outgoing and incoming Ethernet frames. Logically the DEUNA is as shown in Figure 4.11.

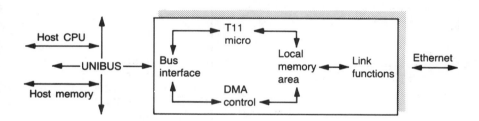

Figure 4.11   DEUNA structure.

The transmission of data to the Ethernet proceeds as follows:

- host CPU tells T11 micro there is a message to transmit
- T11 moves data from host to local memory using direct memory access (DMA)
- link functions transmit message onto Ethernet
- if collision then retry up to a maximum of 15 times
- T11 tells host whether message has been transmitted.

Reception of data from the Ethernet is similar:

- link functions receive and verify data
- data is placed in local memory

- T11 is informed about the presence of data
- T11 uses destination address to start DMA
- DMA moves data from local to host memory
- T11 tells host CPU that a message has arrived.

4.7.7 Programming the DEUNA

A software driver is usually built into the host memory, and its form is dependent on the host operating system as well as on the specific details of the network controller hardware.

In the case of the DEUNA, this has four status/control registers accessible by the host CPU; the registers are memory-mapped into the host address space. These are called PCSR0–PCSR3, as shown in Figure 4.12.

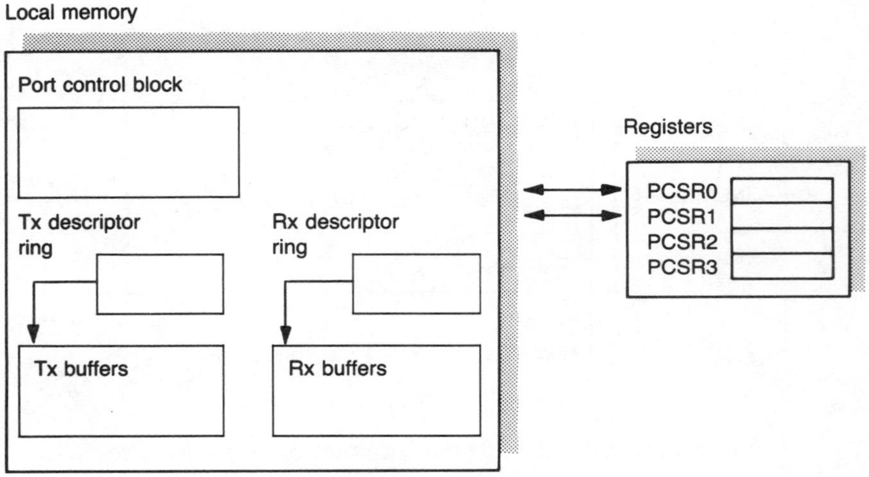

Local memory

Figure 4.12 Programmer's view of the DEUNA.

The DEUNA local memory has a data structure consisting of transmit (Tx) and receive (Rx) buffer pools with a descriptor pointing into each buffer pool. The buffers are chained together in a ring structure. The port control block contains up-to-date details of the status of the current transfers.

The DEUNA provides the following functions:

- *control functions* – attention from either driver or DEUNA
- *port commands* – start, stop etc.

- *data functions* – Tx and Rx
- *ancillary commands* – read/set addresses/counters etc.
- *maintenance functions* – bootstrap etc.

These are used as primitive operations by the software driver resident in the host operating system.

4.7.8 Ethernet chip sets

Several chip sets implementing Ethernet's data link layer and part of the physical layer are now available from different manufacturers, replacing the discrete logic previously necessary, as for example on the DEUNA example outlined above. The numerous small and medium scale integrated circuits on the link board can be replaced by a mere handful of chips, two of which are the Ethernet chip set. The result is that the controller and host interface functions can now be accommodated on a single circuit board, with consequent space, power and ultimately cost savings.

Each available chip set consists of two devices:

- CSMA/CD protocol chip
- serializer chip.

By far the more complex is the protocol chip, typically a 40- or 48-pin VLSI (very large scale integration) device. This deals with the usual link layer functions, including encapsulation and decapsulation of frames and taking retry action following collisions. The reason for the serializer chip being separate is not so much that it is complex, but rather because the technology used to fabricate the VLSI protocol chip is not fast enough to drive a serial bit stream at 10 Mbits/sec. (Actually a 20 Mbits/sec clock is required.) Serializers are built using bipolar logic, a very fast logic family.

The serializer does the Manchester encoding and decoding (see Section 4.3) and passes the collision detect signal to the protocol chip as well as the input/output data. Typically the arrangement of the controller is as shown in Figure 4.13.

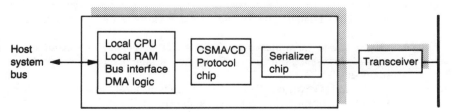

Figure 4.13 Ethernet controller arrangement.

The chip sets have mostly been designed to enable easy interfacing to any 16-bit microprocessor. Either this microprocessor would be used to control the transfer of data frames between a host and the Ethernet, just as the T11 does in the case of the DEUNA, or the microprocessor might itself be the host.

Some chip sets are summarized in Table 4.1.

Table 4.1   Early Ethernet chip sets.

Manufacturer	CSMA/CD protocol chip	pins	Serializer	pins
AMD/Mostek (LANCE)	7990/68590	48	7991/3891	24
Intel	82586	48	82501	24
SEEQ	8001/8003	40	8002	20
Ungermann–Bass/Fujitsu	61301	64	502	24

References

Abramson, N., (1970). 'The ALOHA system – another alternative for computer communications' *Proc. Fall Joint Computer Conference*, 281–285

Abramson, N., (1973). 'The ALOHA system' *Computer Communication Networks* Abramson, N. and Kuo, F.F. (eds.), Prentice-Hall, 501–518

Blair, G.S. and Shepherd, W.D., (1982). 'A performance comparison of Ethernet and the Cambridge Digital Communication Ring' *Computer Networks*, **6**,(1), May

Bux, W., (1981). 'Local-area subnetworks: a performance comparison' *IEEE Trans. Comms.* **COM-29**,(10), October, 1465–1473

Crane, R.C., (1982). 'Ethernet designer's guide' *Microprocessors and Microsystems*, **6**,(8), October, 405–412

Dalal, Y.K. and Printis, R.S., (1981). '48-bit absolute internet and Ethernet host numbers' *ACM Computer Communication Review*, **11**,(4), October, 240–245

DIX, (1980). *Ethernet: a local area network – data link layer and physical layer specifications* Digital, Intel and Xerox Corporations, version 1.0, September

ECMA, (1982). *Local area networks (CSMA/CD baseband) – coaxial cable system* **ECMA-80**, European Computer Manufacturers Association, September

Hutchison, D. and Corcoran, P., (1982). 'Building local area networks to Ethernet specification' *Computer Communications* **5**,(1), February, 12–16

IEEE, (1982). *CSMA/CD access method and physical layer specifications* Draft IEEE Standard 802.3, December

International Standards Organisation, (1985a). *LOTOS – An FDT based on the temporal ordering of observational behaviour* **DP 8807**, Geneva, Switzerland

International Standards Organisation, (1985b). *Estelle – An FDT based on extended state transition model* **DP 9074**, Geneva, Switzerland

Joy, B., (1983). 'Berkeley 4.2 gives Unix operating system network support' *Electronics*, 28 July

Leffler, S.J., Fabry, R.S. and Joy, W., (1983). *A 4.2 BSD Interprocess Communication Primer* Computer Systems Research Group, Dept of Electrical Engineering and Computer Science, University of California, Berkeley

Metcalfe, R.M. and Boggs, D.R., (1976). 'Ethernet: distributed packet switching for local computer networks' *CACM* **19**,(7), July, 395–404

Milner, R., (1980). *A Calculus of Communicating Systems*. Springer-Verlag: New York

Postel, J. (editor), (1980a). 'DoD standard Internet protocol' *ACM Computer Communication Review* **10**,(4), October, 12–51

Postel, J. (editor), (1980b). 'DoD standard transmission control protocol' *ACM Computer Communication Review* **10**,(4), October, 52–132

Roberts, L.G. and Wessler, B., (1973). 'The ARPA network' *Computer Communication Networks*, Abramson and Kuo (editors), Prentice-Hall

Shoch, J.F., Dalal, Y.K., Redell, D.D. and Crane, R.C., (1982). 'Evolution of the Ethernet local computer network' *Computer*, August, 10–26

Tanenbaum, A.S., (1981). *Computer Networks*. Prentice-Hall

Xerox, (1981a). *Internet transport protocols*, Xerox System Integration Standard XSIS 028112, December

Xerox, (1981b). *Courier: the remote procedure call protocol*, Xerox System Integration Standard XSIS 038112, December

Xerox, (1981c). *The Clearinghouse: a decentralized agent for locating named objects in a distributed environment*, OPD-T8103, Xerox Corporation, Office Products Division, October

Chapter 5
Token ring and bus

The token passing LANs form the subject of this chapter. Once again the aim is to show the historical development of these networks and their evolution into standard form. The General Motors MAP initiative also forms an important part of the chapter, and the intention is to show how the token bus technology, together with a choice of higher level OSI protocols, has formed an application driven architecture.

5.1 Overview

The use of token passing as a communications arbitration protocol has been well known for a considerable time. Over 15 years ago Farmer and Newhall outlined the idea of using a token as a dynamic means of sharing a communications medium (Farmer and Newhall, 1969). In the face of typical bursty computer traffic this proves to be more efficient of bandwidth than a static allocation scheme for multiple users. A two-level hierarchy of rings was envisaged, the top level interconnecting a set of secondary rings at different sites. An experimental single ring was built at Bell Laboratories, operating at some 3 Mbits/sec. A single bit represented the circulating token, and a supervisory computer was used for cleaning up faulty packets from the network. These features appear in much later token ring systems. Also, the start and end of the packet were delineated by bipolar violation, a technique used in the new standard token passing systems (see Sections 5.3 and 5.4).

In the early 1970s the University of California at Irvine worked on a token access local area network (Loomis, 1973). This was part of the DCS (Distributed Computing System) project (Farber *et al.*, 1973; Farber, 1975) which originally intended to use an empty slot ring design but used a token ring implementation in the end. The design for the DCS ring interface was developed into an idea for a single-chip device (Mockapetris *et al.*, 1977), which was taken up later at Massachusetts Institute of Technology (MIT) (Clark *et al.*, 1978) and developed into a practical implementation (Saltzer and Pogran, 1979).

IBM's token ring work at their Zurich research laboratory (Bux *et al.*, 1981) was in large measure responsible for the technical details incorporated into the IEEE 802 Project's token ring draft standard (IEEE, 1983), although many detailed alterations were made including the use of long (48-bit) addresses as in the CSMA/CD standard.

A study of ring networks is presented in Liu and Rouse (1983). This includes details of the above work on token rings, and also reports on the Ringnet built by Prime (Gordon *et al.*, 1980). This was probably the first commercially available token ring LAN, and was used for interconnecting Prime computers. More recent work, specifically on low-cost token rings, includes Hutchison and Coffield (1984) and Willis (1983).

The token bus has emerged, alongside the ring, as one of the new draft standards for LANs, despite the fact that nothing significant had previously appeared in print which could be identified as the inspiration for the token bus. Basically, the bus approach uses the same medium access protocol as the ring version but is built on a bus topology. In fact the bus is made to look like a logical ring in order to support the token passing protocol. Each station has a unique address and the addresses are arranged in a logical ordering such that each station has a known 'up station' and 'down station' on the logical ring. The token is passed explicitly from one station to the next using this logical ring ordering. Details follow in a later section.

It seems the case that the IEEE 802 committee introduced the token bus as a result of pressure from groups who were unhappy with the non-determinism of CSMA/CD, yet equally unhappy with the complexities of active repeater elements in the token ring physical system. Token passing on a passive broadcast bus seemed the right compromise – and it was hoped that this combination would be suitable for industrial real-time applications.

In this chapter we begin by looking more closely at the token ring technology, then at that of the token bus. In the case of the ring we can first look at the experimental system at MIT before going on to describe the new standard.

5.2 Tokens

There are two major differences between Ethernet type systems and token rings, namely the access control mechanism and the communication method.

Access in Ethernet is by contention and communication by broadcast whereas in a token ring access is by token and communication is point-to-point.

Problems of rings such as the reliability of the repeater string and provision of distributed initialization/recovery can be overcome, leaving rings with several advantageous features, some of which are:

(1) Token rings are deterministic. If a maximum packet size is decided upon, the maximum time interval between successive appearances of the token can always be calculated, i.e. once a node has sent one packet the time within which the next one will be able to be sent is known.

   Ethernet, on the other hand, can suffer collisions. Collisions mean that the time interval between transmissions cannot be calculated. Though unlikely, it is possible a node may never be able to send if continuous collisions were to occur.

(2) Token rings are point-to-point. This allows fibre optic technology to be used quite easily.

   With Ethernet, however, use of fibre optics presents problems in connecting to the communication medium – no suitable tapping method is presently available.

(3) Token rings use repeaters. This means they can span a much greater physical distance more easily than Ethernet.

   Although such arguments in favour of token rings are attractive, broadcast networks have other equally attractive arguments in their favour. So far, research has not shown any one method to be conclusively 'best'. A good paper on this is by Saltzer and Clark (1981).

5.2.1 MIT token ring

The Massachusetts Institute of Technology (MIT) Laboratory for Computer Science's implementation of a token ring provided many ideas for this type of local network.

To send a packet a node must:

(1)   wait for the token to come by,

(2)   transform it so that no other node will recognize it,

(3)   transmit its packet,

(4)   replace the token.

A node is allowed to send only one packet, which has a maximum length, after which it is required to return the token. This approach guarantees all users fair use of the ring on a 'round robin' basis and ensures no one user can 'hog' the ring.

With a token control mechanism a way must be devised for the token to start moving, and for recovery in case the token gets lost or transmission errors cause two or more tokens to appear.

One other consideration in a token system is that the ring must be large enough 'bit-wise' for a complete token to be accommodated on the ring. To overcome this, a shift register is switched in if necessary.

The MIT design was aimed at being efficient, yet cheap, and with easy add-on facilities. With a ring there are no routing decisions – every packet travels all around the ring and in the MIT version it is removed by the originator.

5.3 Token ring

As with Ethernet, there was significant experimental work with token rings leading up to the specification of a standard. Token access methods were described in technical reports more than 15 years ago (Farmer and Newhall, 1969) but have tended to be overshadowed by the Ethernet activity until the recent international standards work began. The most important interim developments in token rings have taken place at MIT and more recently at IBM Zurich (see Saltzer and Pogran (1979) and Bux *et al.*, (1981)), and these have had a major influence on the draft token ring standard which has been produced in parallel by IEEE (1983) and ECMA (1983). In this section, token rings are described in general terms and details given of the new draft standard token ring.

Figure 5.1 outlines the topology of a token ring. The ring consists of a number of nodes interconnected by segments of the communication medium (typically twisted pair wires or coaxial cable) linking together the

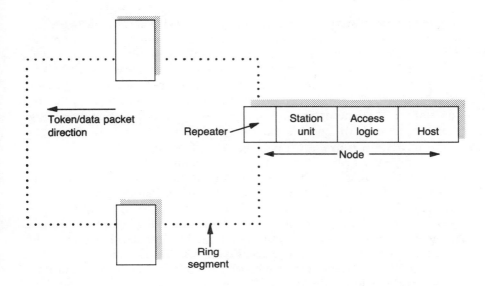

Figure 5.1   Token ring topology.

node repeaters in a loop. These repeaters pass on serial data from one segment to the next, but also allow the attached station to read the information as it passes. In addition, the ring can be broken at a repeater so that the station can write data onto the ring.

Data travels unidirectionally round an individual ring at one of two data rates specified in the standard: 1 or 4 Mbits/sec. The repeaters contain bypass relays which are powered from the station; these are automatically operated when the station is switched on or off to connect it to or disconnect it from the ring. Repeater reliability is expected to be extremely high. The standard requires each repeater to have a mean time between failures of greater than one million hours. As in Ethernet, each station has a unique network address.

A unique bit pattern called the 'token' continuously circulates the ring while no station requires to send a message. When a station is requested by its attached host to transmit a message to another host on the ring, the station must wait for the token to pass through its repeater. When the token has been recognized the station alters one of the bits (say from 0 to 1) so that the token is no longer available to any other station. The station then sends its message, which may be of variable length, addressed to the station specified by its own host. Immediately after the completion of the message, the token is reinstated onto the ring by the transmitting station so that the next station downstream may use the ring.

In the token ring system there is no contention as in Ethernet to use the medium. The right to use the ring passes in a round robin fashion from one node to the next in physical sequence. Furthermore, each node is guaranteed access to the ring within a certain worst case time (worst case when all other nodes on the ring use their right to transmit a message) given one important provision: there is a maximum permitted length of message transmitted by any station. This is necessary both to ensure a fair share of the medium among stations, and also to enable stations to detect a potentially disastrous occurrence – the token going missing, or equivalently being corrupted.

There is a general problem with ring configurations which does not apply to Ethernets or other bus topologies, namely that the electronic length of the ring, that is the number of bits which can be accommodated within the closed loop, is limited. This is due to the fact that each repeater provides storage for only a few bits at a time, and that a bit in transit spans a significant length of the communications medium (at 10 Mbits/sec one bit takes up 20 m, while at 1 Mbits/sec it occupies 200 m).

Obviously, then, the length of the ring in bits depends on the number of attached stations as well as on the physical expanse of the ring. This does not imply a limitation, however, on the length of data packet which can be accommodated but rather on the length of the token. The token must be entirely accommodated within the closed loop to allow it to circulate the ring, but this is not the case for data packets. The reason why ring length is no problem for data packets is that a transmitting station, in addition to inserting its packet bit by bit onto the ring, also drains its own packet from the ring – in other words the ring is effectively broken at the transmitting node. Only when a transmitting station has seen the end of its own packet return does it regenerate the token pattern and cause its own repeater to close the ring once more.

Note that, whereas packets may be as long as thousands of bits, the token need be only several bits long, e.g. 10 bits in the experimental MIT system and 24 bits in the new token ring standard.

Despite the fact that the token may be very short, it would be usual to make no assumptions about the minimum number of attached stations for any network configuration but to have at one place in the ring a shift register of length suitable to accommodate the token. This is called the latency buffer. If the system contains a so-called 'monitor' station, this is a suitable place for the latency buffer.

Another way to look at the token is that it has two states: free and busy. The free token has one of its bits, usually called the token bit, set to 0 (using the example given above) and a busy token, which immediately precedes a message, has its token bit set to 1. It is important to note that a token, whether free or busy, should pass any given node within a time determined by the ring latency, including repeater delays, plus the maximum transmission time for one station. This is called the valid transmission time.

A monitor station is used principally for detecting and correcting errors in the system. Transmission errors due to noise and other factors are a fact of life. A single-bit error affecting the token would be particularly catastrophic if no measures were taken to deal with it. Responsibility for error detection and correction can be assigned in two ways in token rings. In the first, a specific monitor station has the task of ensuring the integrity of the token pattern. It does this by employing a timer which is started whenever the token passes its repeater. The initial value of the timer is chosen to correspond to the expected maximum time between consecutive tokens, whether free or busy, that is the valid transmission time. Should the timer decrement to zero the monitor will deduce the existence of an error. It will initiate the reinstatement of the token pattern onto the ring and may possibly also perform some error logging action.

In the second method there is no specific monitor station but instead a form of distributed control is employed. Recognizing that a single monitor station, like the token itself, is a potential weakness in the system, the strategy used spreads responsibility for missing token detection and consequent regeneration over all the stations on the ring. Each station has a timer with value chosen as before, and each can potentially detect a missing token. The problem in this case is one of arbitrating which station places the token back onto the ring (two or more tokens on the ring simultaneously is just as big a problem as no token at all).

Various possible strategies could be adopted, including one in which stations having expired timers independently send a token onto the ring and then watch for a possible multiplicity of tokens. If there is, each station backs off for a random time interval before trying again, as in Ethernet. However, the method specified in the token ring standard involves a station with an expired timer sending out a special type of data packet which all stations can recognize as a claim token packet. The idea is that of the stations which send out claim token packets, the one having the highest network address should win the bid to reinstate the token. Stations therefore defer to claim token packets containing source addresses greater than their own, and the successful station is the one which receives a claim token packet containing its own source address. The standard for token rings in fact uses a combination of the two monitor methods just described. There is initially a specially designated master monitor node which has a no-token timer, but in case this special node fails all the other nodes contain a backup monitor function which is invoked if a longer timer expires. Following the claim token sequence the node which reinstated the token assumes the role of the master ring monitor. Each node, furthermore, has a backup latency buffer which is switched into the ring whenever that node becomes the master monitor.

The packet format for a token ring, according to the standard, is illustrated in Figure 5.2, along with the format of the token itself. In many of its fields this format is the same as that of the standard Ethernet, but there are important differences.

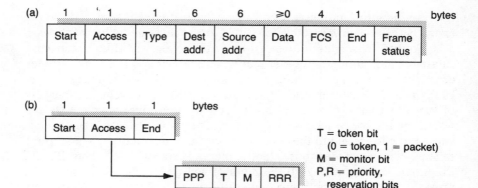

Figure 5.2   (a) Packet format for the token ring; (b) token format.

The access field contains the token bit, although the token is considered to be the sequence start–access–end. There is a monitor bit which is set to 0 by a node transmitting a packet. This bit is set to 1 by the active monitor station. Packets observed by the monitor to have a monitor bit of 1 are considered to be faulty and are aborted. In the access field there are also priority and reservation bits which are intended to be used by nodes having urgent transmission requirements, for example nodes using the ring in real-time applications such as voice transmission. Eight priority levels are provided.

The start and end fields are unique patterns which cannot occur within the body of a packet. In the token ring, as in Ethernet, bits are encoded using a form of Manchester code, which it will be recalled guarantees a transition in mid bit cell. In this case the differential Manchester encoding technique is used. In this form, a zero is encoded by a transition at the beginning and middle of the bit cell; the first half of a one's bit cell takes the level of the preceding cell's second half, followed of course by a mid bit cell transition. The differential form has slightly improved error detection characteristics which may be useful in a ring configuration.

Start and end are made unique by including non-data bits, i.e. bits which have no mid cell transition. End has an error bit which can be set by any node which detects a packet error, and passed to the active monitor station to log and report faults.

Notice that the data field length has no maximum value determined by the architecture of the standard. However, the value of the token holding timer for a station limits the time for which that station can transmit a frame. When a ring system is initialized the value of the token holding and the other timers must be agreed upon. Altogether there are seven timers:

Timer	*Recommended setting*
TRR – return to repeat	2.5 ms
THT – token holding	10 ms
TQP – queue protocol data unit	10 ms
TVX – valid transmission	THT + TRR (= 12.5 ms)
TNT – no token	1 s
TAM – active monitor	3 s
TSM – standby monitor	7 s

The recommended settings have been carefully chosen. Although the system can be initialized using other values, this should be done only for a good reason. As a little thought will show, timer values which are too small cause recovery actions to be invoked too readily, while values which are too large mean that ring bandwidth will be unnecessarily wasted. The THT timer value of 10 ms is equivalent to the transmission of 5000 bytes at the 4 Mbits/sec data rate option. This can be thought of as the normal maximum frame length.

The other timers are designed to deal with exception conditions including the faulty operation of a transmitting station, or of the active monitor, or the disappearance of the token.

The frame status field contains response bits, specifically 'address recognized' and 'packet copied' bits. These are set to 0 on transmission and set as appropriate at the receiving node. Thus, low level acknowledgments are provided, unlike Ethernet, and these can be used to implement low level flow control.

Each ring station contains three finite state machines (FSMs) corresponding to the three separate activities which the station can be operating. These are:

- operational FSM

- standby monitor FSM

- active monitor FSM.

The operational mode is the normal one, and begins when the station is initialized into the ring configuration. Its address is checked to be unique in the ring and its presence made known to its immediate neighbour downstream. The normal functions consist of receiving (and repeating) and transmitting frames. This FSM can be suspended if a monitor FSM is required to operate.

Standby monitor mode is entered after initialization of the station. This FSM checks to see whether the active ring monitor is functioning properly by setting the TSM timer. If the TSM expires then this station will attempt to become the active monitor (and the operational FSM suspended meantime). Under normal conditions every station has its stand-by and operational FSMs running together.

There will be only one active monitor station at any time. This FSM checks for and deals with errors, using the TVX and TAM timers. The active monitor and operational FSMs run in parallel.

5.4 Token bus

The token bus is an implementation of a logical token ring on a bus communication medium (see Figure 5.3). It has emerged from the recent IEEE (1982) and ECMA work on LANs to become one of the standardized architectures, without significant experimental work having been previously reported.

Amongst the token bus advocates, the primary motivation for adopting a bus instead of a ring communications medium was the simplicity and passive nature of the bus cable, which has no active components inserted. In contrast, the ring medium has repeaters in series with cable and is therefore more prone to component failure. Ethernet, however, uses a probabilistic medium access protocol which is not good enough to ensure real-time response across a local network.

The token bus is considered by many to combine the good features of CSMA/CD (namely its passive, flexible medium) and the token ring (its deterministic token access protocol), and therefore it should perform well in factory and other real-time applications. The provision of real-time properties in a LAN is not so easy to assure, however, even in a token bus system because of the possibility of the token 'disappearing', i.e. being corrupted by noise or not reinstated by a faulty transmitting station. Although token passing systems have built-in token recovery features, these too may fail.

According to Le Lann (1985), CSMA/CD protocols are in fact suitable for use in real-time systems when operated in (at least) duplicate, and an algorithm applied to control the parallel channels. One CSMA/CD

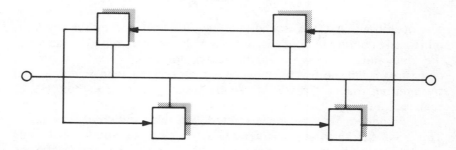

Figure 5.3 Logical ring implemented on a bus.

channel is used for control with the other(s) being for data. This system will handle normal and emergency messages (the latter being messages which require top priority in acquiring a channel). The failure of a channel can also be tolerated: for a system with N channels if $N - 1$ fail then the remaining 1 will operate the conventional CSMA/CD protocol, but determinism can be provided only when two or more channels are working.

The format of a token bus packet is illustrated in Figure 5.4. It has similarities to both Ethernet and token ring packets.

The preamble serves the same purpose as in Ethernet packets, that is it allows the receivers to synchronize onto the bit cells of the transmitted message. Start and end are similar to those of the token ring, using non-data patterns for uniqueness (violations of the Manchester encoding), and including an error bit in end. Source and destination addresses have two possible lengths, like the IEEE 802.3 and ISO 8802/3 CSMA/CD standard, but unlike those of the earlier Ethernet and the token ring. They can be either two or six bytes long, but all addresses on a given LAN must be the same length. The control field combines features of both the access and type fields in the token ring. It indicates packet type, and has priority and reservation bits for certain types of packet. One of the types indicated is that of 'token'. There is no status field containing response bits and consequently no provision for low level acknowledgments.

In the token bus system a token is in fact a whole packet with a zero length data field, but containing destination and source addresses as well as a control field (with the free token pattern) and FCS field. The token is passed round the nodes in decreasing numerical order of network addresses, and to do this each node has to send explicitly a free token packet with appropriate addresses to the next node in sequence. There is no possibility of collisions as in Ethernet, and no problem as in the token ring with disappearing tokens. The node which currently holds the free token (whether it has just finished transmitting a packet or not) has the responsibility for sending the token to its successor node. Should a successor station fail to accept the token the token holder enters recovery procedures to find a new successor and to remove the (presumed) failed station from the logical ring.

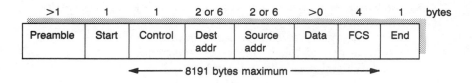

>1	1	1	2 or 6	2 or 6	>0	4	1	bytes
Preamble	Start	Control	Dest addr	Source addr	Data	FCS	End	

◄──── 8191 bytes maximum ────►

Figure 5.4 Packet format for the token bus.

To allow stations to send and accept tokens in this way, each station knows not only its own address on the network (as in Ethernet and the token ring) but also those of its successor and predecessor. These last two addresses are maintained dynamically within stations. The algorithms built into the nodes allow stations to leave and join the logical ring, updating the successor and predecessor addresses as appropriate.

The description so far concerns the token access method but has not given details of the communication technology used. In fact the token bus standard specifies three alternative physical layers, two being baseband systems similar to that of Ethernet and the third being a broadband system which uses well-known CATV (essentially cable television) technology. The first baseband system offers a data rate of 1 Mbits/sec, the second a choice of either 5 or 10 Mbits/sec. The broadband alternative offers 1, 5 or 10 Mbits/sec as its data rates. All three systems use 75 ohm coaxial cable as the communication medium.

As indicated above, the main use of the token bus architecture will probably be in applications which need a guaranteed upper bound on access time for a given node, namely in real-time applications, while still using the simplicity of Ethernet-like communications at the physical level. Section 5.6 outlines the adoption of the token bus in two application domains represented by the PROWAY and MAP communities in process control and manufacturing systems respectively.

5.5 The standard token passing systems

As for CSMA/CD (Ethernet) the IEEE reference numbers for the token passing LAN standards have become ISO numbers as follows:

- 802.4 has become 8802/4 (token bus)
- 802.5 has become 8802/5 (token ring).

The frame structures and other details from the IEEE (and ECMA) work have been carried across to the ISO documentation. From the early drafts some details have been changed in both the bus and ring specifications. Of the two the token bus was the first to become firm. When Project 802 first reported on the specific technologies being 'standardized' it had seemed highly likely that the token ring was well ahead of the bus version in technical maturity.

However, at least some of the delays in work on the token ring lay in a patent dispute on the token ring access mechanism. A Dutch organization called Willemijn Houdstermaatschappij B.V. had filed patents in the USA and other countries and claimed that material in the token ring drafts produced by IEEE was subject to these patents. The origins of Willemijn are somewhat mysterious. In 1983, IEEE 802.5 draft specifications contained a note to the effect that this patent claim had been made and that licences could be obtained under this patent from Willemijn.

The effect of this of course was to force prospective implementers of the standard token ring to consider whether they were willing to pay a licence to a third party for the right to use the IEEE 802.5 specification. In the meantime the computing press were much more interested in whether IBM (who originated the essence of 802.5) would commit themselves to backing the token ring standard; such a commitment was given after a year or more of speculation. This has had the effect of assuring independent implementers that the token ring standard has a secure future.

Because the token bus specification hardened first, and probably because 802.4 had considerable industrial pressure behind it, semiconductor manufacturers had already begun producing 802.4 chip sets, whereas the slowness of 802.5 meant a corresponding lag in committing the token ring specification to silicon.

5.5.1 Service specifications

As for the standard Ethernet the LLC/MAC interface for both types of token passing system offers the following services:

- MA_DATA.request
- MA_DATA.confirm
- MA_DATA.indicate

where the request is by the local LLC asking the MAC to send data to another (remote) LLC. The confirm is given by the local MAC to the requesting LLC to say whether the request was successful. Indicate is passed by a MAC to its LLC to indicate the arrival of data.

At the MAC/physical layer boundary the token ring has the same primitives as the standard Ethernet, namely:

- PH_DATA.request
- PH_DATA.confirm
- PH_DATA.indicate

with the same meanings.

The token bus uses a different set, reflecting characteristics of its mode of operation:

- PH_DATA.request
- PH_DATA.indicate

- PH_MODE.request
- PH_NOTIFY.request

where PH_DATA.indicate provides the requesting LLC with confirmation of its previous PH_DATA.request operation, on a one-bit-at-a-time basis, as well as the usual indication of arriving data bits. PH_MODE.request is for use in stations which can function as both a source of bits and as a bus repeater for the network. When the station is transmitting, the physical layer must send bits to all connected bus segments; when in repeater mode, bits must be sent to all segments except the one which is the source of the bits. PH_NOTIFY.request tells the physical layer that an end-of-frame delimiter has been received and therefore, immediately following, the physical layer should see only silence on the medium (or so-called 'pad idle' bits which constitute a frame's preamble).

In addition to the above, network management services are specified at both the LLC/MAC and MAC/physical layer boundaries. The management services differ for the bus and ring systems, but in general terms include resetting the MAC and physical layer logic, specifying timer values, and detecting errors in operation.

5.6 PROWAY and MAP

PROWAY and MAP are user-driven 'standards' developed for local network industrial applications. This section describes the background and requirements of both initiatives, and shows how the token bus is being used as the basis for these industrial applications.

5.6.1 PROWAY

PROWAY (meaning process control data highway) is intended for process monitoring and control applications and was originally prepared by the International Electrotechnical Commission (IEC), specifically IEC/SC65C/ WG6. The goal of the working group was to specify a method of interconnecting systems in multivendor process control applications meeting the following requirements:

- high reliability
- guaranteed access times for data transmission
- specified performance even under abnormal conditions.

In 1983 the proposed standard was produced. Up to 100 devices over distances of up to 2 km would be supported by a dual-redundant bus. A maximum access delay of 20 ms would be tolerated for maximum configurations (100 stations) in which half the stations are simultaneously requesting access to send messages of 128 bits average length. These are very small message lengths compared to typical network applications in office and software development environments. An average throughput rate of up to 100 Kbits/sec was envisaged in the process control type of application; each bus in the proposed standard would have a capability of 1 Mbits/sec data rates, thus allowing plenty of capacity for unusual peak traffic rates.

The physical layer and communications medium were initially unspecified but the IEC working group kept in close contact with the IEEE 802 local network project and came to the conclusion that the token bus (802.4) standard offered basically the features they required. Together with the Instrument Society of America (ISA) they worked on an extension to 802.4 which would give the essential PROWAY characteristics, including the protocols required at the LLC/MAC boundary.

In 1983 an Appendix (B) appeared in the 802.4 standards document entitled *Extensions for industrial control*. Reasons for trying to ensure compatibility between 802.4 and PROWAY are given. These include the potential benefits of sharing a single communications system for office and industrial applications, a reduced body of knowledge required by development and maintenance staff concerned with the joint network, and the economic benefit of producing a larger volume of a smaller range of chips to implement a single standard.

The extended needs of the token bus standard include the following:

- recovery from transmission errors while the sender continues to hold the token, using immediate acknowledgement and a limited number of retries;
- the ability to request predefined data which is returned from a remote station while the requester holds the token;
- the ability to initialize and control a remote station whose higher layers are out of operation;
- closer control of the upper bound for a station's access time to the shared medium.

An important specific addition to 802.4 would be a new data frame category at the MAC level. This would use reserved symbol patterns to introduce three members of this new category:

- request with no response
- request with response
- response only.

These are in line with the initial PROWAY specification which envisaged five functions at the 'user highway' boundary, i.e. services at the LLC/MAC boundary in IEEE terms. They were:

- *SDA* – send data with acknowledgement; mandatory (to a single remote station; delivery confirmed)
- *MOP* – management of PROWAY; mandatory (local network management facilities)
- *GSD* – global send data; optional (send to all stations; no acknowledgements)
- *RDR* – request data with reply; optional (get data from a single remote station)
- *RSR* – remote station recovery; optional (bootstrap a halted station).

Basically these are connectionless services; connection-oriented operation is not thought appropriate for this type of industrial control application. For more details of the initial PROWAY work and the IEC-proposed standard see Capel and Lynch (1983).

In due course it is expected that details of industrial control local networks will make their introduction formally into the community of ISO local network standards under the names miniMAP and Fieldbus (see Section 3.5).

5.6.2 MAP

An altogether more prominent initiative, MAP (manufacturing automation protocol) is driven by the General Motors Corporation in the USA. It is intended to be the standard basis for a factory-wide communications system supporting the sorts of applications used in this environment, and allowing for multivendor equipment throughout the factory.

The basic idea is to have a backbone network running through the factory onto which are attached management and manufacturing control computers, as well as a variety of other networks controlling individual shop floor manufacturing cells. These other networks would typically be low speed, low cost proprietary systems built for specific purposes and integrated closely with vendor devices such as robots. These networks would be attached to the MAP backbone by means of gateways. Thus, the entire system forms a two-level network hierarchy.

General Motors set up the MAP task force in late 1980 to investigate and identify a common communication standard for plant-floor systems. Its specific objectives were:

(1) to define a message standard supporting application-to-application communications

(2)   to identify application functions to be supported by this message format standard

(3)   to recommend protocols that meet the functional requirements of MAP.

The first MAP document, a general introduction together with implementation guidelines, appeared in late 1982. In early 1984, version 1.0 of MAP was published. This was much more detailed and showed how upward 'migration' paths could be taken from interim to internationally accepted standards. MAP is based on the OSI reference model architecture. Until firm OSI standards for layers above the data link were available, the intention was to use US National Bureau of Standards (NBS) protocols as an interim measure. Later versions (starting with 2.0 in mid 1985) contain more detail on upper layer protocols and also on network management. In summary, the protocol choices for MAP V3.0 (MAP, 1987) are:

- layer 7: ISO application kernel (CASE) + FTAM + MMS
- layer 6: ISO presentation kernel
- layer 5: ISO session kernel
- layer 4: ISO transport class 4
- layer 3: ISO network connectionless
- layer 2: IEEE 802.2 class 1
- layer 1: IEEE 802.4 broadband.

The adoption of the token bus LAN as specified by IEEE 802.4 was made for basically the same reasons as it was chosen for PROWAY: it gives predictable access times and the communications medium is simple and reliable. The use of a broadband medium suited the General Motors strategy for factory communications systems.

From early on, General Motors had planned to install broadband cable in their manufacturing plants. This choice allows for the shared use of the cable for different types of traffic, and provides high bandwidth for future growth in demand. Furthermore, the technology of broadband is well proven. It is used in community access television (CATV) in which components and techniques have been developed and improved over many years.

On top of the broadband token bus is the class 1 (connectionless) LLC layer. Level 3 of MAP is the ISO connectionless network layer. At the transport layer the ISO class 4 service is specified. This builds on the connectionless lower layers to give a full connection-oriented service.

The session, presentation and application layers are represented by the ISO core session and presentation facilities and the common application services elements (CASE) of the application layer. At the application level, specific functions included are FTAM (file transfer and management) and, originally, MMFS (manufacturing messaging format standard). The former is an ISO standard, the latter a MAP-developed format for encoding messages and providing limited file transfer to manufacturing nodes such as numerical control systems, programmable controllers and robots. MMFS has since been progressed by the Electrical Industries Association (EIA) as standard RS-511, and is now called MMS (manufacturing message service) in MAP V3.0.

Unlike PROWAY, the MAP documents present a total systems plan, including application-to-application messaging, and gateways to other (non-MAP) networks.

Recently there has emerged another protocol architecture called TOP (technical and office protocol) designed to complement the MAP work. Originated by the Boeing Corporation of Seattle, USA, TOP is the office application counterpart of the industrially based MAP. TOP also uses the OSI model architecture but is based on IEEE 802.3 Ethernet (TOP, 1987).

General Motors intend MAP to be an open standard, i.e. one which is available to any organization, be they users or implementers of the standard. MAP has support from a variety of other companies, some of whom see the results being applicable to their own environments, while others want to manufacture MAP-compatible components. Already there is a MAP user group, of which many of these companies are members. It is not, of course, a matter of technical advancement for its own sake: the commercial pressure to automate factories is largely the motivating factor behind the creation of MAP. General Motors expects to become much more world-competitive through the deployment of MAP in its own factories. Commentators predict savings in development time of a few years for new vehicle models, improved quality in production and even reduced costs of a couple of thousand dollars per vehicle.

In addition to the so-called backbone MAP architecture document – the main thrust of MAP initially – there is now a MAP cell architecture which defines an end system capable of communicating with other networks attached to the MAP backbone. These may be reduced capability networks for specific factory applications, or PROWAY/miniMAP networks (with reduced layering compared to MAP) suitable for real-time response. MAP bridges are used to connect MAP subnetworks at the data link level. Gateways connect a MAP system to non-MAP networks.

Finally, as will be explained in Chapter 9, network management is also included in the MAP specification and will play a very important part in ensuring the proper operation of factory systems of the future.

References

Bux, W. *et al.*, (1981). 'A reliable token-ring system for local-area communication' *National Telecommunications Conference*, November, A2.2.1–A2.2.6

Capel, A.C. and Lynch, G.F., (1983). 'Proway: the evolving standard for process control data highways' *InTech*, September, 91–94

Clark, D.D., Pogran, K.T. and Reed, D.P., (1978). 'An introduction to local area networks' *Proc. IEEE* **66**,(11), November, 1497–1517

ECMA, (1983). *Local area networks: token ring* Final Draft ECMA-RR, European Computer Manufacturers Association, January

Farber, D.J., Feldman, J., Heinrich, F.R., Hopwood, M.D., Larson, K.C., Loomis, D.C. and Rowe, L.A., (1973). 'The distributed computing system' *IEEE Compcon'73*, February, 31-34

Farber, D.J., (1975). 'A ring network' *Datamation*, February, 44–46

Farmer, W.D. and Newhall, E.E., (1969). 'An experimental distributed switching system to handle bursty computer traffic' *Proc. ACM Symposium on Problems in the Optimization of Data Communication Systems* Georgia, October, 1–33

Gordon, R.L., Farr, W.W. and Levine, P., (1980). 'Ringnet: a packet switched local network with decentralized control' *Computer Networks* **3**, 373–379

Hutchison, D. and Coffield, D., (1984). 'A simple token ring local area network' *Microprocessors and Microsystems* **8**,(4), May, 171–176

IEEE, (1982). *Token-passing bus access method and physical layer specifications*, Draft IEEE Standard 802.4, December

IEEE, (1983). *Token ring access method and physical layer specifications*, Draft IEEE Standard 802.5, April

Le Lann, G., (1985). 'Real-time protocols' *Local Area Networks: An Advanced Course* (Hutchison, D., Mariani, J.A. and Shepherd, W.D., editors) Springer-Verlag

Liu, M.T. and Rouse, D.M., (1983). 'A study of ring networks' *IFIP WG6.4 International Workshop on Ring Technology* University of Kent, September

Loomis, D.C., (1973). *Ring communication protocols* Technical report #26, Department of Information and Computer Science, UC Irvine, January

MAP, (1987). *Manufacturing automation protocol*, version 3.0, MAP/TOP Users Group

Mockapetris, P.V., Lyle, M.R. and Farber, D.J., (1977). 'On the design of local network interfaces' *Proc. IFIP '77*, August, 427–430

Saltzer, J.H. and Pogran, K.T., (1979). 'A star-shaped ring network with high maintainability' *Proc. Local Area Communications Network Symposium*, Mitre Corp., Boston, May, 179–190

Saltzer, J.H. and Clark, D.D., (1981). 'Why a ring?' *ACM Computer Communication Review*, **11**,(4), October, 211–217

TOP, (1987). *Technical and office protocol*, version 3.0, MAP/TOP Users Group

Willis, P.J., (1983). 'The Bath token ring: architecture and early experience' *IFIP WG6.4 International Workshop on Ring Technology*, University of Kent, September

Chapter 6
The Cambridge Ring

This chapter is about the development of the Cambridge Ring in the UK, the main example of a slotted ring technology. Although relatively unimportant in other countries, having arrived on the ISO standards scene late in the day, the research based on this local network has played an important part in progressing local network protocols and distributed computing.

6.1 Introduction

As the name suggests, this network originated in Cambridge, at the University computer laboratory, and has a loop topology similar to that of the token ring. The first notable event in the Cambridge Ring's history was when Professor Maurice Wilkes, then head of the computer laboratory, presented a paper on local ring communications at the PACNET conference in Japan in August 1975 (Wilkes, 1975). What he reviewed and suggested for further development was the **register insertion** system of operation. The idea of register insertion was already being pioneered at the Hasler organization in Switzerland (Hafner *et al.*, 1974) and in the USA at Ohio State University (Reames and Liu, 1975). Wilkes, indeed, references these two sources in his paper. The primary reason for using register insertion was to avoid the problem of hogging whereby one node could constantly transmit packets onto the network. Basically, Wilkes proposed having continuously circulating packets or slots in the network, marked either full or empty depending on whether they were being used.

In December 1976 an addendum to Wilkes' paper was issued, outlining a way in which 'hogging' can be avoided more simply: if each full slot is made to return to and pass its transmitting node before being marked as empty then hogging does not take place. Furthermore, the return journey from destination to source can be used to convey information on whether the data in the slot was accepted at the destination node. Wilkes therefore decided to adopt this new anti-hogging technique and the Cambridge Ring became known as an empty slot ring. Each slot has a small fixed length data field, two bytes in the Cambridge Ring design. Consequently, the slot contains not so much a packet as a minipacket (see Section 6.2 for further details).

In fact, the notion of using the empty slot technique for ring networks was first reported by J.R. Pierce in the Bell System Technical Journal in 1972 (Pierce, 1972). An experimental ring was built, operating at 1.5 Mbits/sec (Kropfl, 1972). Although these early papers put forward the main ideas in this area, credit for carrying the ideas through the difficult path to realization lies firmly with Wilkes' project at Cambridge.

The Cambridge Ring is unidirectional, and has a raw data rate of 10 Mbits/sec. Each node has an active repeater inserted in the ring (as opposed to Ethernet in which the taps are passive). The cable therefore consists of segments linking the repeaters together, each segment consisting of two pairs of wires. Typically, twisted pairs (telephone wires) are used, although in the original ring at Cambridge University one of the segments was a fibre optic link. Faster versions of the ring are likely to make use of fibre optic cable because of its high bandwidth capability.

There is a fixed node called the monitor station which has the responsibility for creating the empty slot structure when the ring starts up, and for clearing corrupt minipackets and reporting instances of errors.

Unlike the case of the token ring, the monitor function is not backed up in any other node.

Devices are attached to the ring repeaters via access logic and a station unit. Each station unit is the same as all others apart from an address plug which uniquely identifies that particular node. Inside the station unit are three registers: the transmission shift register, the receive shift register, and the source select register. This last register is used to limit access to a device. When it contains all ones, the station will listen to a minipacket from any source. If it contains zero, the station is deaf to all sources. Otherwise the station will receive from the device whose address is in the register. Access logic is specific to each type of device and will in many cases be a parallel interface unit onto a computer bus.

In the new UK Cambridge Ring interface specification (see Section 6.9) a 40-bit minipacket is defined: two extra 'type' bits have been added for future use. Work has also progressed to produce special chips to implement the functions of the repeater and station unit, and separately to develop a 'fast' ring operating at 100 Mbits/sec.

Higher level software protocols are required to be built on top of the minipacket basic ring service so that the attached hosts or devices on the network can intercommunicate without having to know all the details of the ring operation. Directly on top of the minipacket layer it is usual to build a 'packet protocol' (PP) (or 'basic block protocol' (BBP)) which deals with packets of variable length similar to those directly transported over an Ethernet.

Above the packet layer can be implemented two alternative types of service – either a virtual circuit or a datagram service, as introduced in Chapter 2, and further discussed in Section 3.6.1. In the experimental ring built at Cambridge both types were provided, the virtual circuit service in the form of the byte stream protocol (BSP), and the datagram facility as the single shot protocol (SSP). See Section 6.6 for further details of these protocols. The recent Cambridge Ring UK standard on protocols (see also Section 6.9) contains specifications of ring minipacket, packet, virtual circuit and transport protocols, called R-, P-, V- and N-services respectively.

6.2 Ring details

In the Cambridge Ring, the bandwidth is subdivided into slots which circulate continuously round the ring either carrying data or ready to accept data, i.e. there can be one or more slots following each other head to tail round the ring (with a small gap between adjacent slots).

Each station is allowed to use a slot to send a single minipacket only. In other words, the slot cannot be immediately reused by that station but must be passed downstream for a subsequent station to use it. Furthermore, the next slot must also be allowed to pass unused. So a station can use at most

1 in 3 slots in a 1-slot ring, or in general 1 in $n + 2$ in an n-slot ring (if no other station is wishing to transmit). If m stations are contending for the bandwidth, each will get access to at least 1 in $n + m$ slots.

In a 10 Mbits/sec standard Cambridge Ring, the data field occupies 40% of the minipacket capacity (slightly more for the 38-bit minipacket), and so the system bandwidth is approximately 4 Mbits/sec, assuming a small head-to-tail gap. Thus the maximum point-to-point bandwidth is 1.3 Mbits/sec in a 1-slot ring, or $4 / (n + 2)$ Mbits/sec in an n-slot ring. When m stations are attempting to transmit, each will get at least $4 / (n + m)$ Mbits/sec of the system bandwidth.

The main aims of the ring's designers were (Wilkes, 1975; Wilkes and Wheeler, 1979):

(1)   to preserve the conceptual simplicity of a ring system in the practical design

(2)   to include a minimum of protocol at the hardware level

(3)   to prevent the possibility of hogging of the ring by one station.

The designers felt that the bandwidth available over short distances was more than sufficient, and therefore making best use of the bandwidth was not one of the aims.

In its simplest form an empty slot system suffers from hogging, but it was realized that, by allowing the minipacket to make one complete revolution and not marking it empty until it had passed the source, this defect could be overcome. Therefore, the empty slot principle was chosen as the basis of the design.

The structure of the ring is illustrated in Figure 6.1.

The minipacket structure shown in Figure 6.2 is designed to minimize delay at the transmitter and receiver, and to maximize timing tolerance.

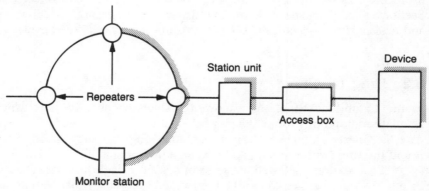

Figure 6.1 Ring structure.

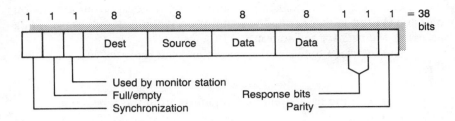

Figure 6.2   Minipacket format.

The first bit is always 1 and is used by the framing circuitry to synchronize with the 'start of minipacket'. The second bit indicates whether the minipacket is full (1) or empty (0). The monitor station uses the third bit to remove erroneous minipackets. This will be dealt with later. Next come the destination and source bytes, allowing 255 different stations, followed by two data bytes. The response bits are used to convey response information and will be mentioned later. The parity bit is used to help with error detection and will be discussed in the section on error recovery. The minipackets follow each other head to tail up to the capacity of the ring, the 'train' being terminated by at least two zeros called the gap digits. Current rings in the computer laboratory at Cambridge have two, three and four minipackets circulating respectively.

6.3   The ring station

The station is shown in greater detail in Figure 6.3.

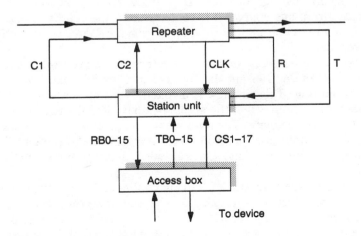

Figure 6.3   Station structure.

The repeater is designed to operate autonomously from the station unit and is used to regenerate the signal at each node, as well as providing access to the ring for the station.

The interface between the station and the repeater consists of five lines:

- *R*: passes the data stream continuously from the repeater
- *T*: this enables the station unit to pass digits to the repeater for transmission
- *C1*: this line carries control waveforms instructing the repeater to either pass on the digits from the ring or insert digits from the station unit
- *CLK*: clock from repeater to station unit.

The fifth line (C2) is a further control line, used only at the monitor station to initialize the ring.

The station unit contains three registers:

(1)   transmit shift register

(2)   receive shift register

(3)   source select register.

It also contains circuitry for framing, parity checking, independent transmission and reception, and circuitry for detecting and interrogating returning minipackets.

Recall that the source select register is used to limit access to a station. When this register contains all ones, the station will listen to a minipacket from any source; if it contains zero, the station is deaf to all sources; otherwise the station will receive from the source whose address is in the register.

When the transmission circuitry detects an empty minipacket it will form the data in the transmit shift register into a minipacket and transmit this onto the ring. This circuitry is invoked by a transmit signal from the access box and assumes that the access box has filled the register with the destination and data bytes. The transmit shift register is circular and retains a copy of the minipacket, allowing the minipacket to be retransmitted, if necessary, without reloading. On transmission the response bits are set to 11.

On the receiving side, a circuit continuously monitors the data stream for minipackets addressed to the station. When one is found, provided the receiving register has been cleared after the previous transmissions, the digit stream will flow into the receive shift register. If the register has not been cleared the response bits are marked '00' (station busy). In the meantime the source is checked against the source select register. If the station is deaf to the source the response bits are set to 10, otherwise shifting ceases and the response bits are set to 01 (minipacket accepted). On acceptance the minipacket remains in the receive shift register until it is cleared by a signal from the access box.

The returning minipacket detection circuitry uses its knowledge of the number of minipackets in the ring to detect a returning minipacket. The control bits of the minipacket are interrogated and this information is made available to the access box, which then takes the appropriate action depending on the protocol. The possibilities are:

Response bits	Interpretation
11	destination absent
01	minipacket accepted
10	destination deaf to this source
00	destination busy

The interface between the station unit and the access box consists of two local 16 bit data busses, TB0 to TB15 and RB0 to RB15, and 17 control lines, CS1 to CS17.

TB0 to TB15 pass data in parallel to the transmit shift register, whereas RB0 to RB15 accept data in parallel, from the receive shift register.

The control lines, CS1 to CS17, are the means by which the access box controls the actions within the station unit:

- CS1 sets the 8-bit source select register from RB0-7

- CS2 gates the first data byte from the receive shift register to RB0-7

- CS3 gates the second data byte from the receive shift register to RB8-15

- CS4 gates the source address from the receive shift register to RB0-7

- CS5 gates the source select register to RB0-7

- CS6 gates a '1' to RB6 if the station has rejected a minipacket from an unselected source at any time since the source select register was last set

- CS7 echoes the logical OR of CS16 (handshake response to access box)

- CS8 sets the first data byte in the transmit shift register from RB0-7

- CS9 sets the second data byte in the transmit shift register from TB0-7

- CS10 sets the destination byte in the transmit shift register from TB0-7

- CS11 gates the response bits for the last minipacket returned to TB0-4; these bits are not valid unless CS14 has gone high

- CS12 echoes the logical OR of CS8-11 and CS13 (handshake response to access box)

- CS13 causes the minipacket in the transmit shift register to be transmitted or retransmitted (transmit command)

- CS14 falls at the end of CS13 and goes high when the transmitted minipacket has returned (minipacket returned signal)

- CS15 falls at the end of CS16 and goes high when a minipacket has arrived at the receiving register (minipacket received signal)

- CS16 discards the information in the receive shift register and prepares the station unit to receive (receive command)

- CS17 indicates that the ring is working normally.

The above constitutes the hardware on which the layered protocols can be built. To prevent congestion of the system with minipackets being repeatedly marked busy, which can happen if devices with varying speed characteristics are interconnected, a further algorithm has been incorporated into the hardware. If a minipacket is returned twice marked busy, a delay in transmission is invoked by delaying the appearance of the CS14 signal from the access box. This delay is dependent on traffic load and is given by $2 \times$ ring delay $\times$ traffic density. Further busies increase this delay to $16 \times$ ring delay $\times$ traffic density.

6.4 Maintenance

Additional hardware has been included to shorten error recovery time by localizing the fault. A paper on this subject was produced by Hopper and Wheeler (1979).

A simple scheme is provided by the monitor station to remove erroneous minipackets. This is done by 'unsetting' the monitor bit on transmission. This bit is set at the monitor station. The monitor station will then mark as empty any minipackets which reach it with the monitor bit already set. Therefore, full minipackets can circumnavigate the ring once, and once only.

In addition, use is made of the parity bit in each minipacket. Each station has two parity circuits, one to check the incoming minipacket, and one to produce a parity bit for the outgoing minipacket. Each station continuously computes the parity of passing minipackets and simultaneously senses and overwrites the old parity (this avoids increase in delay). If the old parity does not match, an error has occurred since the last active station. The station proceeds to launch a reporting minipacket to a logging station. A stream of reporting minipackets from a given station will indicate a serious malfunction, otherwise a spurious noise signal can be assumed. Empty minipackets are also monitored in this way, and therefore a continuous check is carried out on the ring.

Breaks in the ring can also be detected. The leading digit in a minipacket is always one, so an unbroken series of zeros cannot occur. If this does happen a station will emit a continuous stream of reporting packets.

It should be noted that in the scheme above, erroneous minipackets are allowed to be received. There is no error recovery at the minipacket level. This is left to the packet level of protocol (see later) and will normally be backward error recovery (retransmission) on receiving an erroneous check sum.

6.5 Modulation system

The original ring was built using TTL technology, operating at 10 MHz, with a maximum distance of 200 m between repeaters. More recently a chip version of the ring has been developed (see Section 6.8). The signals are transmitted along two twisted pairs. To increase reliability the repeaters are powered directly from the ring. Therefore, repeaters continue to work even if a station loses power.

The use of a two channel/four wire system allows a simple self-clocking modulation technique to be used. In each pulse interval, a change on both pairs indicates a one and a change in one pair indicates a zero, each pair being used alternately for signal changes.

This scheme was considered superior to the more common phase or frequency modulation techniques. The advantages of the four wire system include: no half pulse ambiguity, it is fully balanced, little encoding or decoding delay, and it is easy to detect some errors (e.g. no transition in a given pulse interval).

The delay in the repeater is approximately three bits, and the electronic delay in the cable is roughly six bits per 100 m. This gives a ring

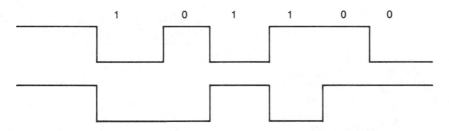

Figure 6.4 Four wire system of modulation.

delay of approximately 10 μs, or 100 bits, in a system with 12 stations, 100 m apart.

In the prototype system, one segment of the ring used fibre optic cables. Wire segments are currently limited to 200 m, but because of the low signal/noise ratio of optical fibres, fibre segments could easily be extended to several kilometres without the need for additional repeaters.

6.6 Ring protocols

This section describes the original ring protocols developed at the Cambridge University Computer Laboratory; the recent standards work which has aligned these original protocols to the LAN/RM interface requirements is the subject of Section 6.9. Although communication on the ring can be achieved using the minipacket protocol described above, in practice most communicating is done using protocols above this level. At present there are three higher level protocols used on the ring. These are the packet protocol (PP), the single shot protocol (SSP) and the byte stream protocol (BSP). BSP allows the setting up of a virtual circuit for communication between transmitter and receiver, whereas the other two support datagram type communication.

6.6.1 Packet protocol

The PP normally sends data in larger quantities than can be held in a single minipacket and has the additional advantage that the data can be directed to a notional port on the destination station. The block sent is known as a basic block, or packet.

A packet has the structure shown in Figure 6.5(a) and commences with a header of the form shown in Figure 6.5(b).

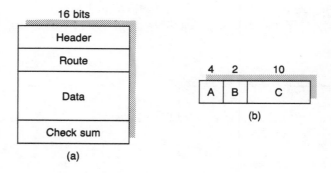

Figure 6.5 Packet structure: (a) packet; (b) header.

Field A is the binary pattern 1001.
Field B is

- 0 long packet with check sum
- 1 long packet with check sum field set to zero
- 2 this packet consists of this single minipacket carrying data C
- 3 reserved for further expansion.

A long packet consists of: route packet, C + 1 data minipackets and a check sum minipacket.

A route minipacket consists of a port number in the bottom 12 bits, the packet being notionally directed to that port at the destination station.

The C + 1 data minipackets conform to the protocol that is currently agreed to be in use at the port identified in the route part.

The check sum minipacket for type 0 packets consists of a 16 bit end-around-carry check sum over the entire packet, commencing with the header minipacket up to and including the last data minipacket. In type 1 packets, the notional check sum packet is sent as zero, and checked to be zero.

The method of reception is as follows (Walker, 1978):

(1)   While a station is totally unable to receive anything it keeps its select register to zero.

(2)   When a station is potentially capable of receiving input it sets its select register to 255.

(3)   It then listens for a valid header minipacket ignoring anything else.

(4)   When a valid header minipacket has been found, if the station wishes to receive from the station from which the header came, then the receiving station sets its select register to that source, thus rejecting input from any other source.

(5)   The receiving station must operate either a per-packet timeout or a per-minipacket timeout in order to recover from a packet being sent which is shorter than the header minipacket suggested. The time-outs commence with reception of the header minipacket. If the timeouts expire at any time henceforth, the input thus far accumulated is ignored, and the station is reset to state (2) above, ignoring the incoming packet.

(6)   The next minipacket after the header is the route minipacket. If interpretation of this leads the receiver to believe that it cannot process the remainder of the packet (e.g. specific port not active) then it may reset itself to state (2) above, ignoring the incoming packet.

(7)   On reaching the end of a packet the check sum minipacket is received and checked. If, for type 1 packets, the check sum is

incorrect, or for type 2 packets, it is non-zero, then the entire packet must be ignored as if it had never been received.

(8)   After reception of a packet, the selection register may be restored to 255 if more input is possible, otherwise zero.

(9)   As an alternative to resetting immediately to state (2), if a partially received packet is to be rejected, the selection register may be set to zero for a short time in an attempt to cause the transmitter to stop sending. The selection may either be for a fixed time, or until the station hardware indicates that a minipacket has been rejected 'unselected'. When the latter strategy is used, a timeout is also required.

For transmission:

(1)   When transmitting the first minipacket (the header) of a packet, due allowance must be made for the possibility of the receiving station being busy or unselected owing to it being in the process of receiving a packet from another source. Attempts to transmit the header should be maintained at least as long as the longest possible packet can take at the reception station. Any other ring failure can be regarded as fatal.

(2)   Having successfully transmitted the first minipacket (header), allowance may have to be made for certain reception stations to perform certain setup operations for the packet, during which time the station will reject as busy.

(3)   After that, the number of busy rejects that may be expected per-minipacket should be very low, as the receiver is supposed to be concentrating on one source only. It will be necessary for transmitting stations to have a timeout or repeat count on a per-minipacket or per-packet basis in order to recover from a reception station crashing in the middle of a packet. A timeout is also necessary to recover from certain ring errors (such as power off) which result in a minipacket never returning to its sender.

6.6.2 Single shot protocol

A number of transactions on the ring consist of a single packet request to which the response is a single packet reply. See Figure 6.6. Such transactions do not require the setting up of a virtual channel as provided by the byte stream protocol (BSP); see below. The single shot protocol (SSP) provides a standard way of handling these simple transactions. It provides for data to be sent and results received; in addition, a return code can be sent in the reply to indicate any error that might have occurred.

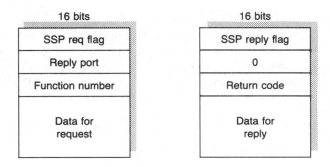

Figure 6.6 SSP packet layout.

The SSP defines the return code to be zero if and only if successful. It is important to note that SSPs must be repeatable.

6.6.3 Byte stream protocol

The byte stream protocol (Johnson, 1980) is built on top of the packet protocol. It provides a pair of synchronized byte streams, and corrects all errors detected by the packet protocol. It assumes that undetected errors will be sufficiently rare to be ignored, although there are facilities for resetting to a standard state if otherwise unrecoverable errors do happen. Acknowledgements are used to ensure data integrity. All erroneous packets are ignored, and the timeout mechanisms of the byte stream protocol repeat unacknowledged packets.

The acknowledgements also provide flow control in order to ensure that a transmitter does not send more data than the recipient has committed itself to accepting. In order that the timeout mechanisms should not lead to futile communication during periods when there is no data to send or nowhere to put it, it is possible for either the transmitter or the recipient to stop the traffic (and assume responsibility for restarting it).

The protocol is designed in such a manner that simple machines can have two fixed buffers, one for transmission and one for reception. On receiving a packet into the reception buffer, the command it contains may be processed independently, and the appropriate parts of the transmission buffer updated. During this operation, it is decided whether or not the updated packet should be transmitted. This technique may lead to some unnecessary repetition of non-essential elements, but this is defined to be harmless.

Each packet that is sent consists of a command referring to the reception of data, a command referring to transmission of data, and the data itself. Alternatively, it can consist of a control command referring to the transaction as a whole. In order that repetitions of packets can be identified as such, commands are given sequence numbers. For example RDYn indicates that packets with sequence number less than n have been successfully received and that the recipient is now ready to receive packet n. An example of a control command is CLOSE which winds up the transaction.

In the implementation of BSP at Cambridge the initial connection consists of sending a single packet in each direction. These packets are called the OPEN and OPENACK packets. An OPEN packet is sent by the originator of the connection and it contains the port number to be used in reply and a number of BSP parameters. These parameters indicate the maximum packet size that the originator is prepared to receive and the largest packet it will send. The OPENACK packet is directed to the station from which the OPEN came and contains a port number for the connection, a return code which will be zero if successful, and a number of BSP parameters. The parameters again indicate packet sizes that will be used.

6.7   The Cambridge Distributed Computing System

The Cambridge Ring is used to support a local area network within the computer laboratory at the University of Cambridge. The network consists of a number of committed computer systems which are ordinary time sharing computers and have their own internal resource control mechanisms outside the control of the network. There are a number of shared servers on the ring including: a nameserver, a printing server, and a fileserver (Dion, 1980). These servers provide a general service for other devices using the ring.

There is also a terminal concentrator that allows a number of terminals to be conected to the ring and is capable of making connections between terminals and computers. In addition there is a processor bank which consists of a number of uncommitted microcomputers, most of which have no local peripherals except for a connection to the ring (Wilkes and Needham, 1980). Part of the system is shown schematically in Figure 6.7.

The Cambridge Distributed Computing System (CDCS) implements the concept of personal computers, not by the provision of a computer in every office, but by providing mechanisms whereby a user at a terminal within his office can either log onto one of the committed computer systems or, more important, gain control of a machine in the processor bank to run an exclusive choice of software (Herbert, 1981; Needham, 1979; Needham and Herbert, 1982).

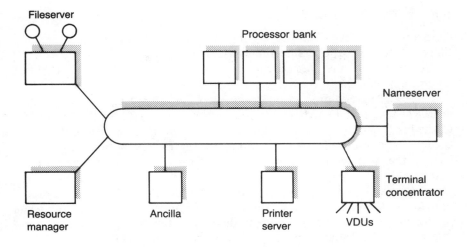

Figure 6.7 The Cambridge Distributed Computing System.

The computers in the processor bank rely primarily on the servers in the network to provide them with essential services such as terminal connections, filing systems and printing. Each machine is provided with a microprocessor-controlled intelligent ring interface. The interface provides the programmer with a channel to the ring and also facilitates remote bootstrapping and debugging.

To obtain a machine a client will indicate to the resource manager the type of machine required, the identity of the bootstrap image to load, and the total time for which the machine is required. The resource manager will check to see if a suitable machine is free and if so pass the names of the bootstrap image and the free machine to the Ancilla (Shepherd, 1981). The Ancilla will then load the bootstrap image into the machine and start it executing. For every different type of machine in the processor bank there is an Ancilla service. This is because different machines have different loading properties and the object of the Ancilla service is to conceal these differences behind a uniform, simple interface.

Control is then passed back to the resource manager which connects the client to the appropriate machine. At the end of the session the user logs off and the machine is returned to the pool.

The CDCS processor bank and its associated services provides a powerful and convenient alternative to the personal computer model of distributed computing. The mechanisms support a framework for the allocation of computers in a manner similar to that of online sessions in a timesharing system. In addition, the services required for the management of the processor bank can be duplicated to guard against hardware failures.

6.8 Ring developments

Chip versions of the Cambridge Ring are now available. These substantially reduce the cost of connecting devices to the ring. In addition the chip version will allow the data part of the minipacket to be set to a variable length, between 2 and 8 bytes.

A UK-agreed draft standard for the Cambridge Ring was produced in 1982, resulting in two documents specifying interfaces (Sharpe and Cash, 1982) and protocols (Larmouth, 1982). This new version of the ring specified a 40-bit minipacket, providing two extra control bits for general use. In the next section the resulting standard ring is described in more detail.

Research has been carried out into the design and implementation of a 'fast' ring which has a raw data rate of 100 Mbits/sec, high performance intelligent interfaces for connecting devices to the ring, and bridges for interconnecting Cambridge Rings. This work was undertaken at both the computer laboratory in Cambridge University, and also independently by British Telecom's research laboratory. At British Telecom a fast slotted ring is under consideration as the basis for an integrated services local network (ISLN) carrying both voice and data. A new slotted ring protocol called Orwell has been designed (Falconer and Adams, 1985). This incorporates two new features, namely the release of minipacket slots at the destination node rather than back at the sending node, and a load control mechanism which keeps ring access delays within a limit (2 ms) acceptable to a voice carrying system.

Considerable research work is being carried out at the Cambridge computer laboratory on the CDCS especially in the areas of protection, processor interaction, and the implementation of dynamic services. The CDCS also provides computing power for other researchers in the laboratory.

A large-scale project, called Universe, to link up a number of Cambridge Rings on different sites throughout England by means of a satellite has recently been completed. One of the main aims of this project was to see how far the characteristics of a local area network could be preserved across the whole system (Wilbur, 1983).

6.9 The standard Cambridge Ring

In 1982 it was decided to produce a specification of the Cambridge Ring for all ring suppliers to work to. Already there were slightly different implementations of the 38-bit ring becoming available which were incompatible. The specification produced was in two parts: *Cambridge Ring 82 – interface specifications* which described the ring hardware and the device interfaces which could be used (Sharpe and Cash, 1982), and *Cambridge Ring 82 – protocol specifications* (Larmouth, 1982). These documents collectively became known as CR82.

Apart from extending the minipacket length to 40 bits the most notable feature of CR82 was the rationalization of the existing ring protocols as follows:

Previous	CR82
Minipacket	R-protocol
PP	P-protocol
BSP	V-protocol
TSBSP	N-protocol

(TSBSP – transport service BSP, an enhanced version of the BSP, dealing in particular with transport level addressing; see Dallas (1980) for a description of a TSBSP implementation at the University of Kent.)

However, these were not essentially different protocols, more a formalization of what already existed. The CR82 documents were sufficient for internal British consumption and served to unify the implementation of the ring by independent manufacturers.

In the spring of 1983 the British community decided to take seriously the fast growing local network initiative in the USA run by the IEEE 802 group, and began to consider ways of moulding the CR82 specifications into a form compatible with the LLC, MAC and physical layering of the LAN reference model. The idea was clearly to make an effort to have an international standard for the Cambridge Ring, albeit a late attempt to do so.

With the cooperation of the British Standards Institution (BSI), draft specifications were prepared in the correct format in time for the ISO meeting in Beijing, China in September 1983. These drafts were given an encouraging reception and the British decided at a Department of Trade and Industry meeting in November to align the P-service with the IEEE MAC-service and to leave the higher layers (V- and N-services) out of consideration, since the IEEE LAN specifications deal only with physical and MAC layers. The technology-independent LLC layer would reside above the new aligned P-service in common with the MAC-service of the other LAN technologies.

In March 1984 two new draft British standard documents were produced, one dealing with physical matters, the other with the MAC layer. The hardware document essentially contains the CR82 hardware details plus optional extensions made possible by the imminent arrival of new ring chips. The new documents do not refer to a 'Cambridge Ring' but rather to a 'slotted ring' LAN in the same way as IEEE 802.3 refers to 'CSMA/CD' and not 'Ethernet'.

An interesting insight into the problems of writing such specification documents was given by the release of a commentary introduction to the drafts. The aim of removing any ambiguities from the specifications was not easily achieved, particularly since several 'products' are in fact specified in the documents, the products going to make up the whole slotted ring system. The documents have been carefully arranged to make clear which parts of the specification apply to which products, in an attempt to remove the possibility of conflicting interpretations, which as the introduction points out, lead to incompatibility when the products are made by independent suppliers.

The major differences from the CR82 are, first, that the new standard gives a choice of basic class or enhanced class nodes, the first corresponding to the CR82 40-bit hardware, the second to hardware with alternative length minipackets and enhanced functionality at the interface between the ring node and the attached device. In the enhanced system, the minipacket can be 40, 56, 72 or 88 bits long, corresponding to data field lengths of 2, 4, 6 or 8 bytes.

Second, the slotted ring standard protocol specifications conform to the usual IEEE LAN distinction between service and protocol, and to the layering into physical and MAC layers with the standard LLC layer above MAC. The slotted ring fits into the ISO document hierarchy as standard number 8802/7. The basic MAC/physical and LLC/MAC services are, briefly:

- P_PACKET.request
- P_PACKET.confirm
- P_PACKET.indicate

- MA_DATA.request
- MA_DATA.confirm
- MA_DATA.indicate

(parameters not shown).

The protocols within the MAC and physical layers correspond to the previous P- or packet protocol (PP) and R- or ring minipacket protocol respectively.

Lastly, the station management activities to monitor and control the station's healthy operation require a set of service primitives at the LLC/MAC and MAC/physical layer boundaries, as for the CSMA/CD and token passing systems.

References

Dallas, I.N., (1980). *Transport service byte stream protocol (TSBSP)*, Computing Laboratory Report, University of Kent at Canterbury

Dion, J., (1980). 'The Cambridge Ring fileserver' *Operating Systems Review* **14**,(4), October, 26–35

Falconer, R.M. and Adams, J.L., (1985). 'Orwell: a protocol for an integrated services local network' *British Telecom Technology Journal* **3**,(4), October, 27–35

Hafner, E.R., Nenadal, Z. and Tschanz, M., (1974). 'A digital loop communication system' *IEEE Transactions – Communications* **COM-22**, June, 877–881

Herbert, A.J., (1981). 'The user interface to the Cambridge model distributed system' *Proc. 2nd International Conference on Distributed Computing Systems*, Paris, April, 503–508

Hopper, A. and Wheeler, D.J., (1979). 'Maintenance of ring communication systems' *IEEE Transactions on Communications* **COM-27**,(4), April, 760–761

Johnson, M.A., (1980). *Ring byte stream protocol specification*, Systems Research Group Note, Computer Laboratory, University of Cambridge

Kropfl, W.J., (1972). 'An experimental data block switching system' *BSTJ* **51**, July/August, 1147–1165

Larmouth, J., (1982). *Cambridge Ring 82 – protocol specifications*, UK Science and Engineering Research Council, November

Needham, R.M., (1979). 'Systems aspects of the Cambridge Ring' *Proc. 7th Symposium on Operating Systems Principles*, December, 82–85

Needham, R.M. and Herbert, A.J., (1982). *The Cambridge Distributed Computing System*. Addison-Wesley

Pierce, J.R., (1972). 'Network for block switching of data' *The Bell System Technical Journal* **51**,(6), July/August, 1133–1145

Reames, C.C. and Liu, M.T., (1975). 'A loop network for simultaneous transmission of variable-length messages' *Proc. 2nd Annual Symposium on Computer Architecture*, Houston, Texas, USA, January, 7–12

Sharpe, W.P. and Cash, A.R., (1982). *Cambridge Ring 82 – interface specifications*, UK Science and Engineering Research Council, September

Shepherd, W.D., (1981). 'Ancilla – a server for the Cambridge model distributed system' *Software – Practice and Experience* **11**, 1185–1195

Walker, R.D.H., (1978). *Basic Ring transport protocol*, internal report, Computer Laboratory, University of Cambridge

Wilbur, S.R., (1983). 'Initial experience with Universe at University College London' *Local Networks: Strategy & Systems*. Online Publications: London, 297–309

Wilkes, M.V., (1975). 'Communication using a digital ring' *Proc. PACNET Conference*, Sendai, Japan, August, 47–55 (plus a one-page Addendum dated December 1976)

Wilkes, M.V. and Wheeler, D.J., (1979). 'The Cambridge digital communication ring' *Proc. Local Area Communications Network Symposium*, Mitre Corp., Boston, May, 47–60

Wilkes, M.V. and Needham, R.M., (1980). 'The Cambridge Model Distributed System' *Operating Systems Review* **14**,(1), January

Chapter 7
Internetworking

The aim of this chapter is to introduce the reader to the problems, and some of the solutions, of internetworking between networks of various types. The OSI network and transport layers are briefly described, but much of the chapter is based on two specific examples, which illustrate different ways of providing internetworking given different circumstances.

7.1　Introduction

In general, local area networks will be open systems in the sense that they will exchange information with systems at other locations. This of course depends on the application in which the local network finds itself. It is likely that closed LANs will appear in large numbers in industrial, automotive and domestic applications – particularly once standards become established, VLSI parts are produced in large quantity and prices fall substantially in consequence – but our main concern here is with open LANs.

In many cases the open LAN will be connected to systems elsewhere by means of a wide area network, probably one based on the national packet switching system. The combination of local and wide area networks connected in this way is termed an **internetwork**. Each component network is termed a **subnetwork** in the ISO/CCITT/ECMA standards documents. (See ECMA, 1982a and 1982b in particular for an overview; Ware (1983) and FOCUS (1984a) explain and interpret the ISO network standard.) Many LAN and WAN subnetworks may be joined together; in fact some forecasters see the ultimate connection of virtually all networks in one large **global** internetwork. One consequence of this possibility is that network designers (and standards bodies) have usually been concerned with providing for a large enough address space in packet address fields to accommodate the global internetwork. Dalal and Printis in their paper on 48-bit absolute internet and Ethernet host numbers (Dalal and Printis, 1981) argue that 48 bits are more than sufficient for this purpose (see Chapter 4 on Ethernet).

7.1.1　Bridges and gateways

Where two local networks are joined together at the data link level, the connecting element is called a **bridge**. A connecting element which joins two networks at a higher level of protocol is called a **gateway**.

Because a bridge joins two networks at a low level, it is in concept (and practice) simpler than a gateway. In general, a gateway or bridge may need to perform a variety of functions, including:

- address mapping
- protocol conversion
- segmentation of packets
- reassembly of packets.

These, and other technical issues in internetworking, are discussed in the context of the OSI network layer in Callon (1983). Section 7.2 describes the OSI network layer approach to internetworking.

Formally, the IEEE 802 LAN architecture stops at the LLC/internetworking boundary. However, it can be assumed that the higher layers, including internetworking, will be based on the ISO OSI model's layers 3–7. MAP and TOP, as explained in Chapter 5, are prominent examples of LAN-based architectures which make use of IEEE 802 physical, MAC and LLC layers, with OSI higher layers. The issue of internetworking centres on the network layer of OSI.

Within OSI, the network layer effort has mainly been involved with a connection-oriented network service (CONS). The influence of the IEEE LANs work has resulted in more recent investigations into a connectionless service (CLNS) which complements the CONS. Network builders can choose between the two classes of service at this level. As was seen at the LLC level, the choice of CO or CL service cannot be made without considering the effects of and on the adjacent layers, in this case the LLC and transport layers.

Whereas in wide area networks the network layer has a responsibility for routing within the network, the simple bus and ring topologies of the standard LANs present network layer requirements only at the bridge or gateway between the LAN and other networks. Within an individual closed LAN the network layer is effectively null; apart from adding and removing a standard network layer header the functionality required is zero. Where a LAN is open, the network layer will have to deal with internetwork addresses at least, ensuring that addresses of stations on different networks are resolved and that messages to stations on remote networks are routed through the LAN's appropriate bridge, gateway or relay.

The term 'relay' indicates a network interconnection achieved at a higher level of protocol, either at the network, transport or even the application level. This would usually involve protocol conversion between the networks on either side. Typically, LANs are joined into the nationwide WAN by means of relays. The LAN protocols are built up within the relay to match the transport layer's upper interface at the WAN side. Typically, electronic mail is also sent by means of relays between networks of different types, where the destination address is mapped at a level above the transport layers of the respective source and destination networks.

In this chapter we also include the transport layer, and consider the form of addresses needed in an internetwork so that stations can be uniquely accessed. The transport layer offers different classes of service to meet the demands of the user at the higher layer and to build appropriately on the facilities offered by the network layer beneath.

7.2 The OSI network layer

The network layer is complex because of the possibility of having to route messages through intermediate subsystems and via gateways/relays. Unfortunately existing subnets are not all the same (and never will be despite the efforts of the ISO) and they vary greatly in the functions or services offered. This wide variation is allowed for in the architecture of the ISO OSI network layer, shown in Figure 7.1.

Each end system will in general be connected to other end systems via subnetworks and intermediate (relay) systems. The structure of the ISO 'NL entity' is further broken down into:

- relaying and routing functions
- subnetwork-independent convergence (SNIC) functions
- subnetwork-dependent convergence (SNDC) functions
- subnetwork access (SNAC) functions
- functions done by subnetworks ('subnet service').

The first two of these are independent of the subnetworks being used, while the last three are subnet specific. ECMA has a slightly different view of the structure of the network layer, suggesting three sublayers:

- internet sublayer (3c)
- subnet enhancement (3b)
- subnet specific access protocols (3a)

where (3c) is equivalent to ISO's SNIC and relaying/routing, (3b) is equivalent to SNDC, and (3a) corresponds to SNAC functionality.

In both ISO's and ECMA's cases the idea is that the network layer bridges the gap between the underlying service provided by the subnetwork layer and the service that is to be offered to the transport layer. The functions used to bridge the gap are the above subnet enhancement elements: these may add to the existing subnet service or else restrict the

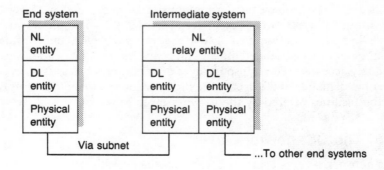

Figure 7.1 Structure of OSI network layer.

use of the functions available. The problem of interworking across a number of subnets has two solutions: hop-by-hop enhancement and use of an internet protocol. In the first approach, each subnet is enhanced separately and mappings made between them in gateways. In the second, an internetwork protocol is implemented over every subnet and uses only the minimum elements from each subnet, building up each to provide all the required services of the network layer.

The internetwork in which the ISO network layer will perform is any interconnected set of subnetworks. The variety of subnet types may include:

- X.25 packet switched networks
- circuit switched networks (i.e. based on the telephone network)
- LANs
- satellite networks.

An internetwork protocol is required which allows users on any two different subnets to communicate. In general it is complicated by the wide variation in quality of service (QOS) offered by the various subnets – in terms of throughput rate, delays incurred, and reliability.

The ISO first developed a connection-oriented (CO) network service, then later produced a connectionless (CL) protocol addendum and proposals for network layer addressing. Relevant ISO documents dealing with the network layer include:

- CO-network service: IS 8348 (CCITT equivalent is X.213)
- CL-network protocol: IS 8473 (includes DAD1, Addendum 1 to IS 8348)
- Network layer addressing: IS 8348 DAD2 (i.e. Addendum 2 to IS 8348)
- Internal organization of the network layer: DP 8648.2 (in draft proposal form)
- Use of X.25 to provide the CO-network service: DP 8878.

For the CO-network service, the following parameters are available to negotiate the desired performance, quality of service etc.:

Performance, QOS parameters	Other parameters
Connection establishment delay	Connection protection
Establishment failure probability	Priority
Throughout	Maximum acceptable cost
Transit delay	
Residual error rate	

Performance, QOS parameters	*Other parameters*
Connection resilience	
Transfer failure probability	
Connection release delay	
Connection release failure probability	

A summary of the primitives offered by the network layer is as follows:

CO-NS:

Network connection phase	*Service elements*
Establishment	N-CONNECT
Data transfer	N-DATA
	N-DATA-ACK
	N-EXPEDITED-DATA
	N-RESET
Release	N-DISCONNECT

CL-NS:

Service element
N-UNITDATA

7.3 LAN bridges

In this section we discuss the specific problem of linking a number of Cambridge Rings together. The solutions described can easily be extended to solve the problem of linking any number of LANs of the same type together including Ethernet systems.

7.3.1 Cambridge Ring bridges

The task of joining two Cambridge Rings together is simpler than that of joining different types of networks since there is no need to perform protocol conversion. In addition, by keeping the propagation delay through the gateway joining the two rings to a minimum, it is possible to create a larger network with the properties of a local area network. This section discusses the problem of joining two Cambridge Rings which are on the same site and outlines the solution which has been implemented at Cambridge University computer laboratory (Leslie, 1983).

It is obvious that there is a need to join separate networks together to allow users on each network to use resources on the other networks as well as allowing data to be transferred between all the networks. What may not be so obvious are the advantages of splitting a large ring network into a number of smaller ones. The advantages of a multiple network over a large single ring can be divided into two areas: reliability and performance.

The most obvious improvement in reliability offered by a multiple ring network is that a failure on one ring, for example a break in the transmission medium, does not have a serious effect on the rest of the network. A second advantage is that physical reorganization of the network can be carried out one ring at a time, so that the whole network need not be out of operation for a long time. This is particularly important in a research environment where there is constant upheaval, but it will also be of some importance in any large application.

Two slotted rings have twice the system bandwidth of a single ring (see Section 6.2). In addition, the maximum point-to-point bandwidth on each of the single slotted rings is one and a third times that of larger ring, assuming an anti-hogging policy. This is important because the basic block delay (at the next level of protocol) is related almost directly to the point-to-point bandwidth. This means that if the system bandwidth being used by hosts on the ring causes a significant degradation in traffic throughput, or if some hosts are being limited by point-to-point bandwidth of the ring, dividing the ring can result in improved performance.

Care must be taken if a ring is divided into subnetworks to ensure that the traffic through the bridge is minimized. For instance, it would not be advisable to have a large processor and its backing store service on separate rings. In this case the degradation would be the result of congestion in the bridge. However, two hosts each on a one-slot ring communicating through an otherwise idle bridge with a delay of a few slot revolution times would be able to transfer a basic block faster than if they were on the same two slot ring. This is simply because the point-to-point bandwidth limit would be that of a single slotted ring rather than a two slot ring.

7.3.2 Design approaches

The main design goal for the bridge connecting the rings is that the delay through it should be as small as possible so that the resulting network will maintain local area network properties. If possible, an extra layer of protocol to deal with addressing of nonlocal hosts should be avoided, since this layer adds overhead even in localized transactions.

However, some means for hosts on one ring to communicate with those on another ring must be provided. Some strategies for achieving this are outlined below, and for each of these is given an indication of the complexity of the bridge required to implement the strategy.

Minipacket bridges

Bridges could be made to accept minipackets for a number of destinations. To achieve this a ring number would have to be added to both the destination and source addresses and have the bridge accept minipackets for a set of rings. An alternative would be to have the bridge accept minipackets for a set of destinations by using a simple table lookup. The major problem with the minipacket bridge is preserving the response bits as described in Chapter 6. These response bits are used as a flow control mechanism within the transmission of basic blocks. To preserve these response bits across a bridge would involve major changes in the ring.

Globally addressed datagrams

In this scheme the basic block is changed to include the global address of both the source and destination hosts. A global address would consist of a ring number as well as a station number. Bridges would contain routing tables to enable them to forward basic blocks either to the destination or the next bridge on the route. This is similar to the approach taken by the PUP internetwork (see Section 7.4 below). Blocks could arrive in an order different to that in which they were sent. Host software would thus have to resequence blocks, deal with the change in address size, and perform part of the binding of an address to a route. (In practice this would be done by a nameserver).

In addition, the guarantee which the ring hardware gives source addresses would be lost. It would be possible for a host to forge a source address within a basic block. In order to have the same degree of security as the single ring a host would have to know where all the bridges on its ring were. It could then trust all traffic coming from bridges and perform its own check on traffic from local stations.

Lightweight virtual circuits

Another possibility, which requires bridges to retain some state information about connections, is to use lightweight virtual circuits. These circuits are termed lightweight because bridges would perform no error control or flow control. This alternative is described in some detail as it forms the basis of the solution adopted by Cambridge University.

The example of an initial connection setup used in this section is that of the byte stream protocol (BSP) described in Chapter 6. Briefly, an OPEN-OPENACK exchange takes place. A host sends out an OPEN block and waits for an OPENACK reply block to return. The OPEN block contains a reply port and the OPENACK includes a connection port number, as shown in Figure 7.2. After the blocks are exchanged, the

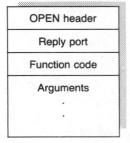
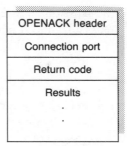

Figure 7.2 OPEN and OPENACK blocks.

reply and connection ports are used until the stream is closed. The station and port number to which an OPEN block is sent is obtained from the nameserver.

The advantages of virtual circuits are that blocks arrive at the destination in the same order as they were sent, and that the extra addressing information need only be sent in the block establishing the connection, in this case OPEN blocks. After a connection is set up, blocks will follow the same path as the block which set up the path, either in the forward or reverse direction.

The state information maintained in the bridges in this scheme consists of six components:

- direction
- reception port
- source station
- next station
- next port
- mapping status.

Mapping status is either 'O', meaning setting up a virtual circuit, or 'N', meaning a circuit has been set up and traffic passes normally through the bridge.

To make a virtual circuit connection the steps could be as follows. The caller uses a nameserver to find out the global address of the service it wishes to use. The global address returned contains the destination ring (network) number, station number on that ring, port number at that station, and also the 'first hop' port number at the first bridge on the route to the destination. This bridge port number is standard for receiving OPEN blocks and is the same on all bridges. Then the caller sends to the first hop port on the first bridge an OPEN block containing (a) this global address and (b) a reply port at the calling station.

The first bridge sets up its own reply port for the returning OPENACK and establishes a mapping from this port to the caller's reply port. The bridge then replaces the reply port in the OPEN block with its own reply port number and sends the block on to the next bridge to the destination, using the standard port number for receiving OPEN blocks.

The next bridge does the same procedure as did the first. This continues to further bridges until the routing tables take the OPEN block to its destination. The destination then allocates a connection port and sends an OPENACK block back along the path traced by the OPEN block, through the ready ports at the intermediate bridges.

An alternative to sending a global address in the OPEN block is for the path to be set up by the nameserver as a side effect of the name lookup procedure. Thus, when the caller in the above example looks up the address of the required service, the nameserver would carry on a transaction with the first bridge, which in turn would carry on a transaction with the next, and so on. The nameserver would respond to the caller, telling it the address of the service which would be a port on the first bridge. The caller would then send an OPEN block to this port and a process similar to that described above would take place.

There must be a way of closing down mappings set up in the bridge. This can be done as soon as an OPEN block is received on the port, or by a timeout following inactivity.

The nameserver scheme has the advantage that hosts do not have to cope with the new address space, or bind an address to a route since the nameserver will perform these functions.

7.3.3 Implementing the bridge

If the delay through the bridge can be kept to the order of a few ring delays, basic block throughput between two rings can approach that of the larger ring. It is desirable, therefore, for the ring–ring bridge to transmit a basic block while receiving it. This has a direct influence on the hardware required for the ring–ring bridge. The hardware responsible for reception on one ring must be closely coupled to the hardware responsible for transmission on the other.

It is normal for hosts to select one transmitter while they are receiving a basic block. If a bridge selects one transmitter during reception of a basic block then other hosts would be locked out. The selection of one source by the bridge would cause a bottleneck in the network. In particular, a slow transmitter could lock out a fast transmitter for a considerable length of time. It is therefore desirable for bridges to multiplex both the transmission and reception of basic blocks.

To implement this multiplexing some modification to the current Cambridge Ring stations used by the bridge would be necessary. A table of response bits with an entry for each source station would be necessary.

One of the aims behind the design of the Cambridge Ring bridge was as far as possible to allow existing protocols to remain unaltered. However any protocol which has actual addresses embedded in the data part of an SSP or OPEN connection will not work through a bridge.

An example of this is the feature in the byte stream protocol known as REPLUG. REPLUG allowed a host with two byte streams open to plug one stream into the other simply by passing an appropriate station address to the users at the other end of each byte stream. This will obviously not work through a bridge. This is now accomplished at a higher level in the protocol structure by passing a service name to the end which reestablishes the connection rather than a station address. It is interesting to note that this is probably the way that it should have been done in the first place. Another example is the protocol for the fileserver (Dion, 1980) which makes use of multiple ports in one connection. These ports distinguish data from control information. This protocol had to be modified to allow it to be used through a bridge. These problems arise because the original ring was designed to work in a single ring rather than a multiple ring environment.

7.4   The PUP internetwork architecture

The purpose of an internetwork architecture is to provide a uniform framework for communication within a heterogeneous computing, communication, and applications environment. In this section we describe one such architecture known as PUP (PARC universal packet) which has been developed at Xerox PARC, Palo Alto (Boggs *et al.*, 1980). This was briefly introduced in Chapter 4, since the architecture was developed on the experimental Ethernet.

7.4.1   The PUP internet

An important feature of the PUP model is that most hosts are directly connected to a local area network, rather than a switch. Gateways are simply hosts that are willing to forward packets among constituent networks. As we will see later, even hosts that do not act as gateways must be able to handle some part of the routing protocol. This is in direct contrast to the approach taken in the bridges described in the previous section.

Because of the requirement to implement the internetwork protocols in the host machines, which are typically quite small, the guiding principle in designing the PUP has been simplicity. This has enabled the design to be kept open ended which in turn makes it easier to incorporate existing local area networks and to accommodate new technologies as they arise.

The basic function provided by the PUP internet is the transport of **datagrams**. The datagrams are called PUPs. Because the internet does not guarantee reliable delivery of a PUP, higher level protocols must take this into account. Each PUP is transported directly and the internet has no notion of a connection. Keeping end-to-end state out of the packet transport system is a major contribution to reliability and simplicity.

PUP protocols are organized in a hierarchy. Level 0 is a packet transport mechanism which depends on the network being used. A typical network would be Ethernet. Associated with each packet transport mechanism is a convention for encapsulating PUPs. Level 1 is an internet datagram. This is the layer of commonality which unifies all the different networks that might be used at level 0. It is the purpose of this layer to provide media independence. Higher levels provide file transport, byte stream and applications protocols.

7.4.2 Protocol details

One of the main aims of the designers of the PUP was to develop a protocol that could be easily implemented on a wide range of different network architectures. The addressing schemes, error characteristics, maximum packet sizes, and other attributes of networks vary greatly. There is an internetwork packet transport mechanism which moves PUPs between hosts and it is the job of the network driver to interface the network to the internetwork packet transport mechanism (IPTM).

A host connected to a single network has one network driver, and a gateway will have one driver for each directly connected network. Only the driver knows about the characteristics of the network's hardware interface and low level protocol.

The interface between the IPTM and the driver is very simple. The IPTM passes down a PUP and a network specific host address, and the driver encapsulates the PUP and does its best to deliver it to the specified host. When a PUP arrives at the host, the driver decapsulates it and passes it up to the IPTM. If for any reason the PUP looks erroneous it is discarded by the driver. Every IPTM must be able to accept a maximum size PUP; if the network cannot directly encapsulate a packet of that size for transmission, the driver must include some form of intranetwork fragmentation. For instance, the Cambridge Ring would have to split the PUP into a number of basic blocks.

A network driver must also be able to broadcast a packet to every station on the network. On some networks, such as Ethernet, this is straightforward; on others it may require replication of the packet to each destination.

A number of major types of network have been integrated into the PUP architecture, each with a different driver. They include Ethernet (Metcalfe and Boggs, 1976) and Arpanet (Kahn *et al.*, 1978).

7.4.3   Internetwork datagrams

PUP format

The standard PUP format is shown again in Figure 7.3. A brief description of the various fields is as follows.

The PUP length is the number of octets in the PUP, including the network header (20 octets) and the check sum (2 octets).

The transport control field is used as a scratch area by the gateways and as a way for the source processes to tell the internet how to handle the packet. (This is equivalent to the functions field in the Cambridge Ring protocols.) The hop count subfield is incremented every time the packet is forwarded by a gateway. If this field overflows the packet is assumed to be looping and is discarded. A trace bit is specified for potential use in monitoring the path taken by a PUP.

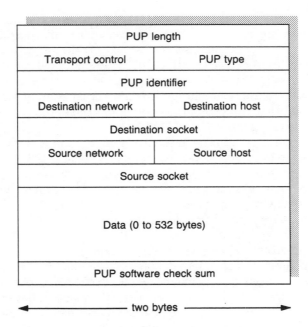

Figure 7.3 PUP datagram.

The PUP type is assigned by the source process for interpretation by the destination process and defines the format of the PUP contents. The possible types are divided into two groups. Some are registered and have a single meaning across all protocols. The unregistered types are a matter of agreement between the source and destination processes.

The PUP identifier is used by most protocols to hold a sequence number. Its purpose is to permit a response generated within the internet to identify the PUP that caused it in a manner that does not depend on knowledge of the higher level protocols used by the end processes.

PUPs contain two addresses: a source port and a destination port. These addresses include an 8-bit network number, an 8-bit host number, and a 32-bit socket number. (Note that the terms host and socket are equivalent to station and port in the Cambridge Ring.) Hosts are expected to know their own address, to discover their network numbers by locating a gateway and asking for this information, and to assign socket numbers in some systematic way.

The data field and the check sum field are self-explanatory.

7.4.4 Routing

Each host, whether or not it is a gateway, executes a routing procedure on every outgoing PUP. This procedure examines the destination port field of the PUP and decides to which of the directly connected networks the PUP is to be transmitted and it yields an immediate destination host. This host will either be the ultimate destination or some gateway en route to the destination. Each routing step employs the same algorithm based on local routing information, and each PUP is routed independently.

Routing information is maintained in a manner very similar to the Arpanet-style adaptive procedures (McQuillan, 1974). The initial item used for selecting routes is the 'hop count' – the number of intermediate networks between source and destination. The protocol for updating the routing tables involves exchanging PUPs with neighbouring gateways and rests logically at level 2 of the protocol hierarchy.

A host which is not a gateway still implements a portion of this level 2 routing update protocol. It initially obtains an internetwork routing table from a gateway on its directly connected network, and it obtains updated information periodically. If there is more than one gateway providing connections to other networks, the host can merge their routing tables and thus be able to select the best route for the packets directed to any network.

7.5   Alternative approaches

Although the PUP internetwork architecture enables different types of local area networks to be linked together, there is no attempt to preserve the performance characteristics of a single local area network across the resulting internet. Each of the stations linked to the network has to be able to deal with the encapsulation and decapsulation of the PUP packets and the gateways have to hold a large amount of routing information. In this section, we first discuss the design of a simple low cost, high performance gateway for linking local area networks of different types together. Secondly, we briefly describe the Universe project which linked several Cambridge Rings by means of a satellite to form a wide area network exhibiting the characteristics of a local area network.

7.5.1   An Ethernet–Cambridge Ring gateway

At first sight the operation of the two systems would appear to be entirely different, i.e. the small packet size of the ring compared with the large packet size of the Ethernet. In practice the differences of the two systems are not so marked. Virtually all of the traffic on a Cambridge Ring used to support a typical computing environment is done using a basic block protocol. In fact it is not sensible to try to support the low level minipacket protocol of the ring across a gateway even when the gateway is being used to link two Cambridge Rings together.

Any gateway must be designed with the following requirements in mind. The Ethernet access processor must be able to accept whole blocks and must always be ready to accept packets sent to it. This is because the transmitting station hardware cannot recognize when the destination is not ready to receive. It will be up to the higher level software to deal with this condition if it arises by 'timing out'. The Cambridge Ring access processor must accept minipackets from the ring and build them up into blocks for transmission to Ethernet. It must also split blocks accepted from the Ethernet interface into minipackets and transmit them to the ring. It need not provide the same speed of response as the Ethernet access processor because a transmitting station can recognize if a destination is either unselected between blocks or busy during a block. The use of these delaying mechanisms allows the processor to carry out additional processing.

These requirements lead naturally to a gateway of the form shown in Figure 7.4 (Shepherd and Corcoran, 1982). Each of the local networks will have a processor based interface to the gateway to deal with receiving and transmitting packets. There will be sufficient local memory to accept a complete block on the Ethernet side and to block and unblock minipackets on the Cambridge Ring side. A central processor system will be needed to hold the routing information and this should have a bank of shared memory that can be accessed by either of the network interfaces.

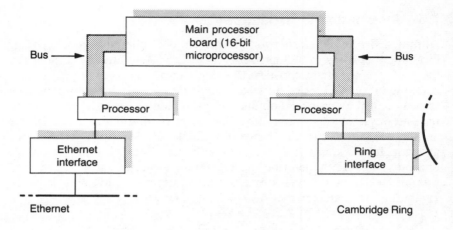

Figure 7.4   Ethernet–Cambridge Ring gateway.

Work on these types of gateways (Shepherd and Corcoran, 1982) has shown that the network interfaces can be divided into a network-dependent and network-independent part. The network-independent part, which forms the major part of the gateway, will be the same for both networks. This greatly simplifies the design of the gateway. As chips for the most common types of local area networks become available the difficulty of modifying the interfaces for different types of networks will become minimal.

The same gateway architecture can be used to link a local network with a wide area network, in particular to build a gateway between an Ethernet (or Cambridge Ring) and an X.25 network (Grant *et al.*, 1983a). This LAN–WAN gateway may involve protocol translation, particularly at the LAN side to build the datagram protocols up to the level of the transport service on the WAN (Grant and Hutchison, 1982; Grant *et al.*, 1983b); it should be described as a relay.

7.5.2 The Universe project

Project Universe (Kirstein *et al.*, 1982; Wilbur, 1983) used a network made up of several Cambridge Rings linked together by a high speed satellite link. The Cambridge Rings were located at several sites in the UK. Each site had an earth station which received from and transmitted to the satellite. The ring bridges described in Section 7.3 of this chapter were part of the Universe system.

The satellite used in the Universe project is the Orbital Test Satellite (OTS). The link consists of two 2 Mbits/sec half channels centred at 11 and 14 GHz. The earth stations transmit at 14 GHz and receive at 11 GHz.

Access to the channel is controlled by a master station (Waters and Adams, 1982). The channel time is divided by the master into 135 ms frames. Traffic arriving at an earth station which is to be transmitted over the satellite link will experience an average delay of approximately half the frame size. The propagation delay over the link is 0.25 s, so the delay on an idle channel will be distributed over the range 0.25 s to 0.385 s. The total configuration is referred to as a satellite bridge.

The bandwidth and error rate of the satellite link are similar to those of a single Cambridge Ring. The major difference is the magnitude of the delays across the system. This means that some of the protocols which are suitable for the single ring will perform badly across the satellite bridge. For instance, the byte stream protocol with a window size of one block (see Section 2.12.1 on HDLC windows) will not perform well over the satellite channel. However, the fileserver read protocol (Dion, 1980) in which a client sends a request to the fileserver which responds with a large number of blocks would work well over the satellite link.

A way to overcome the problems of mismatch between some of the single ring protocols and the delay in the satellite bridge is to provide a protocol converter. This converter would transform the 'window-of-one' block protocol used on the local network into the 'multiple-block' protocol used over the satellite link. The protocol converter could be provided as a special server on the local network. This method, together with the scheme outlined in Section 7.3 of this chapter, was the initial approach taken in the Universe network.

A Universe address consists of four fields: the site number, the subnet, the host, and the port. The first two fields are eight bits wide and the remaining two 16 bits wide. The site number corresponds to a satellite bridge. The address format need only be known by the nameservers and bridges on the system. A datagram very similar to the PUP datagram is also supported but we will not describe this in any detail.

Path setup is performed as before by interaction between a name-server and a bridge, but no further interaction between other bridges takes place. This is to avoid carrying out a series of transactions across the satellite link each of which would be subject to delay. The bridge, therefore, must be able to map the incoming packet onto a full network address. When an OPEN block is received by a bridge it is transformed into a BRIDGEOPEN block which will contain the full network address. The block is passed to other bridges which use the network address to route it towards its destination. The last bridge on the route transforms the BRIDGEOPEN into a standard OPEN block before delivering it to its final destination. SSP requests are dealt with in a similar fashion. Only bridges are aware of the existence of these types of blocks. The algorithm for deleting paths is based on port inactivity. A bridge keeps a timer for each path and when this timer expires it is entitled to delete the path. Paths to ports are treated in a similar fashion but the timeouts vary depending on the status of the port (Adams *et al.*, 1982).

We have described a number of approaches to solving the problem of linking local area networks. The choice lies between very general gateways, which must hold large amounts of routing information and also require all hosts on the network to be able to handle some part of the routing function, and less general gateways, which try to preserve the characteristics of the local network and at the same time make the internetworking completely transparent to the hosts. In the immediate future there is likely to be a need for both types of gateways, one dealing with essentially local requirements, the other with wide area networking.

7.6 The OSI transport layer

The purpose of the transport layer, as introduced in Section 2.3, is to provide a network-independent service to the application-oriented layers above it in the OSI model. To be more specific, this layer takes the network service available and provides the session layer with data transportation facilities at a required quality of service and in an optimum manner. The transport layer bridges a quality of service gap between what the session layer wants and what is given by the network layer.

The ISO have produced two standards documents for the transport layer:

- DP 8072: transport service
- DP 8073: transport protocol.

A basic function of this layer is to perform multiplexing, which it does in order to achieve the necessary quality of service at the optimum cost. For example, several network connections may be required to provide the required rate of service for a single transport layer user. Alternatively, one network connection may be sufficient to support more than one transport connection.

It therefore follows that the transport layer must know the quality of service provided by the underlying network layer.

Basically the transport layer is connection-oriented, although there is now an ISO document describing a connectionless protocol which builds on either the CL- or CO-network service (ISO DP 8602).

The following summarizes the CO-transport layer service:

Primitive	Parameters
T-CONNECT-REQUEST	dest addr, src addr, options, QOS, TS-user data

Primitive	Parameters
T-CONNECT-INDICATION	dest addr, src addr, options, QOS, TS-user data
T-CONNECT-RESPONSE	responding address, options, QOS, TS-user data
T-CONNECT-CONFIRM	responding address, options, QOS, TS-user data
T-DISCONNECT-REQUEST	TS-user data
T-DISCONNECT-INDICATION	disconnect reason, TS-user data
T-DATA-REQUEST	TS-user data
T-DATA-INDICATION	TS-user data
T-EXPEDITED-DATA-REQUEST	TS-user data
T-EXPEDITED-DATA-INDICATION	TS-user data

There are five classes of transport protocol:

- 0: simple class
- 1: basic error recovery class
- 2: multiplexing class
- 3: error recovery and multiplexing class
- 4: error detection and recovery class.

The types of underlying network connection (NC) over which these classes of protocol will operate are identified as:

- *Type A*: NCs with acceptable residual error rate and acceptable rate of signalled failures, such as most local area networks.
- *Type B*: NCs with acceptable residual error rate but unacceptable rate of signalled failures (e.g. disconnect or reset), such as X.25 networks typically.
- *Type C*: NCs with residual error rate not acceptable to the transport service user.

Briefly, the five classes of protocol are now described.

Class 0 is the simplest, intended to operate over Type A networks, and supports:

- connection establishment
- data transfer
- (with segmenting)
- error reporting.

There are no functions for:

- multiplexing
- disconnection
- flow control
- error recovery
- expedited data transfer
- user data exchange during connection establishment
- explicit disconnect (NC does this).

Class 1 provides for recovery from network disconnects or resets, or from loss of data, without having to correspond with the session layer, and is intended to be used with Type B networks (such as X.25).

Class 2 provides for multiplexing transport connections onto network connections. It also allows for flow control by means of a window technique (as in HDLC), and is intended for use over Type A networks.

Class 3 is a combination of classes 1 and 2, intended to be used over Type B network connections.

Class 4 is the most elaborate, being for use over Type C networks, and aims to be able to recover from any damage to or loss of control of data packets. In practice, however, networks of Type C unreliability are not likely to be found.

For further details on the standardization activities for the transport layer, see Knightson (1983) and FOCUS (1984b). Information on UK developments can be found in PSS (1980) and Dallas (1980) which describe respectively the transport service offered on the JANET (joint academic) network and an implementation of TSBSP (see also Chapter 6, Section 6.8). There is also an ECMA transport protocol, described in ECMA (1982c).

References

Adams, G.C., Burren, J.W., Cooper, C.S. and Girard, P.M., (1982). 'The interconnection of local area networks via a satellite network' *New Advances in Distributed Computer Systems*, Beauchamp, K.G. (ed.): Reidel, 201–210

Boggs, D.R., Shoch, J.F., Taft, E.A. and Metcalfe, R.M., (1980). 'PUP: an internetwork architecture' *IEEE Transactions on Communications*, **COM-28**,(4), April, 612–624

Callon, R., (1983). 'Internetwork protocol' *Proc. IEEE* **71**,(12), December, 1388–1393

Dalal, Y.K. and Printis, R.S., (1981). '48-bit absolute internet and Ethernet host numbers' *ACM Computer Communication Review* **11**,(4), October, 240–245

Dallas, I.N., (1980). *Transport service byte stream protocol (TSBSP)*, Computing Laboratory Report, University of Kent at Canterbury

Dion, J., (1980). 'The Cambridge Ring fileserver' *Operating Systems Review* **14**,(4), October, 26–35

ECMA, (1982a). *Network layer principles*, report TR/13, European Computer Manufacturers Association, September

ECMA, (1982b). *Local area networks – layers 1 to 4 – architecture and protocols*, report TR/14, European Computer Manufacturers Association, September

ECMA, (1982c). *Transport protocol*, Standard ECMA-72 (2nd edition), European Computer Manufacturers Association, September

FOCUS, (1984a). *Intercept recommendations for the OSI network layer*, FOCUS: standards for IT, Technical Guide TG 100/1, UK Dept of Trade and Industry, March

FOCUS, (1984b). *Intercept recommendations for the OSI transport layer*, FOCUS: standards for IT, Technical Guide TG 102/1, UK Dept of Trade and Industry, March

Grant, A. and Hutchison, D., (1982). 'X.25 protocols and local area networks' *Computer Networks* **6**,(4), September, 255–262

Grant, A., Hutchison, D. and Shepherd, W.D., (1983a). 'A gateway for linking local area and X.25 networks' *Computer Communication Review* **13**,(2), March, 234–239

Grant, A., Hutchison, D. and Shepherd, W.D., (1983b). 'Implementation of a local network – X.25 gateway' *Local Networks: Strategy & Systems*, Online Publications, London, 149–163

Kahn, R.E., Gronemayer, S.A., Burchfiel, J. and Kunzelman, R.C., (1978). 'Advances in packet radio technology' *Proc. IEEE* **66**,(11), November

Kirstein, P.T., Burren, J.W., Daniels, R., Griffiths, J.W.R., King, D., McDowell, C. and Needham, R.M., (1982). 'The Universe Project' *Proc. Sixth International Conference on Computer Communication*, September, 442–447

Knightson, K.G., (1983). 'The transport layer standardization' *Proc. IEEE* **71**,(12), December, 1394–1396

Leslie, I.M., (1983). *Extending the local area network*, Technical Report no. 43, University of Cambridge, Computer Laboratory

McQuillan, J.M., (1974). *Adaptive routing algorithms for distributed computer networks*, Harvard Ph.D. Thesis, Report no. 2831, Bolt, Beranek and Newman, May

Metcalfe, R.M. and Boggs, D.R., (1976). 'Ethernet: distributed packet switching for local computer networks' *CACM* **19**,(7), July, 395–404

PSS, (1980). *A network independent transport service (Yellow book)*. PSS Study Group Three: UK, February

Shepherd, W.D. and Corcoran, P., (1982). 'A gateway development system' *Microprocessors and Microsystems* **6**,(1), January/February, 21–24

Ware, C., (1983). 'The OSI network layer:standards to cope with the real world' *Proc. IEEE* **71**,(12), December, 1384–1387

Waters, A.G. and Adams, C.J., (1982). *Satellite transmission protocol, implementation specification* Universe Paper 125.2, Rutherford Appleton Laboratory, UK, March

Wilbur, S.R., (1983). 'Initial experience with Universe at University College London' *Local networks: strategy & systems*. Online Publications: London, 297–309

Chapter 8
Higher level protocols

The intention of this chapter is to introduce and briefly describe the OSI upper layer architecture, namely the session, presentation and application layers, in order to show the standards approach to providing higher level protocols.

8.1 Introduction

Moving up in the seven-layer OSI model, from the transport layer towards the user level, the aim is to provide a truly network-independent and easy-to-use network interface. All problems concerning the network connection between end nodes should be well and truly hidden from the user. Yet the OSI transport layer gives a true end-to-end service, providing the ability to send and receive information reliably. What remains to be done to provide the user with a better service?

The OSI standard defines three more layers above the transport layer:

- session (layer 5)
- presentation (layer 6)
- application (layer 7).

The importance of these layers lies in the additional facilities with which the network user can build distributed applications. Briefly, layers 5, 6 and 7 allow users to break up their dialogues into sessions, and to provide common formats and protocols for specifying the syntax and semantics of the user data. In this chapter, we look at each of these layers in a little more detail, concentrating on the services offered by each.

In the local networks developed in the late 1970s – especially Ethernet and the Cambridge Ring – protocol architectures evolved which were rather simpler than that of the OSI model. The relatively elaborate higher levels of OSI are not matched in these LAN-based architectures, and users can interface to many LAN systems directly at the protocol level they think appropriate to their needs. Most often the users of such LAN systems are researchers and systems programmers – not at all 'users' in the sense of the user of the OSI model architecture. This point will be taken up again in Chapter 10.

Whereas the LAN user tends to be closely familiar with the lower level protocols in the network, and is more than willing to exploit the LAN characteristics directly, the OSI user is expected to be someone who does not want to know anything about networks, but wishes to carry out a transaction with a remote entity as simply as if that entity were in the same local computer.

However, there is a problem with the OSI approach. Layers 5, 6 and 7 are quite complex, and it is not transparently clear how to use them to build distributed applications. The standards documents themselves offer little help in this direction. What is required is an associated guide to assist the designer and implementer to use the standards. In the UK, the Department of Trade and Industry FOCUS initiative (introduced in Chapter 2, Section 2.2) has produced 'Intercept recommendations' which interpret some of the standards documents. These go part of the way to providing a user guide of the type suggested. For LAN standards, they are being reprinted in the British Standards Institution *Draft for Development* series of documents, as Part 2 of each standard.

Until sufficient experience has been gained by a variety of designers and implementers, it will not be certain that the uppermost three layers contain the correct facilities. At present there is some doubt about this, particularly amongst the LAN community. Recent work within ECMA, CCITT and also ISO on remote operations service (ROS), is aimed at producing standards for transactions between remote entities, particularly in interactive applications (see Chapter 10, Section 10.4 for further discussion). This work may serve to answer some of the criticisms of OSI's uppermost three layers.

8.2   User requirements

The most common user requirements in using network communications at present are for:

- file transfer
- remote log in
- remote job submission.

These apply particularly to the use of wide area networks. In local networks there are increasingly many applications which take advantage of the high speed and high reliability of LANs to build closely coupled systems for dedicated applications. Many of these are in the domain of the so-called 'real-time' application, where it is essential for messages to be delivered within a critical time limit or else dire consequences may result. In such systems the user requirements may include file transfer but will principally consist of interprocess communication (IPC). Processes or tasks running either in the same or different computers may need to pass information or indeed to activate one another; these activities are variously achieved by message passing or by placing information in shared memory.

It may well be that the OSI model is unsuitable for applications of this nature, and that further research is necessary to develop an alternative model. Such distributed computing applications based on local networks are further discussed in Chapter 10.

8.2.1   Upper layer architecture

The OSI model architecture is designed to be totally general purpose, to apply to any networked system. As such, it necessarily contains all the ingredients to enable user applications of any variety to operate across the network.

Whereas the network and transport layers together can be seen to provide internetworking and a true end-to-end service, the combination of the session, presentation and application layers gives a full user interface to the underlying network, providing for:

- synchronized dialogue (session)
- standardized user data representation (presentation) (i.e. common syntax)
- common user semantics (application).

It is logical to view layers 5, 6 and 7 together (Larmouth *et al.*, 1984). They are distinct from the lowermost four layers, which provide a transport service of the required quality over particular networks. Following the publication in 1983 of ISO 7498, the basic reference model of OSI, it was decided to create a special upper layer architecture group within WG6 of ISO TC97 SC21. Its remit is to work on the architectural details of layers 5, 6 and 7, which until 1984 had been insufficiently developed. The ISO, in setting up this new study group, acknowledged that the uppermost three layers should be considered together.

One of the early results of their work was the notion of **pass-through** services (see Figure 8.1). All session services are available to the application layer. Some of these are directly mapped, i.e. the presentation layer adds no value to the session layer service, but it is made available to the application layer looking as if it were a layer 6 facility.

Another result of the upper layer group's work is that request and response protocol data units (PDUs) from the application, presentation and session layers are embedded together. It was found that only in this way can the setting up of application connections be made to work

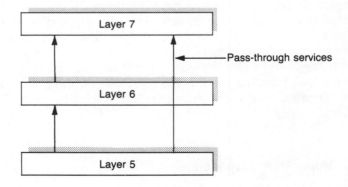

Figure 8.1 Pass-through services.

efficiently, because there are so many interdependencies between the three layers. Embedding minimizes the number of PDUs exchanged, and ensures the appropriate interaction between the layers during connection setup.

However, it is difficult to see why such complexity is needed at the higher protocol levels. Indeed, some system implementers are looking for the provision of ways in which vertical paths (paths of least resistance) can be made through the OSI layers, cutting out the unnecessary complexity for specific applications. Unfortunately much less work has been done on the higher layers and there is presently little user experience to give a suitable explanation for these layers using applications as examples.

In the next few sections we look at each of layers 5, 6, and 7 in turn, in an attempt to explain these in more understandable terms than can be found in the standards documents.

8.3   The OSI session layer

The session layer provides uniform mechanisms for controlling data exchange between end user applications. In doing so, it aims to reduce variations in the ways in which applications and their supporting protocols operate.

This layer has its origins in work done largely by CCITT on Teletex (for the S.62, now T.62, standard). Early work was also provided by ECMA in their ECMA-75 session protocol and this has been carried over to the OSI documents.

Teletex is one of the 'telematics' applications, or in other words office document communications applications. Other telematics areas include videotex, facsimile and message handling systems. The word 'teletex' was originated by Siemens in West Germany, but has been made available to the CCITT as a reserved term. In addition to the CCITT and ECMA work in this area, the ISO's TC97/SC18 on text and office systems is doing a considerable amount of work on office document structures and text communications services.

Teletex combines features of word processing, telex and communications and is concerned with automating the office handling of text documents, particularly transmitting copies to remote locations. It is a direct terminal-to-terminal service, using either the public switched telephone network, or X.21/X.25 networks. Special word processing terminals having teletex communications capability have been developed by manufacturers. These will automatically set up calls, send information and clear calls, and also automatically receive and store a number of documents.

Compared with telex, teletex is faster and more versatile. Compared with facsimile, which sends bit mapped pictorial images of documents, teletex is suitable only for text, and uses character codes to send information. There is a so-called 'mixed mode' being standardized which deals with a combination of teletex and facsimile techniques for text and images.

The definition of standard teletex is equivalent to the OSI transport and session layers, and as indicated above has influenced the session layer standard, mainly because it is one of the few available applications which could be used to shape the upper OSI layers (ITSU, 1986). Below the transport layer, it is open which sort of communications facility to use for sending teletex information. Above the session layer, it is the subject of ongoing study how to integrate teletex with other applications, including electronic mail. An obvious difficulty is that each application has its own specific requirements at these highest layers.

While the early work on defining the session layer was in progress, several candidates were proposed as the basis for the OSI session; this necessitated cooperation amongst ISO, CCITT and ECMA. At a SC16 meeting in June 1982, in Tokyo, a decision was reached to combine CCITT's S.62 and the ECMA-75 session protocol to produce a single OSI standard.

The work involved took a year or so to complete, and at a meeting of SC16/WG6 in Vienna, in March 1983, the following documents were approved:

- DP 8326 session service definition.

- DP 8327 session protocol specification.

In common with the other OSI layer specifications, the session layer uses service and protocol data units (in this case SSDUs and SPDUs) to communicate with the session user layer and peer protocol layers respectively. Further details of the OSI session layer are given in (Emmons and Chandler, 1983).

The session user (i.e. the presentation layer) exchanges SSDUs with the session layer across its service interface; SPDUs are exchanged with remote peer layers.

The fundamental operation of the session layer is that of setting up, managing and closing down connections. There is a one-to-one corre-spondence between presentation and session layer connections, and in turn between session and transport layer connections. A connectionless form of

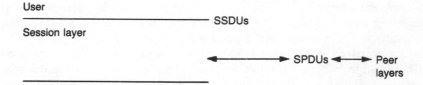

OSI is being studied, and has made progress, but will involve the session layer only to the extent of mapping addresses through from the transport to the presentation layer.

The session layer provides two alternative styles of protocol operation: half duplex and full duplex. These reflect the two choices in designing application layer protocols, where the two schools of thought are either to use a two-way simultaneous data flow between the partners in the exchange (the full-duplex method), or a one-way-at-a-time approach (half duplex). With the latter approach the use of **tokens** controls the current direction of data flow – the token holder has the right to transmit.

Both styles of operation can use facilities for recovering from failures, based on **synchronization points**. These are placed as required within the session layer dialogue, and can be used to roll back the session to a point where both parties agree on a common state of their dialogue. If these are not used, then a failure during a session may leave both parties unsure about the state of the other party, and the session may have to be restarted from the beginning.

The functions provided for the local session user to manage and control dialogue with remote users are:

(1)   normal data exchange

(2)   expedited data exchange

(3)   token management – the right to exclusive use of services

(4)   dialogue control – half and full duplex

(5)   synchronization

(6)   resynchronization

(7)   activity management

(8)   exception reporting

(9)   typed data

(10)   capability data.

These are grouped into three subsets, called:

- basic combined subset (BCS)
- basic synchronized subset (BSS)
- basic activity subset (BAS).

The BCS includes the fundamental part of the session layer services, called the **kernel**. It can use either the half or full duplex functional unit, and is intended for use in applications which do not require synchronization facilities.

The BSS adds synchronization facilities to the BCS, and is intended for more complex applications which require recovery mechanisms.

BAS includes BCS, and adds so-called activity management as well as some exception reporting facilities. Activity management is an extended form of synchronization intended specifically for use with certain telematics applications.

A summary of the session layer service primitives is as follows: (P = provider; U = user)

S-CONNECT	session connect
S-RELEASE	orderly release
S-U-ABORT	U-abort
S-P-ABORT	P-abort
S-DATA	normal data
S-EXPEDITED-DATA	expedited data
S-P-EXCEPTION-REPORT	exception reporting
S-U-EXCEPTION-REPORT	
S-TYPED-DATA	typed data
S-TOKEN-GIVE	token management
S-TOKEN-PLEASE	
S-SYNC-MAJOR	session synchronization
S-SYNC-MINOR	
S-RESYNCHRONIZE	
S-ACTIVITY-BEGIN	activity management
S-ACTIVITY-END	
S-ACTIVITY-INTERRUPT	
S-ACTIVITY-DISCARD	
S-CAPABILITY-DATA	capability data exchange

There are different options for carrying user data at the session level. S-DATA is the normal type, whereas S-TYPED-DATA and S-EXPEDITED-DATA are provided as alternatives to this and are not subject to token control. The difference between the latter two is that S-TYPED-DATA can be blocked by flow control action (as can S-DATA) but S-EXPEDITED-DATA gives a means of communicating information when the flow control mechanism has blocked the main channels. S-CAPABILITY-DATA is used to find out the capability of the remote partner before a session is begun.

8.4   The OSI presentation layer

Applications using OSI require to send information to remote locations across a network or internetwork. The meaning of this information (its semantics) is the concern of the application layer. However, the form in which the information will be carried (its syntax), is a presentation layer matter, so that the session layer can be presented with a user data bit pattern for transportation.

This layer provides a protocol by means of which communicating systems can exchange information about the syntax of applications. In the connection-oriented form, this involves setting up a connection, handling the syntax definition between systems for the duration of application transfers, and of course closing down the connection.

Initially three requirements were studied:

- virtual terminal data streams
- file transfer data streams
- job transfer data streams.

When the OSI model was in its early stages, file and job transfer protocols were considered to belong to the application layer, while virtual terminal protocols were placed in the presentation layer. This has now changed. All three protocols are part of the application layer, and are called specific application service elements (SASE). See Section 8.5 for more details.

The standard introduces the notions of **abstract** and **concrete transfer syntaxes**. The concrete transfer syntax is easy to understand. It is simply the bit pattern used in the session layer to exchange messages between systems, in other words an implementation of the meaning of the user data. The abstract transfer syntax, however, is the means by which the application layer defines the data structures it requires to send to another system. It makes available primitive structuring elements to enable the definition.

This is just the same as defining data structures in a programming language, for example Pascal, using types like integer or character as basic building blocks for the definition. Of course, implementation of these data structures, i.e. how they appear as sequences of bits, can be done in different ways. Thus the requirement that communicating systems agree on a specific concrete transfer syntax.

Presently, many applications define their data down to the level of a sequence of ASCII characters or perhaps a stream of binary octets, and in such cases the need for the presentation layer disappears. However, it is thought desirable to separate semantic and syntactic descriptions so that applications would not have to be concerned with matters of implementation. In the long run it is hoped that a sufficiently rigorous notation will be developed which will enable semantic descriptions to be automatically transformed into a suitable syntax for implementation by the presentation layer protocol. Meanwhile, the use of an abstract syntax is a sort of halfway house between this goal and a full implementation description (as in ASCII or binary) by the application itself.

It must also be recognized that variations in bit patterns must be allowed for, even for a given application at different times in its use. Examples include the need for encryption of various sorts when confidentiality is required, and the use of data compression to minimize data transfer costs. These are seen as presentation layer concerns.

The relevant standards documents are:

- DP 8822 presentation service definition
- DP 8823 presentation protocol specification.

See Hollis (1983) for an introduction to the OSI presentation layer standard.

A specific abstract syntax notation called ASN.1 has been developed in conjunction with the standard, allowing applications to define information they need to transfer using the presentation service. ASN.1 gives a notation for specifying values of a defined type. ISO DIS 8824 specifies the notation itself, while DIS 8825 gives basic encoding rules for use with DIS 8824's notation. These encoding rules enable a concrete transfer syntax to be produced from an abstract syntax definition written using ASN.1. ASN.1 was originally developed by CCITT for their message handling systems (MHS) recommendations, and is published as X.409. The two ISO documents are equivalent to X.409, but have been rewritten.

It is not mandatory to use the ASN.1 syntax. Other methods may be used, for example an ISO character set standard such as ISO 646 (ASCII).

Note that each application protocol (such as file transfer or virtual terminal) has an associated abstract syntax which matches its own data transfer requirements. This will be true also for new applications, as they arise, in the areas of graphics, videotex and even voice communications.

A **presentation context** is the pairing of an abstract syntax with a 'compatible' transfer syntax. A transfer syntax is compatible if it can express all the information described in the abstract syntax. Some transfer syntaxes may provide data compression, while others may provide encryption. Such options may perhaps be decided when the two parties negotiate a suitable transfer syntax.

8.5 The OSI application layer

This layer, the uppermost in the OSI architecture, deals with the semantics of information exchange between application processes (recall that the presentation layer provided for common syntax). See Bartoli (1983) for an introduction to the application layer.

Important concepts within the application layer are:

- *SASE* – specific application service elements
- *CASE* – common application service elements.

The CASE is intended to be independent of the nature of the application, and contains protocols which, it is intended, will be commonly useful in building OSI applications. The protocols include, most obviously, those for setting up and closing down 'associations' (or connections) between parties.

In the long run there will be many different applications, each of which has specific protocol requirements in order to carry out its task. The idea of the SASE is that it contains protocols which have been found to be useful for specific applications – a sort of library of useful protocols. At present the SASE includes VT (virtual terminal), FTAM (file transfer and management) and JTAM (job transfer and management) protocols. In the future this list will grow as experience with OSI applications develops.

The ISO's internal structure of the application layer is quite complex. It uses a model consisting of four parts:

(1)   an application process model

(2)   an application entity model

(3)   a model of the application association and its relationship to application processes, application entities and presentation service access points (PSAPs)

(4)   a model of application contexts and their relationship to application service elements and the user element.

We explain these terms, and the model components, as follows. A process is the natural view of an application, and exists in the user's domain.

An application entity (AE) is the representation of an application process (AP) within OSI, and is bound at any time to a particular PSAP at the presentation layer boundary. There may be more than one AE within an AP: see Figure 8.2, which shows that for each PSAP there is a corresponding SSAP at the session layer boundary.

The AE consists of a collection of application service elements and an associated user element. The user element acts as an interface layer into the application process. Application service elements are protocols consisting of application-specific and common protocols, in other words taken from the SASE and CASE.

In general, an ASE (application service element) is a part of an AE that provides some well-defined OSI environment capability. An ASE can use the services of another ASE in the AE, use the services of the presentation layer directly, and may provide services to other ASEs and to the user element in the AE.

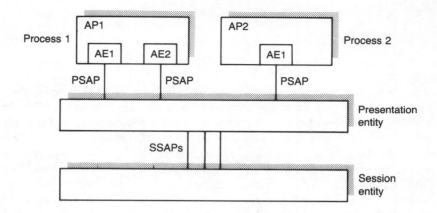

Figure 8.2   Upper layer application model.

For further reading on specific protocols at the application level, the following may be useful. The *Green Book* (PSS, 1981) contains a description of character terminal protocols on the PSS (1980) wide area network provided in the UK by British Telecom. This is an interim protocol, one of the so-called *coloured book* UK protocols produced in advance of OSI. For an introduction to SASE protocols, Lowe (1983) gives a description of the OSI virtual terminal service, and Lewan and Long (1983) a description of the OSI file service.

In Cunningham (1983) there is an introduction to message handling systems and their protocols (X.400 etc.). This topic is explained further in Chapter 10, in Section 10.3 on electronic mail. See the *Red Book* (JTP, 1980) for details of the UK job transfer and manipulation protocol (JTMP) used over the JANET (Joint Academic Network), and Langsford *et al*. (1983) for a description of the OSI management and job transfer services.

In the UK the *Blue Book* (High Level Protocol Group, 1981) file transfer protocol has been developed to work over the JANET and PSS wide area networks, and is the basis on which local network users (for example using Ethernet) transfer files between remote sites.

References

Bartoli, P.D., (1983). 'The application layer of the reference model of open systems interconnection' *Proc. IEEE* **71**,(12), December, 1404–1407

Cunningham, I., (1983). 'Message-handling systems and protocols' *Proc. IEEE*, **71**,(12), December, 1425–1430

Emmons, W.F. and Chandler, A.S., (1983). 'OSI session layer:services and protocols' *Proc. IEEE*, **71**,(12), December, 1397–1400

High Level Protocol Group, (1981). *A network independent file transfer protocol* (*Blue book*), UK, revised edition, (February)

Hollis, L.L., (1983). 'OSI presentation layer activities' *Proc. IEEE* **71**,(12), December, 1401–1403

ITSU, (1986). *OSI and Teletex: relationships and interworking study report*, Report TG 106/1, UK DTI's ITSU, London

JTP, (1980). *A network independent job transfer and manipulation protocol* (*Red book*), JTP Working Party of the DCPU, UK, April

Langsford, A., Naemura, K. and Speth, R., (1983). 'OSI management and job transfer services' *Proc. IEEE*, **71**,(12), December, 1420–1424

Larmouth, J., Curtis, G.E. and Pearson, H.J., (1984). *An introduction to the technical content of OSI layers 6 and 7*, available from the UK DTI's ITSU, London

Lewan, D. and Long, H.G., (1983). 'The OSI file service' *Proc. IEEE* **71**,(12), December, 1414–1419

Lowe, H., (1983). 'OSI virtual terminal service' *Proc. IEEE*, **71**,(12), December, 1408–1413

PSS, (1980). *PSS Technical User Guide*, No. 17, Issue 1, British Telecom, November

PSS, (1981). Study Group Three. *Character terminal protocols on PSS* (*Green book*), UK, revised edition, February

Chapter 9
Network management

This chapter sets out to cover the emerging area of network management and its development into distributed systems management. Management is a key part of the OSI reference model although being progressed rather later than the seven protocol layers themselves. Some attention is also given to other views of management, notably those of the IEEE and the MAP community.

9.1   Introduction

This chapter introduces and describes the subject of network management. For local area networks this is a relatively new idea, but forms of network management have been used for many years in wide area networks. To explain the developments now active in local networks we look at a range of activities including standards work and also examples of wide area network management. But first we briefly recall some basic material about networks and their classification.

Networks are generally classified into one of two types:

- wide area networks (WANs)
- local area networks (LANs).

In WANs, machines communicate via a series of switching nodes. Data to be transferred is broken up into a series of packets each of which is sent from the source host to the destination host via the switches. Packets may travel by the same route or by completely different routes – it depends on the rules, or protocols, that the individual network uses.

There are now hundreds of different WANs in use throughout the world. In the USA one of the largest is the DARPA (Defense Advanced Research Projects Agency) Catenet which is an example of an internetwork – a collection of interconnected packet switched networks. In the UK, British Telecom's PSS (Packet SwitchStream) is widely used and JANET (Joint Academic NETwork) serves the academic community.

LANs are a fairly recent development encouraged by the general fall in the cost of computer hardware, by the increasing number and variety of peripheral devices available and especially by improvements in chip technology. Unlike WANs, which are usually operated by a country's telephone companies, LANs belong to the user organization that installs them and are therefore 'free' as regards operational tariffs. They possess much faster transmission speeds than WANs. This is due to the physical media that LANs use and the fact that only localized distances are spanned, typically confined to a single building or a campus environment – say up to a maximum of 10 km. LANs also possess high reliability, again due to the media used and the fact that many LAN technologies make use of passive components.

The usage of LANs is increasing, especially in office automation and real time process control environments.

9.2   Network management of wide area networks

The term 'Network management' as applied to WANs is generally understood to refer to functions such as auditing and accounting. This is because users, in using the network for communication, are consuming a service provided by a common carrier. The carrier has to know how much to charge users per time period and therefore has to have statistics on who sent how many packets, and when. Charging is primarily related to the number of hops a packet has made in travelling to its destination node and, as this route is not necessarily the most optimal one, on any 'regional boundaries' crossed on the way.

Gathering of statistics will also enable the carrier to determine how adequate the facilities provided are, e.g. if congestion is a frequent problem between two particular nodes then perhaps another route between them should be arranged.

Therefore, there is a need for network management in WANs, hence the increasing number of available monitoring tools and software for them.

9.2.1 Survey of work in the area

A detailed examination of other work that has been done is outside the scope of this chapter, but it is mostly WAN based. This work includes:

- University College London's work in managing their distributed service environment (Winfield *et al.*, 1984). They have a large network configuration consisting of interconnected Cambridge Ring and gateways to JANET and to Arpanet in the USA.
- Bell Laboratories' network management is described in Coates and Mackey (1982), giving details of the Bell Labs network expansion and the consequent necessity for network management.
- Digital's network management in DECnet (Stewart and Wecker, 1980) is an actual layer specified in their network architecture. DEC seem to have realized the importance of network management prior to OSI, IEEE *et al.* which are now busy defining standards to allow its implementation.
- The Hatfield Polytechnic network monitoring work is described in Vassiliades (1984). They use a Cambridge Ring and run WAN protocols (digital data communication message protocol – DDCMP) on top of basic Cambridge Ring protocols.

A description of network management facilities for JANET (previously known as SERCnet) can be found in Kummer (1980).

9.3 Managing local area networks

Network management for LANs is a recent area of investigation in which there is now considerable interest, although little work has yet been done.

This section discusses the management of LANs in general terms. Although the 'high level' aims of management systems are similar for all LAN architectures, the 'low level' methods of achieving them are not. The high level ideas discussed here are relevant to all LAN architectures.

There are two main application areas in which LANs are being put to use:

(1)   The loosely coupled interconnection of computers and devices in a local area. This provides the basis for resource sharing types of application.

(2)   The distributed computing system where the LAN plays the part of an extended backplane to distributed nodes that make up a more closely coupled computer system.

Ethernet is currently the main LAN technology being used by systems manufacturers in both classes of application.

LAN systems typically consist of a number of autonomous, multi-vendor, interconnected machines. As such, with differing operating systems at end nodes and a variety of protocols in use over the cable not all the networked systems can (easily) interwork. It may be that complete interworking of systems is not required. However, this leaves a number of logical networks in operation over a single LAN. One of the first problems facing the network manager is how to deal with several logical networks.

Also, today's operating systems do not provide sufficiently good networking software interfaces on which to base network management. The International Standards Organisation basic management framework standards documents, currently in draft form, describe how to achieve management of the communication service through additions to the existing seven layer OSI model (ECMA, 1984; ISO, 1985a). Such draft standards are not recipes for implementation.

A major problem is that most modern day operating systems were not designed with networking in mind. UNIX, for instance, predated the LAN era, and networking software was added as an afterthought. (Note: we do not include UUCP in our deliberations as it was intended for something quite different and is of little use in the environments we anticipate.) Recent releases of UNIX, e.g. 4.2 BSD, have been shipped with implementations of the US DoD TCP/IP protocol suite. However, no layered structure is evident that can be cleanly altered and added to.

Recently, several management domains have been identified for study, and standards bodies are examining these with a view to standardization:

- network management
- LAN management
- systems management

- OSI management
- management of distributed application processing (MDAP)
- distributed systems management (DSM).

The COST (Cooperation Scientifique et Technique) 11 *bis* LAN Management group (Sloman, 1984) in Europe has been looking at network management for real-time applications although many of their ideas are applicable to other application areas such as office automation. The COST 11 group argues that the ISO management model is not quite good enough because it appears to be aimed at 'systems management' activities such as resource control, application process management and commitment control. The difference between 'systems management' and 'network management' is subtle. For effective systems management there has to be effective LAN management. It could be argued that they are one and the same, but it is probably better to consider distributed systems management as an application built on the lower level LAN management. Having defined their own management model, the group then split systems management (their definition) into the categories:

- configuration
- maintenance
- performance measurement and optimization.

However, for the casual observer of this work it is somewhat unclear where, and how, these areas fit together – especially as the remit of one management domain may overlap with several others.

This chapter aims to work from the 'bottom up' towards a model that brings the various domains together. In the following sections we examine LAN management, in particular the standards work of the US Institute of Electrical and Electronics Engineers (IEEE). Next, the OSI basic management framework and the wider issue of distributed systems management are discussed; this is being studied in a European COST-11 *ter* project and, in the UK, in a special interest group on distributed systems management (SIGDSM). Then a model is proposed that attempts to bring the domains together coherently. The final section, in the light of this model, summarizes the various areas of work in progress.

9.4 Goals and philosophies

LAN management is at the lower layers of our model. The IEEE term for what we call LAN management is 'systems management' (IEEE, 1985). LAN management has one basic goal – to allow continuous and efficient operation of the LAN communications subsystem. This somewhat broad definition may be subdivided into five subtasks:

(1) *Configuration management*: this includes the capabilities for remote initialization, reset, and close down of both the whole LAN system and single entities within the LAN. Part of configuration management is also to provide for software distribution and installation, e.g. new releases of protocol software.

(2) *Fault management*: covers fault detection, diagnosis and correction. The following capabilities are seen as necessary to provide these functions:

- error reporting
- confidence testing
- alarms of potential faults
- hardware repair
- software repair
- reporting of repairs
- software dump.

(3) *Performance management (monitoring)*: to assist in the evaluation of the LAN system, requires the collection of various traffic statistics (number of packets sent, collisions and so on). Counter set/reset functions are needed here.

(4) *Access control management*: for monitoring the integrity of a LAN, this is a security related function.

(5) *Accounting management*: closely linked to (3), this is to assist in the distribution of costs that, on a LAN, may be notional. Accounting management correlates the statistics collected by (3) to help with capacity planning.

The IEEE work is based on the premise that many of the devices, e.g. bridges and repeaters, that make up the communications subsystem are too primitive to support seven OSI layers. IEEE management information is mostly collected from the lower layers. The IEEE, therefore, define a systems management protocol that can use only the services of the lower communications layers.

The split of tasks defined by the IEEE is similar to that of the General Motors manufacturing automation protocol (MAP) although, again, the terms differ. In MAP V2.0 the management is divided into: monitoring, control, configuration, problem determination, and recovery (General Motors, 1985).

9.5 Architectures

LAN (or system) management architectures all tend to conform to the same principles. With the layer abstraction (of the OSI model) as a basis, management is divided into layer management and systems management. Layer management is achieved via processes resident within the individual layers responsible for collecting management information. These processes are called layer management entities (LMEs).

Layer management is generally brought together via a system management application process (SMAP). SMAPs communicate among themselves to provide management of the general LAN system. SMAPs, therefore, make use of the LMEs to discover information about the layer in which they reside. An LME can enquire about another layer via the SMAP – so both SMAPs and LMEs use each other's services. The arrangement is depicted in Figure 9.1.

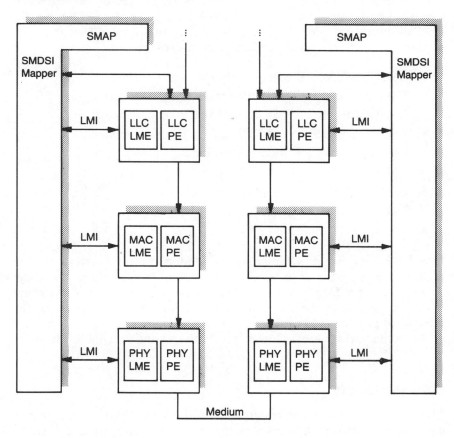

Figure 9.1 System management architecture (IEEE).

Figure 9.1 shows the SMAPs of two open systems and the means by which they interface to the data link and physical layer management entities and protocol entities. The SMAPs communicate with the LMEs via Layer Management Interfaces (LMI) and with each other via a System Management Data Service Interface (SMDSI). Each interface provides a set of primitives. The SMDSI provides:

- SM_DATA.request
- SM_DATA.indication

and these are used to pass systems management protocol data units (SM_PDUs) for transmission to remote SMAPs and to receive incoming SM_PDUs from remote SMAPs. In other words, these are the primitives that allow the SMAP to interact with the protocol entities (PEs).

The LMI is used by the SMAP to make specific management requests to a layer, by the SMAP to inform the layer of an event, by the layer to inform the SMAP when events occur, and by the layer to make requests to the SMAP. The associated primitives are:

- LM_SET_VALUE.request/indication
- LM_SET_VALUE.confirm/response
- LM_COMPARE_AND_SET_VALUE.request/indication
- LM_COMPARE_AND_SET_VALUE.confirm/response
- LM_GET_VALUE.request/indication
- LM_GET_VALUE.confirm/response
- LM_ACTION.request/indication
- LM_ACTION.confirm/response
- LM_EVENT.indication

As explained in Chapter 2, user primitives are 'request', which requests the provision of a service, and 'confirm', which returns the result of the previous request. Provider primitives are 'indication', which informs of the request for service, and 'response', which reports the outcome of the attempt to provide the service.

In the next section we look at protocols, staying with the IEEE work.

9.6 Protocols

The protocol used is expressed within the SM_PDUs. Management exchanges are defined in terms of managers, the requesters of information, and agents, the responders to requests. Eight types of SM_PDU have, so far, been identified. These are:

- a PrivatePDU can be sent either by a manager or an agent; this type is implementation specific

- a LoadPDU specifies that the PDU is defined within the load protocol (which is under study)

- a RequestPDU is sent from manager to agent to request an operation

- a ResponsePDU is sent back by an agent that has received a request to the originating manager with the results of the operation

- an EventPDU is sent from agent to manager informing the manager that some event has occurred

- an EventAckPDU is an acknowledgment for the above

- a TraceRqPDU (Trace Request PDU) goes from manager to agent to another agent; this PDU tests the operation of the station in which the last agent resides as well as links to the station

- a TraceRspPDU (Trace Response PDU) is sent by an agent to a manager as an acknowledgment of receipt of the TraceRqPDU.

The 'manager–agent' model is also endorsed by MAP where the network manager and manager–agents exchange **network messages** containing management information.

9.7   Applications

Applications of LAN management are various, and the degree of management required depends on the individual usage of the LAN. We will return to the latter point in the next section. LANs are increasingly used as the backbone to implement a distributed system and a good example is in the expanding area of factory automation. The General Motors MAP defines a standard for LAN communications between various factory devices. GM envisage a more-or-less automated factory environment based on a series of interconnected LANs, where a broadband token bus (to the IEEE 802.4 specification) forms the backbone of the system. The subnets are connected to this backbone via gateways or bridges making up the complete network system. Each subnet, called a manufacturing cell, generally has a specific task to perform, for example engine assembly. Successful operation of such a complex system depends on reliable transfer of data and information around the network. Therefore the communication system itself is a potential weak link – and this is where LAN management is useful.

In the interim period, while management standards are under development, General Motors have defined their own network management scheme, mentioned briefly at the end of Section 9.4. As MAP provides input to ANSI and IEEE the General Motors management approach is much the same as the IEEE/ANSI draft standards – based on layer managers, system managers, and network manager. MAP concepts differ a little from those drafts, however. The **network management entity** is the entire set of programs and data used to effect network management and the humans that control them. The network management entity is the combination of the network administrator, the person with ultimate responsibility for network management decisions, and the network manager, the application programs that direct network management operations themselves. The intention is that all nodes participate in network management, via the layer and system management, and all network management functions access and use a common database.

In the MAP V2.0 specification five elements of network management were identified: monitoring, control, configuration, problem determination, and recovery. However, in the V2.1 specification to allow General Motors to get some degree of network management up and running the scope has been narrowed. In the V2.1 specification they concentrate on:

- configuration management
- performance management
- event processing
- fault management.

Each of these is a distinct management application that lives in the network manager node. These applications correspond with related manager–agents that reside in each node. As far as V2.1 goes only the tools to accumulate the required management are considered; the human interface is not defined. Also, the decisions to be made from the information are left to a human operator. Ultimately, perhaps, these will largely be the responsibility of an expert system.

MAP addresses 'network management because the automated factory environment must be based on successful, integrated and, above all, highly reliable communications between machines. Therefore General Motors have recognized the importance of managing the enabling medium and components that allow communication to take place.

9.8 Automated management

Many of the functions of LAN management could be automated, with human intervention on a management-by-exception basis. Each node on a LAN can run a management process that performs node management for the local users. Each node can, in turn, report to a dominant node that has complete control of a single LAN – this echoes a common setup in a WAN environment where one node is usually designated as the 'network control centre' and performs in a supervisory role. We can envisage each LAN being a 'domain' with a node acting as network management centre (nmc) for that domain. In a large internetwork a hierarchy of nmcs might exist, each in correspondence with the others and with a 'root' node as a central control and monitoring point. Ultimately a decentralized control system based in all the nmcs might be a better solution. Network management packets of two classes, status and control, will travel along the LAN(s).

Each node is responsible for monitoring its own traffic – this can largely be done in hardware. Every so often it can report to its nmc, enabling the nmc to do performance management. Likewise, the nmc can regularly poll each node on the LAN for a status report.

The use of expert systems techniques can be seen as a way to automate management. Fault management is one area where expert systems techniques are potentially useful. Faults may occur in both hardware and software. Local node management processes can monitor the local node's software and hardware. Any unusual event may be checked against a small rule base and appropriate action taken. Software faults such as corruption after a node crash are correctable – the node can request reload via the nmc. Hardware faults are more complex. Without having component redundancy one method would be to place a limited process, in firmware, at the access level. Should the base system fail, the access process may probe to determine the nature of the fault. If an insufficient reply or no reply at all occurs, the access process can send a 'help' packet to the nmc which may either attempt to rectify the fault or request human intervention.

Configuration management is another area where a degree of automation is possible. A new node that has been added would have the management process already resident. On connection to the network a broadcast 'here-I-am' packet could be sent as part of some initialization process. Other nodes could note this and update appropriate tables.

Automated management is of most obvious use in dedicated, critical, real-time types of application – factory automation and process control systems for example.

9.9 ISO OSI basic management framework

The IEEE systems management framework is based on the OSI basic management framework so there is much in common between the two, but terminology varies, as usual. The remit of the OSI standard is to form:

> 'the basis for the definition and specification of services and protocols which enable the planning, organizing, supervising and controlling of the communication service that forms a part of a complete distributed

information processing system. It is recognized that OSI management is a subset of the general management of distributed information processing'.

(The last sentence of that quote agrees with the management model proposed in the following section.)

OSI provides the communications basis for distributed application services. OSI management is concerned with the management of the communication service (i.e. network management). The two main areas that the OSI framework sets out to standardize are:

(1)   the information that needs to be communicated
(2)   the protocols for the transfer of management information between open systems.

A set of **management requirements** is defined:

- standard, easy to use, functions to plan, organize, supervise and control the communication service, e.g. configuration management, monitoring and accounting
- flexibility to adapt in a dynamic environment, e.g. reconfiguration and name handling
- predictability, i.e. open systems should support applications in a secure and predictable manner
- security – use of passwords, encryption
- fault management, i.e. error alarms, diagnosis of faults, recovery
- good human–computer interface – appropriate command–response languages.

OSI management performs three tasks with information:

- processing
- storage and retrieval
- communication.

The reference model for OSI management is an extension of the IEEE one, given earlier, in that it spans all seven layers of the OSI reference model. Instead of SMAPs we have OSMAPs (OSI management application processes). Layer managers (LMs) exist also. Within OSI, management is divided into two activities:

(1)   OSI management which is the interworking of OSMAPs across open systems

(2)   open system management which is concerned with individual open systems.

Figure 9.2 shows the OSI management model. Although this figure is a little dated, it illustrates the principles involved. Three open systems are illustrated. The leftmost system demonstrates the layer managers (LM) and management information base (MIB) tied together via open system management. The other two open systems are the same. All three are united via the OSMAPs, through which OSI management is provided.

9.10 A complete management model

In the UK, there have been two related management groups: MDAP and SIGDSM. The MDAP (management of distributed application processing) group was concerned with the development of standards to assist users in the management of distributed applications. SIGDSM (special interest group on distributed systems management) has no affiliation but is formed from those in industry and universities in the UK with a common interest in

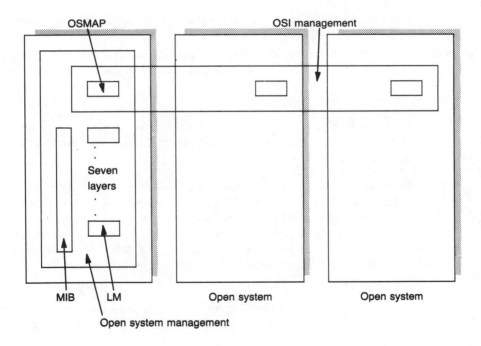

Figure 9.2 OSI management.

management and user requirements. The DSM group aims to define such management needs, and the necessary tools to effect it, over a wide variety of distributed systems, with the aim of providing input and feedback to the standards making bodies. We now look a little more closely at the remit of the two groups and present an integrated management model.

9.10.1 MDAP

One of the original MDAP documents stated the following needs of users of computer systems:

(1) management support in order to plan, organize, supervise and control their information processing needs

(2) languages to specify and configure their application

(3) the ability to accommodate changes of requirement or to introduce new applications to meet new needs

(4) distributed processing systems which run their applications in a secure and predictable manner

(5) mechanisms to authenticate the source of information and validate the destination of information transfers

(6) reliable reports whenever failure renders their applications unavailable or unreliable

(7) information which helps them specify performance criteria, establish a given quality of service, and control cost (ISO, 1985b).

In a companion document MDAP is defined to be

> 'a series of management services and the inter-computer communications required to maintain the desired state of distributed applications' (ISO, 1985c).

A problem with MDAP is that many of the services listed for investigation are already covered by network management and other standards. In our opinion MDAP is concerned with end system resource management, more than anything else, and may build on, or interact with, information and services provided by network and other management standards. This belief fits in with the accepted definition of distributed application management:

> 'the name given to the set of functions which helps users meet the requirements of controlling and monitoring the execution of their distributed applications'

where there is emphasis on the 'controlling and monitoring'.

9.10.2 Distributed systems management

In this chapter, a distributed system is a collection of systems interconnected by a LAN/WAN/internetwork. A system is generally a node with some processing capability. Distributed systems management (DSM) is the highest level of management. Whereas OSI/LAN management is operating system-to-operating system and MDAP (management of distributed application processing) is process-to-process, DSM is total system-to-total system – DSM is perhaps the 'sum' of MDAP plus OSI/LAN management.

The SIGDSM group has the aim of looking at the necessary tools to provide this highest level of management. With a knowledge of the evolving standards the best way of using the information collected and identifying 'gaps' in the standards is being considered. For example, many of the relevant standards define what is to be done but do not specify what to do with the result; the human interface is often not defined. Often the information collected could be put to use in planning tools and decision making models. These are a few of the things the group is concerned with.

9.10.3 The model

Figure 9.3 illustrates our management model. Again, three open systems are pictured; the layer and system management present in each are pictured on the rightmost one. The individual systems are 'connected' by OSI management alongside which sits MDAP. The entire, 'whole' system that results is the domain of DSM.

It may be difficult to perceive the difference between DSM, MDAP and OSI management. In fact, the difference between 'distributed system' and 'distributed application' may be somewhat unclear. (A 'distributed

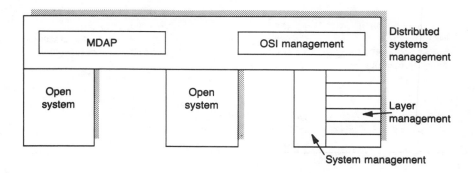

Figure 9.3 A conceptual model of management domains.

application' is a set of processes that perform a distinct task. It is, therefore, a subsystem of a larger distributed system.) However, if we list some examples of distributed systems applications:

- air traffic control
- airline reservations
- mail (MHS)
- process control
- factory automation
- banking
- EFTPOS
- IPSE
- automotive
- resource sharing

and then attempt to classify them, according to the degree of management required we arrive at Figure 9.4, showing a possible management spectrum.

In this figure, we classify management under three headings: DSM, MDAP and 'Limited'. DSM and MDAP are as discussed. 'Limited' management applies to environments with a typically small number of interconnected machines where management is largely unnecessary. We assume that all possess OSI management (or equivalent).

It is important to note that a system could possess varying degrees of management functionality. For instance, a system may be truly distributed

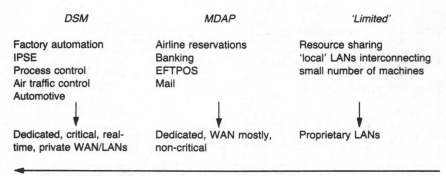

Figure 9.4   Management spectrum.

but may not possess a DSM capability. It might have LAN management of some sort to look after the communications links, but may leave other management tasks to be performed manually by the user.

The degree of management that a distributed system needs to exhibit is related to the use to which that system is put and how closely coupled the individual nodes are. For instance factory automation is an example of a dedicated, critical, real-time application. In the MAP environment where ultimately some thousands of programmable devices may interact, a high degree of automated management is required. At the other extreme are small micronets where a few micros share a quality printer. Virtually no management is necessary in this case.

9.11 Conclusion

More recently, the Advanced Networked Systems Architecture (ANSA) research project based in Cambridge, UK has developed a model of management which encompasses the organization within which the networked or distributed system is situated. Four layers of management are identified: (from the highest level to the lowest) policy, administration, activity and operation. The entire model is presented as a control system in which the higher layers exert authority on the lower ones, while results from the lower layers are fed back up to the higher to effect possible changes in management (ANSA, 1987). The SIGDSM activities correspond roughly to the lowermost two layers only, namely the activity and operation layers. Future work is likely to include collaboration between ANSA and SIGDSM to attempt to integrate the management views of the two groups.

Several key areas in information processing have been identified from the management point of view. Work is in progress within various standards bodies, and research is under way to design tools to assist in the general area of distributed systems management and distributed processing. However, several of the areas overlap causing confusion in both terminology and functional responsibility.

As upper layer OSI standards stabilize, and 'catch up' with lower layers, as vendors start to offer OSI products and hence true open systems become more of a reality, distributed processing will be more commonplace and more complex, and management will be a key necessity.

References

ANSA Project, (1987). *ANSA Reference Manual*, Cambridge, UK

Coates, K.E. and Mackey, K., (1982). 'The evolution of network management services in the Bell Labs network: throes and aftermath' *Compcon 82 – High Technology in the Information Industry*, IEEE Computer Society, February, 220–230

ECMA, (1984). *OSI management architecture*, ECMA TR/YY European Computer Manufacturers Association, December

General Motors, (1985). *Manufacturing automation protocol*, MAP V2.0 and V2.1, General Motors Corp., Michigan, USA, February and March

IEEE, (1985). *Draft IEEE standard 802.1: part B, systems management*, IEEE Computer Society Revision I, September

ISO, (1985a). *OSI basic management framework*, ISO/TC97/SC16, Geneva, Switzerland

ISO, (1985b). *Management of distributed application processing*, ISO/TC97/SC21 N389, Geneva, Switzerland

ISO, (1985c). *UK Comments on document SC21 N389; management of distributed application processing*, ISO/TC97/SC21/WG5, Geneva, Switzerland

Kummer, P.S., (1980). *Management and operation of a wide-area network*, Network Development Group, SERC, Daresbury Laboratory, Warrington, UK

Sloman, M., (1984). *Management of Local Area Networks*, Part 2 of Final Report of COST 11 bis Local Area Network Group, October

Stewart, R.L. and Wecker, S., (1980). 'Network management in DECNET', *Compcon 80 – Distributed Computing – 21st International Conference* IEEE Computer Society, September

Vassiliades, S., (1984). *Measurements on the Hatfield network*, School of Information Sciences, Hatfield Polytechnic, UK

Winfield, B., Daniel, T. and Hall, B., (1984). *Network management in a distributed service environment*, INDRA Note 1577, University College London, April

Chapter 10
Distributed computing systems

The last chapter deals with distributed computing systems based on local area networks. The aim is to review the research which has been done in this area, to describe the results produced, and to look at work in progress, emphasizing that distributed computing is an active and growing research field.

10.1   Introduction

Local area networks are communications subsystems used to support higher level applications of various kinds, as briefly discussed in Chapter 3. In that chapter, rough classifications of office and industrial applications were introduced. These sorts of applications are based on distributed computing systems involving several processing sites interconnected by a network (Enslow, 1978; Stankovic, 1984).

Distributed computing systems can be categorized as either open or closed. Open systems possess gateways to link them to the world beyond, so that potentially they can communicate with any other open system. Closed systems, on the other hand, are self-contained and have no need to communicate beyond their own boundaries. In the case of open systems it is clear that adherence to the OSI model is a considerable advantage, although not absolutely essential within the system. Protocol conversion between a private internal form and the OSI standards could take place in the external gateway.

Less clear altogether is the case for closed systems to adhere to OSI layering. Indeed many LAN implementers and users currently claim that specially tailored protocols are necessary to achieve efficiency in distributed LAN-based systems, and that use of OSI protocols leads to unacceptably slow implementations.

In cases (even in open applications) where full OSI layering is evidently unnecessary, it is possible to make use of null or subsetted layers to trim down the implementation size and also the runtime figures. Now that LAN chips are available for the standard technologies it is sensible to consider building distributed systems from these parts and then to decide whether the higher level protocols (from the network layer and up) will be standard or special purpose.

In the long run, as more protocol functionality appears on LAN chips, the decision whether to go standard will be made at higher and higher layers – and presumably with silicon implementations will come acceptably high performance from higher OSI protocol layers, as well as the availability of low cost building blocks. It is then possible that the need for specially tailored protocols for LANs will diminish, except for those who wish to continue the search for top level performance for their own applications, and for research projects wishing to explore non-standard techniques within LANs.

In this chapter, we survey briefly the sorts of application being run across local area networks, and internetworks, the tools and techniques developed to build distributed systems, and some of the issues and problems in the distributed systems area.

What, broadly speaking, are the issues involved? We begin with a brief coverage of the scope of distributed computing systems.

10.1.1 Enabling factors

The two key factors which led to the feasibility of distributed computing are both technological. In the mid to late 1970s there were considerable advances in the cost-effectiveness of processing through the rise of the microprocessor, and corresponding improvements in fast, cheap communications technology through the advent of LANs. The combination of the two technologies enabled distributed computing to become a reality.

This coming together of processing and communications was not a new idea – plans in this direction were already taking shape in the late 1960s – but never before was the cost element sufficiently low. Significant developments were made in the USA, particularly at Xerox PARC, as Chapter 4 has pointed out, and also in the UK at Cambridge University as outlined in Chapter 6.

10.1.2 Motivations for distributed computing

What is the attraction of distributed computing? The answer consists of several parts, which may be grouped as follows:

- flexibility
- performance
- availability.

(a) *Flexibility*: a distributed system consists of a number of modules which may be increased or decreased, in principle, without affecting the operation of the entire system. This can allow for growth in capacity or even variety of modules, for improvements in technology (e.g. upgrading a particular processor), and for maintenance of modules. Such a system also gives scope for moving processing power to where it is required. These goals, however, are not generally easy to achieve. How easy or otherwise will depend on the model used to design the distributed system, as well as on other factors including whether the system is homogeneous or heterogeneous.

(b) *Performance*: the ability of a single processor to cope with increasing workloads is strictly limited, given that users will demand response times that are within some reasonable expectation. It has long been realized that the way forward is to provide multiple processors. Indeed, multiprocessor computers have been designed and built for many years, traditionally based on a parallel bus communications system. Work is continuing on the design of computers containing a large number of processing elements, in some cases having architectures significantly different from the conventional von Neumann machine (in particular the dataflow class of architecture).

Whereas such computers are candidates for replacing the present-day large mainframes, centralized in one location, in this chapter we are concerned with geographically dispersed computing. Multiple microcomputers can provide greater computing power than a single large computer costing the same. When multiple processors are interconnected by a network, greater benefits can result. These include the possibility of sharing resources such as filestore, printing and plotting facilities, and the ability to locate computing power where it is most useful to the user. These benefits apply to programming development environments, and equally to dedicated applications such as factory shop floor and process control systems.

Where the interconnected processors need to cooperate together to achieve a common goal or set of tasks, it is not an easy matter to build a satisfactory distributed system. In that case some of the processing power, and much of the complexity, goes into dealing with intercommunication.

(c) *Availability*: a distributed system gives the opportunity to build configurations having extremely high levels of availability, i.e. the percentage of time for which the system is providing a satisfactory service. When designing systems for high availability, it is sensible to assume that failures – whether of hardware or software – will occur, and to take measures to cope with these. This method of providing highly available systems is called **fault tolerance**.

Some applications, such as telephone switching and air traffic control, have demands for 100% availability. Presently, these tend to be built using multiprocessor systems in which every functional unit (hardware and software) would be duplicated at least once. This approach puts cost at a much lower level of importance than availability, and is appropriate for such critical applications. These applications could equally well be based on LAN communications, using the same approach of replicating major components.

Other sorts of application, with less stringent availability requirements, can potentially be built very cheaply (using much lower levels of redundancy) by providing a pool of processors to which software processes can be allocated dynamically. The failure of one, or a few, of these processors would not alter the functionality of the total system. Failures, of course, may downgrade the system's response times, but the provision of a small amount of redundant processing power in the pool could counterbalance the failure of, say, one or two processors.

Where resources other than processing power are concerned, namely filestore and peripheral devices, once again the provision of a certain amount of redundancy is the natural approach to improving availability. But there is considerable interest in viewing distributed systems design not from the point of physical resources but instead in terms of logical resources or objects. Presently, the design of highly available distributed systems is still a research topic. One of the choices to be made is what model the design should be based on.

10.1.3 Models

The design of a distributed system is, implicitly or explicitly, based on a model of the system or of the application which will run on the system. Essentially this is the designer's view of the way the distributed components should be arranged in relation to the computing tasks to be run. The model is very important because it determines many of the characteristics of the resulting system. Recently, some research attention has been focused on finding better models for producing the desirable properties of flexibility, good performance and high availability.

The following models have proved to be useful:

- the hierarchy
- the processor pool
- the client–server model.

(a) *The hierarchical model* is often used in applications which have a hierarchical or tree structure. Most often this is found to be the case in industrial and commercial organizations. Take the example of a factory, where a shop floor reporting application is typically structured in a three-level hierarchy. The lowest level is the shop floor itself, where microprocessor-based devices will be placed for gathering information about the progress of the manufacturing work. (These may collect data automatically, or else operators may input data using specially designed keypads.) At an intermediate level will be medium-sized computers which collect information about a cluster of shop floor activities, and do some processing. The highest level will be the management computer, usually a large machine having the capacity to deal with all the processed data from the clusters. At this level, an overview is maintained of the total system, and management decisions taken as appropriate to the state of the application at any time.

It is natural in this example to build a hierarchical distributed system, even to the extent of using a star topology for the communications subsystem, between both the top and mid levels, and the middle and lowest levels. In process control applications a similar hierarchy would be evident in the model used. In either application, an alternative to a star between the middle and lowest levels is the multidrop bus, using a protocol such as HDLC (see Chapter 2, Section 2.12.1).

More recently, local networks of the bus or ring variety have been introduced in factory and process control environments, particularly between the top and middle level computers. The General Motors MAP initiative will clearly bring token bus LANs in particular into widespread use in these sorts of application (see Chapter 5, Section 5.6). Nevertheless, the assignment of tasks to computers, and the relationships between the computers, will likely continue to be modelled as a hierarchy.

(b) *The processor pool*: quite in contrast are applications where there is no obvious tree structure, but a dynamically varying set of tasks which require to be assigned to a processor as one becomes available. Examples of this sort of application are programming development environments and telephone switching systems. In the former case, users initiate log in sessions, compilations, text processing jobs, and so forth. In the latter, telephone transactions at various stages of completion, and new calls, are being handled simultaneously.

Obviously these could be, and are frequently, implemented by a single processor. However, a pool of processors to which task assignments can be made dynamically would clearly be beneficial for coping with growth in demand, for good performance, and for high availability. In the case of telephone switching, each telephone transaction is separate from any other and can easily be assigned to a processor arbitrarily. Some global control over the system's resources is necessary, and would be the responsibility of an operating system, or resource manager, which is active over the whole network of processors.

One of the ideas of having a pool of processors is that processing power appropriate to the needs of a task will be allocated, in other words not just running a job on a single processor but allocating several as necessary, e.g. to meet a particular response time demanded by the user. The partitioning of a task into separately runnable parts would presently have to be the responsibility of the user submitting the job, as there would be no way for the system to decide how to do this.

In fact, there is presently little experience of programming distributed user applications, and relatively little use of programming languages developed for this purpose, such as concurrent versions of Pascal, and occam.

(c) *The client–server model* is the best known in the distributed computing literature. It came to prominence through the development of the personal computer or workstation, and was used as a basis for designing the Cambridge Distributed Computing System (Needham and Herbert, 1982), and also for the Grapevine (Birrell *et al.*, 1982) and later distributed systems work at Xerox PARC.

The model is based on the idea that resources are not contained within a single large computer but are instead distributed across a number of smaller machines interconnected by a local network. The user, or a program acting on his behalf, is the client. Servers are agents with which the client makes contact to use the appropriate service. It is rather as if the shared resources within a large computer were taken out and each assigned to its own machine: these include the printer spooler (with the printer), and the file system handler (with the file system). Much has been written about file servers as a key component of distributed systems designed to the client–server model, for example Mitchell and Dion (1982) and Muir *et al*. (1985). A good account of the various servers in the Cambridge Distributed Computing System is given in Needham and Herbert (1982).

Each user has a processor of his own, but there are two different views of how this is achieved. In the Xerox PARC approach, each user has a desktop workstation, or personal computer on which much of his everyday work can be done. The workstation configuration will include sufficient disk filestore to support the user's everyday set of working tools – his programming environment. To access a shared resource such as the printer, or the large capacity filestore (used perhaps for archive purposes), the user resorts to the network.

At Cambridge, the model is slightly different. Each user is assumed to have only a relatively simple terminal, perhaps a VDU (still a true reflection of the level of equipment in the UK!). A processing server maintains a pool of processors, and allocates the user to one at the beginning of a log in session, or as required by a client for some processing task. With this approach, a processor of a type appropriate to the user's needs can be allocated. Thus the Cambridge Distributed Computing System, although essentially a client–server system, uses the pool processor model for allocating processing power.

10.1.4 The object model

Another way of viewing distribution is in terms of the logical resources in the system. In this view, known as the **object model**, the correspondence between logical resources and their physical realizations is made as late as possible. This allows a model to be built without the constraints of a particular physical configuration, a model which can attempt to satisfy two of the three aims – flexibility and availability – leaving performance considerations until the configuration is known. (Performance has always been the easiest criterion to satisfy, in the sense that one can select from a choice of technologies having different speeds, and if a fast enough one is not available now, it will be developed next year.)

The mapping from logical to physical resources can be made in one of two ways: statically and dynamically. In the simpler static method, a permanent allocation of logical to physical is made when a distributed system is being set up ready to run, in the same way as (logical) software is ordinarily loaded into (physical) computers following compilation and linking. In this approach, the distribution remains permanently set up on a particular hardware configuration. Good availability would be achieved by replicating logical resources on separate physical components. Some flexibility is inherent in the modular construction of the system.

More difficult to realize, but offering potentially greater benefits, would be a dynamic allocation of logical to physical resources. This is an area for research, and offers the possibility of very high availability indeed, as well as flexibility beyond the confines of the static approach. The idea here is that while the system is running, logical resources can be remapped from one physical site to another. This might be done in cases of failure of a hardware component, or during the maintenance of a component, or when it is required to reconfigure the system for reasons of growth (or some other evolution strategy).

A way ahead to enable the realization of these difficult goals is to have some global control over the resources of the entire system, although this does not imply that the control should be centralized within one component. Rather, global control should be decentralized, that is control spread throughout the components, logical and physical, so as to cope properly with effects of failures. This approach is being taken in research work to develop **distributed operating systems**, using the object model. This is discussed further in Sections 10.5 and 10.7.

10.1.5 Building blocks

Whatever model is used as a basis for designing distributed systems, the implementation of their distributed nature calls for suitable building blocks, in other words some means for communication between the distributed parts of the system. In terms of the OSI model of networks, this means using protocols provided by the uppermost three layers, which in turn map down onto the lowest four layers for transportation of data.

10.2 Higher layer protocols

Higher layer protocols, that is protocols above the LLC layer, are left undefined in the IEEE 802 local network standards documents. The assumption is that they are left for the clients or user of a network to define, which in most cases is exactly what they wish to do.

It is convenient to some extent to leave these higher layers undefined because local networks have in the main been designed from the bottom up. Most effort has gone into the physical and medium access layers, which is where local networks are chiefly to be distinguished from their wide area counterparts. The logical link control layer is the uppermost formal layer in the LAN reference model. It is also the layer which brings together the various LAN technologies to a common interface.

In the distributed systems examples introduced in Chapters 4 and 6, based on Ethernet and the Cambridge Ring respectively, the higher layer protocols were devised by the system developers to suit their needs. In fact, in both cases, the protocols developed have had a considerable influence on the subsequent LANs protocol work, including that of the standards bodies.

A key building block for distributed applications is the remote procedure call (RPC), which is described in more detail in Section 10.4.

Although only lately part of their work, the ISO is putting significant effort into this area, which they call remote operations service, or ROS. CCITT and ECMA were already working on remote transactions services, and some of this has resulted in the X.410 document as part of the X.400 message handling services (see Section 10.3 following).

There is now significant interest in developing a model of open distributed processing (ODP) which would be based on the interconnection model of OSI but would incorporate protocols suitable for building distributed systems. The starting point for these protocols are RPC and ROS as mentioned above. The UK ANSA project introduced in Chapter 9 (Section 9.11) has begun developing a framework for ODP, and is working together with ECMA on a distributed applications support environment (DASE). A key element of DASE is the REX or remote execution protocol which is a generalization of RPC and supports both synchronous, reliable calls (as in RPC) and asynchronous, unreliable calls, i.e. datagrams (ANSA, 1987).

The DASE work aims to unify support environments for a wide range of distributed applications including office and factory systems, and is putting a strong emphasis on the quality of the resulting distributed system in terms of its levels of performance and reliability.

10.3   Electronic mail and X.400 message handling systems

In this section, we discuss the important and widespread application of electronic mail, which spans both local and wide area networks, and which is becoming the subject of standardization through the CCITT X.400 series of standards documents. In electronic mail, computer systems are connected together only very loosely, compared to the more closely coupled distributed systems applications to be discussed in Sections 10.4, 10.5 and 10.6.

Electronic mail is a system whereby text messages may be passed from one computer user to one or more people. (Occasionally, electronic mail is used to send mail to programs instead.) The recipients may be on the same computer or another one (accessible by one or more connecting networks). The messages passed are stored at the receiving computer until the recipient deals with them. At that time he may use a program to read and perhaps reply to or otherwise act upon his mail. This has important consequences since the two users do not need to use their computers at the same time: problems which plague telephone conversations, such as different time zones and peculiar working hours, are solved.

The method used to transfer the mail messages from one site to another differs between different computer systems and networks.

A mail system typically consists of two separate parts to reflect the two distinct parts of the mail operation: the user agent, which deals with mail preparation and mail reading, and the mail delivery agent. This is essentially the structure used in the message handling system (MHS) model described in the CCITT X.400 series of standards documents. In that standard model the MHS consists of user agents (UAs) and message transfer agents (MTAs).

The user agent program is responsible for communicating with the user of the mail system in order to allow him to read and send mail. Essentially, this program has the task of hiding the implementation details of the mail system from the user while providing all the mail perusal and editing facilities that he might need.

The mail delivery agent program is responsible for delivering the mail messages which have been prepared by the user agent in communication with the user. It always communicates with the user via the user agent.

The delivery agent receives the preformatted message from the user agent and makes some decision about how best to deliver it and which networks, if any, should be used to connect to the mail recipient's machine. This decision is often based upon the format used for the message address (described later). Having decided the next network to use, the delivery agent then, if necessary, reformats the message to conform to some of the standards used on that network. Having done this, the delivery agent calls the program responsible for the required network and allows this to initiate the mail transfer.

In addition, the system may also be receiving mail from other sites or users via connecting networks. These messages are received by the programs monitoring and controlling those networks and are passed directly to the delivery agent. They are then examined to ascertain whether they are intended for users registered at this site. If they are, then they are passed to a local-mail delivery program which usually delivers them to the user's **mailbox** (simply a file where incoming mail is always placed). If they are not intended for this site, then the delivery agent treats them as if they are incoming messages, reformatting and retransmitting them as necessary.

An electronic mail message is usually constructed to conform to a particular format in order to allow the reading of messages to be, to a certain extent, automated. However, as the sender of a message can have no idea of the complexity of the software which will be used by the reader of the message, the format used must, necessarily, also be human readable.

Almost all mail systems divide the mail message into two sections, the message header and the message body.

10.3.1 The message header

The message header contains various information concerning the message, arranged as a series of lines or header fields. Each header field has a name which specifies, in a human readable format, the use of that line. In normal use the header field of a message is very similar to:

From: David Hutchison <dh>
Date: Tues, 15 Jan 86 10:25:32 gmt
Message-Id: <34452.6675786222@dcl-csvax.comp.lancs.ac.uk>
To: doug
Cc: stephen,jon
Subject: research

Note that the message header contains the names of both the sender and the recipients of the mail, in the 'From' and 'To' lines respectively, in a readable format. In addition, the 'Cc' field holds the names of recipients of carbon copies of the message. The 'Message-Id' field simply contains a unique identifier which refers to this message and is produced automatically by the mail delivery agent when the message is sent. It can be used to trace lost mail messages, to delete duplicates or as a search string in a file of messages. The 'Subject' field merely contains a string which may be used by the user agent program to provide a summary of the message.

10.3.2 The message body

In contrast to the message header, the message body has no fixed format at all and is simply a sequence of lines of text which make up the message itself.

10.3.3 Domain-oriented addressing

In the **domain-oriented addressing** system the address of a site is built in a hierarchical form. Thus, for example, the Lancaster site is registered as 'comp.lancs.ac.uk'. This address may be expanded to read:

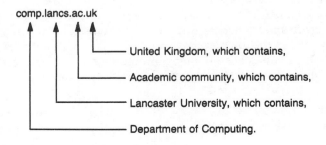

The whole system is based upon a tree structure in that each site (or word in the address) is a node or subdomain. There is one person (or organization) at each node of the tree responsible for assigning the names of the subdomains attached directly to that node. This means that a large central regulatory body is not required.

It is possible for a site other than 'lancs' to register the names 'comp', 'vax1' and 'vax2' as the registration specifies only that the sites directly attached to a node have different names (this is particularly useful with names as imaginative as vax1, vax2, ..., vax$N$, etc.).

Using this system it is also possible to specify only as much of a domain name as is necessary. The mailer is then able to expand it to the full domain name.

Thus, if we were to specify the partially-qualified domain:

'cs.strath'

the mailer would try the following expansions (in order):

'cs.strath.comp.lancs.ac.uk'
'cs.strath.lancs.ac.uk'
'cs.strath.ac.uk'
'cs.strath.uk'

This works on the assumption that, the more local the machine, the more mail messages will be sent to it from that site. Although this works in the majority of cases, it is sometimes necessary to specify the fully qualified domain name in order to be unambiguous. Therefore, if a program is the sender of the mail, it should always use the full form. The partial form is recognized to save users' typing.

This system seems to satisfy all the criteria which have been required of the addressing system. However, the owners of the UK domain have decided that, within the UK, names should be displayed in the reverse order to that used elsewhere in the world. In this way, the name 'comp.lancs.ac.uk' (in little-endian form), which is valid anywhere in the world should, in the UK, be converted to 'uk.ac.lancs.comp' (i.e. in decreasing hierarchical order – known as big-endian form).

It is intended that gateways to and from the UK should automatically convert to and from these forms but, in addition, many other UK sites have to perform the operation as well (as part of their mail relaying system). This then leads to many problems due to ambiguities. For example, given the address 'vax1.strath', do we convert it to:

'vax1.strath.ac.uk' or
'uk.ac.lancs.vax1.strath'?

There is, in general, no easy way to resolve these problems, as the sending site may have no knowledge of the receiving site's sub-domains (and thus not be able to see that an address is clearly nonsense). This is a great handicap to the automatic expansion of names for the domain-oriented addressing system. Although use of the full domain name circumvents most of these problems, it fails when the bottom level subdomain matches a top level domain. For example, the address 'uk.ac.rl.earn' gives problems because both 'uk' and 'earn' are top level domains.

Many sites (should) make use of the **smarter mailer** technique. Thus, if the mail delivery agent is presented with the address 'joe @basser.oz', it should determine that 'oz' is the top level domain for Australia, and pass it by the 'quickest' route to the nearest Australian site. To give another example, given the address 'ann@ihnp4.uucp', and given that the route to 'ihnp4' is not known, we would pass the mail to a site that *does* run the software to determine the route. Naturally, if that site determines that the route is via us, we run into a mail loop problem. This is partially alleviated by returning an error mail message if the hop count exceeds a certain value (usually 30). Of course, if this error message is also undeliverable (possibly due to another mail loop), there are problems!

10.3.4 The X.400 standards

The standards documents referred to as the X.400 message handling systems (MHS) basically describe a standardized electronic mail system, and are published by the CCITT. This is an application in which there is plenty of implementation and user experience, and of which heavy use is made and will continue to be made, particularly in conjunction with office automation and telematics applications. See Cunningham (1983) for an introduction to the X.400 series.

The characteristics of the MHS are as follows:

- standard message header format similar to an office memo
- store-and-forward delivery of messages to multiple recipients
- conversion of message contents to allow message transfer between dissimilar terminal types
- delivery time control
- submission and delivery time stamping
- notification of delivery/non-delivery
- standard service access controls.

The major components of X.400 are:

- an interpersonal messaging service
- a message transfer service.

In the functional model illustrated in Figure 10.1, these components are represented by user agents (UAs) and message transfer agents (MTAs) respectively. There is one UA for each user registered with the MHS. Although the UA facility provides an interpersonal messaging service, the MTA system on which the UA is built provides a general store-and-forward information delivery service. With this structure, alternative types of agent could be provided for different messaging activities, such as directory services, or even remote sensing applications.

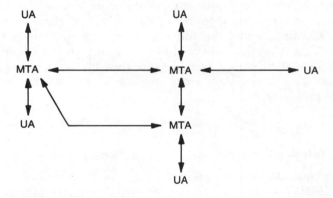

Figure 10.1   Functional X.400 model.

The protocol relationships between these components are illustrated in Figure 10.2.

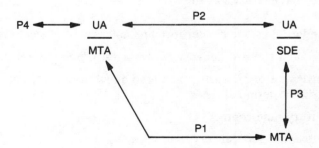

Figure 10.2   Protocols in the X.400 model.

The protocols are briefly described as follows:

- *P1*: store-and-forward message transfer protocol between MTAs
- *P2*: end-to-end protocol and message format specification between UAs (SDE: communications facility with restricted access to a MTA, e.g. over a communications link)
- *P3*: restricted access protocol to MTA by UA/SDE
- *P4*: protocol between user terminal and UA, e.g. X.29 (this is not defined in X.400).

These protocols will, in due course, become part of the SASE suite within the application layer of OSI. The documents produced for the X.400 MHS are briefly introduced next:

- *X.400*: system model service elements
  - this is a tutorial document
  - it deals with naming and addressing
  - and gives an overview of layer architecture
- *X.401*: basic service elements and optional user facilities
  - defines service elements of inter-personal messaging service and message transfer service
- *X.408*: encoded information type conversion rules
  - gives the rules governing conversion of document types: currently telex, IA5 text, teletex, G3 fax, text interchange format 0, videotex, voice, simply formatted documents.
- *X.409*: presentation transfer syntax and notation
  - defines the way protocol elements are expressed in other X.400 documents
- *X.410*: remote operations and reliable transfer service
  - presents concepts and definition of methods to describe interactive protocols (similar to RPCs – see Section 10.4, following)
  - describes a reliable transfer service
- *X.411*: message transfer layer
  - defines the P1 protocol used to connect message handling systems (with message transfer agents within systems)
  - also defines the P3 protocol between user agent and message transfer agent
- *X.420*: interpersonal messaging user agent layer
  - defines the P2 protocol between user agents (essentially this is a standard message header format)

- *X.430*: access protocol for teletex terminals

  - defines necessary protocol elements and gateway functions to enable teletex terminals and X.400 MHS to be connected together.

It is likely that significant further work will be done in the MHS area before the detailed structure of X.400 is considered mature, and before it is finally integrated into the OSI architecture. The prediction has been made that X.400 will consolidate electronic mail standards to the extent that X.25 did for packet switching several years ago.

10.4   Remote procedure call (RPC) protocols

An important distributed systems building block developed relatively recently (Nelson, 1981) is the remote procedure call (RPC) protocol, designed to make the activation of remotely situated software as easy as local software. A RPC transaction consists of a call message being sent from the calling to the called computer, followed by the requested remote action being carried out, and finally a reply message returning to the calling computer with the results of the action.

The idea is to provide the syntax and (possibly) the semantics of a local procedure call for the RPC, so making it convenient for the designer/ programmer to construct a distributed application. There are however, some difficulties with RPCs, principally:

- achieving local semantics
- achieving transparency of performance
- recovery from communications or node failures.

Recently, RPC protocols have been included in protocol standards work, notably as X.410 (remote operations protocol) within the X.400 message handling systems CCITT protocols, as indicated in Section 10.3 above. RPCs were briefly mentioned in Chapter 4 (on Ethernet) in the context of the Xerox protocol architecture (Xerox, 1981) and the TCP/IP architecture (Postel, 1980a and 1980b).

The RPC is considered to be a useful building block for pro- gramming of distributed applications. Embedded (as an extension) in a programming language (such as the SUN RPC for the C language), a distributed programming version of the language becomes available. The well known Courier RPC protocol developed for the Xerox Network Systems (XNS) is intended to facilitate the construction of distributed applications (Xerox, 1981).

Basically, the RPC protocol is an interprocess communication (IPC) facility, where the calling and called processes are located in machines remote from each other. It is the potentially high performance of LAN protocols which led to the idea of adding the RPC protocol layer on top of the data transport mechanism of the LAN. The underlying protocols used can be either datagram or virtual circuit based. RPC protocols have been fully explored by Nelson (1981) and concisely presented by Birrell and Nelson (1984).

The idea is to provide the appearance of a local procedure call but where the call and its reply (or return value) travel over a communications network between the communicating processes. The underlying network should not be apparent to the user of the RPC, except in the matter of performance, and in the event of failure. Even for high speed LANs, providing transparency of performance for RPCs is difficult, particularly if based on a virtual circuit which has first to be set up, managed during the call and return, then closed down. Users with particular performance aims in mind should make careful estimates of RPC timings when designing their applications.

If a failure occurs during a RPC transaction, the action which was lost can be restarted, but in this case performance will suffer considerably further. This should be taken into account when estimating timings, at least to the extent of considering restarted actions as possible, if exceptional, events.

Failures can occur due to the calling or called process crashing, or because the call or return message is corrupted or disappears. From the viewpoint of the calling process, the last three of these events are indistinguishable, and manifest themselves by the absence of a return message (following a timeout period). In this case, restarting the RPC involves resending the original call message.

When failures do occur, a more serious problem is ensuring the semantics of the RPC (i.e., what meaning is associated with a reply message when one returns from the called process).

For normal, local procedure calls, the return of control to the caller means that the call was obeyed, once and once only. For RPCs we cannot make the same deduction. In fact the semantics of RPCs can be classified into two main divisions (Nelson, 1981):

- exactly once
- at least once.

Exactly once semantics is the ideal, being the same as for a local procedure call. Implementation is moderately complex, and involves labelling each call message with a unique sequence number composed of the originating network node number plus a time stamp. Return messages are labelled with the sequence number of the corresponding call. In addition, the called machine must maintain a history list of previous messages and the action taken for each one. Using these mechanisms, the caller can resend messages safe in the knowledge that the called process will not repeat its actions, thus preserving the once only semantics required.

At least once semantics is considerably easier to implement, but can produce undesirable effects. The meaning of a successful reply message is that the remote action has been carried out one or more times, but the caller does not know how many times. Generally this is acceptable only if the actions being repeated produce the same result each time (a so-called 'idempotent' action). If not, the result produced may well be wrong.

For either class of semantics, should no reply message be received, even after a number of retries, the caller may assume a catastrophic failure of either the communications subsystem or the called machine, and would typically report the presumed failure to the user or to a higher level of software.

In addition to the standards work on remote operations, further technical progress on RPCs will include their integration into programming languages and programming environments for distributed applications.

10.5 Distributed operating systems

In many applications which make use of communications networks, the component computers are essentially independent, exchanging information as and when requested by users. Examples include MHS (electronic mail), telematics applications and distributed banking systems. In these cases, each computer is responsible for managing its own resources, which it does by means of its own local operating system. The coupling between computers across the network is rather weak.

High performance local area networks, however, give the opportunity of much more closely coupled working. This technology is being used to build distributed computing systems in which resources can be shared on a network-wide basis, and, increasingly, so that the computers can cooperate on a common set of tasks (Tanenbaum and van Renesse, 1985). For such applications, a distributed operating system (DOS) is required, to manage the network of computers and the resources they offer. The aim is that applications have the impression of a single, large computer, and are unaware of the distributed nature of the system.

There are two routes to building a DOS. In the first, each computer already has its own local operating system. A layer of software is placed between each operating system and the application software running on the machine. System calls are trapped by this layer and checked to find the location of the resource to be used. If local to the machine, the call is passed to the local operating system. If remote, the call is sent across the network to be obeyed on the appropriate machine. The result is termed a network operating system (NOS). This technique has been used to build the well-known Newcastle Connection (or UNIX United) (Brownbridge *et al.*, 1982), and other systems involving the interconnection of UNIX-based computers across local networks, e.g. Blair *et al.* (1982 and 1983).

In these UNIX-based NOS cases, the filestores are the key to unifying the individual operating systems. Resources are represented as files of various types, including runnable programs, text files and input/output devices. The appearance of a single, large filestore is given by imposing a so-called 'super root' to link together the naming trees of each filestore. RPCs are used to communicate requests to access resources which are located on remote machines. This occurs within the NOS layer and is intended to be invisible to the application programs.

Because distribution is not built into the kernels of the constituent operating systems, but is added as a separate layer, this approach may suffer from unacceptably high overheads, and give poor performance. It is also likely to prove a difficult route to developing highly available systems.

The second route, a much more ambitious one, is to design the DOS from first principles, integrating distribution into the system from the start. Existing local operating systems are discarded in favour of the DOS kernel. With this approach, sometimes called a global operating system to distinguish it from the NOS, it is hoped that all the potential advantages of a distributed system can be realized.

Currently, there is insufficient evidence to prove that this approach offers significant improvements over the NOS, but there is plenty of active research work attempting to do so. Examples of global operating systems based on the object model are Amoeba (Tanenbaum and Mullender, 1986) and Cosmos (Nicol *et al.*, 1985). In their survey of DOS work, Tanenbaum and van Renesse conclude simply that this is an interesting and fruitful area of research, and will continue to be so for a number of years (Tanenbaum and van Renesse, 1985).

Some of the important research issues in distributed computing directly affecting the development of DOSs will be discussed in Section 10.7.

10.6 Distributed databases

An important application on which much work in distribution has been done is that of distributed databases. Communications networks provide the opportunity to distribute data, but what are the reasons for wishing to do so?

Perhaps the most obvious reason is because organizations maintain distributed data in the normal course of their business. Banking and insurance, the health service, the public libraries, and retail organizations are examples. In some of these cases, where partitioned data already existed, network connections allow greater freedom to communicate and share data between geographically separate sites. In others, the arrival of network technology may have provided a business opportunity which did not previously exist.

Other motivations for distributing data include cases where there is simply too much information for a single computer system to deal with, or where user access times will be improved by partitioning data onto separate machines. In this latter case, regionalizing data to places where it will be most often needed is a common strategy. Also, distribution of data along with processing can, it is hoped, lead to the goals of greater flexibility and high availability as discussed in Section 10.1.

In order to improve availability, data can be replicated at several sites. However, this in itself brings the problem of maintaining consistency across the several copies. This problem of multiple copy update has been the subject of much research, and algorithms have been developed which provide solutions. Section 10.7 describes this problem further.

A good coverage of the technical issues in distributed databases is given in the book by Ceri and Pelagatti (1985). A good many specific distributed database systems are described in the research literature. Two such systems are IBM's R* (Lindsay et al., 1983), a distributed version of the R relational database, and the Genesis project which attempts to integrate distributed database operations within a distributed operating system (Page et al., 1985).

Much of the technical development of distributed databases centres round the notion of a transaction. This is also further discussed in Section 10.7.

10.7   Research issues in distributed computing

Considerable effort in the software engineering domain has been focused on the development of more advanced programming environments. Vital to the longer term success of this research is the existence of distributed systems bases having high availability.

Distributed computer systems have much greater potential for high availability than single machine systems, as explained in Section 10.1. This is due to the fact that resources can be provided redundantly at different sites. Because of this they should, in theory, be capable of continued operation in the face of failures. However, it is extremely difficult to realize this potential for high availability in practice. The distribution of computer systems introduces several new problems, which must be overcome if high availability is to be achieved. These problems make it very difficult to maintain the consistency of data in the distributed environment, and present an unreliable working environment to the user. Three important problems that occur in distributed systems are:

- the possibility of partial failure (more difficult to deal with than total system failure)
- the higher level of parallel activity
- the unavailability of accurate global state information.

In such an environment, it is vital to have a mechanism to simplify the treatment of these problems and to maintain the consistency of data. Distributed atomic transactions are intended to achieve this aim and to present the user of a distributed system with a reliable working environment.

Much research has been conducted on the development of atomic transaction mechanisms. Most of this research has related specifically to database systems. The application of the transaction concept to distributed systems in general imposes a new set of requirements on the transaction mechanism. Conventional database techniques lack the flexibility and efficiency needed to meet these requirements. The transaction model must therefore be extended for use in distributed systems environments.

The transaction concept originates from the field of contract law. Contracts (transactions) can only be broken if the individuals involved are willing to break the law. Legally transactions can only be broken if they were illegal in the first place. Illegal transactions are undone by compensating transactions. Transactions must be:

- *consistent*: they must obey the law
- *atomic*: they either happen in entirety and all parties are bound by them or they do not happen and none is bound
- *durable*: once committed they cannot be cancelled.

When the transaction concept is applied to distributed computing, transactions are considered to cause changes to the system state. Not all distributed system states are consistent, however, so some changes should be disallowed. The rules governing permissible changes in the system are called the consistency constraints.

The operations provided by a system can be generalized to reads and writes. Reads leave the system state unchanged, but writes cause changes. A collection of operations which together comprise a consistent change may be grouped to form a transaction. The consistency property of transactions requires that they preserve the consistency constraints of the system. That is, they change a consistent state into a new consistent state. The atomicity property requires that a transaction either completes all its operations successfully and commits, or none of its effects survives and it is cancelled. The durability property requires that once a transaction has committed it cannot be undone.

10.7.1 Consistency

It is important to distinguish between three different forms of consistency: **mutual** consistency, **internal** consistency and **application-dependent** consistency.

Mutual consistency refers to the consistency which exists between replicas of a data item. Replicas are mutually consistent if and only if they are all identical. Internal consistency refers to single objects in the system. Internal consistency is maintained for an object if updates to that object are atomic (partial updates can lead to the object being left in an inconsistent state). Application-dependent consistency is involved with relationships between the values of multiple objects, and is determined by the application.

Application-dependent consistency relies on both mutual and internal consistency, and makes further assertions about the relationships between object values. Atomic transaction mechanisms should maintain application-dependent consistency. In doing so they must honour the consistency constraints of the system. This would be easy to achieve if the constraints could be listed. The transaction mechanism could then check proposed new system states against the consistency constraints and disallow any that did not conform. In reality, however, the consistency constraints for a system are usually too numerous to list and, in fact, most of them are probably unknown to the transaction system. In this environment the transaction mechanism undertakes a slightly easier task of providing mechanisms that, if used properly, enable the application program to maintain its consistency constraints. This can be achieved by ensuring that transactions are atomic with respect to failures and other concurrent transactions.

Transactions usually consist of multiple operations which cause a complex change of the system state. These complex changes usually result in the production of temporary inconsistent system states. Temporary inconsistency is inherent in all serial computation and therefore consistency constraints cannot usually be enforced before the end of the transaction. The intermediate states of a transaction may become visible as a result of two related and fundamental problems, **synchronization** and **recovery**. It is the job of the transaction mechanism to stop these inconsistent states from becoming visible to other transactions in the face of these problems. Synchronization relates to the control of concurrently running transactions to avoid conflict. Two transactions conflict if their operations are interleaved in an order which results in the production of an inconsistent system state. The recovery problem relates to the recovery of data objects after errors and system failures. The two mechanisms must work together to maintain consistency. The problems of synchronization and recovery are discussed in the following sections.

10.7.2 The synchronization problem

The general problem of synchronization can be divided into two separate problem areas. The first is known as the **mutual exclusion** problem. Mutual exclusion is concerned with ensuring that only one transaction operates on a data object at any one time. Solutions to this problem include locks, semaphores and monitors. The second problem is concerned with ordering the operations of transactions over multiple objects such that the operations of conflicting transactions do not become interleaved in the wrong order. This is termed **event ordering**.

The event ordering problem could be solved simply by forcing transactions to execute serially, i.e. by disallowing a new transaction from starting until the previous one has finished. This approach would severely limit the performance of the system though (through loss of concurrency) and, in many cases, it would be unnecessary since not all transactions conflict. Synchronization mechanisms should not restrict concurrency unnecessarily and should only disallow the interleaving of operations in an order that would otherwise result in conflict.

The interleaved ordering of the operations of a set of concurrently running transactions is called a schedule. A schedule is consistent if it gives each transaction in the set a consistent view of the system state. A sufficient condition for a schedule to be consistent is that the effect of running the schedule is equivalent to the effect of running the transactions serially. This is the property of serializability. For transactions to be serializable they must appear to be indivisible with respect to other concurrently running transactions.

10.7.3 The recovery problem

The recovery problem for transaction systems is concerned with returning the system to the last consistent state or advancing the system to the next consistent state, when a failure or error occurs.

The occurrence of a failure or error during the execution of a transaction, but before the final commit, results in the transaction aborting. When a transaction aborts, all the effects of the transaction must be undone and the system must be returned to the state it was in at the time the transaction started. This is called backward error recovery, and involves undoing any tentative writes that have taken place during the first part of the transaction. Failure to do this would mean that intermediate inconsistent system states resulting from partial execution would become visible outside the transaction.

When a failure or error occurs after the final commit but before the transaction has finished executing then the transaction mechanism must ensure that all the operations of the transaction are completed. This is called forward error recovery, and involves accumulating enough information at commit time to complete execution and make all the required updates.

Recovery mechanisms should also be capable of surviving errors and failures during their execution.

The issues discussed in this section are being tackled in particular by research groups developing distributed operating systems, on which many applications in the future will be based.

10.8 Concluding remarks

In this chapter we have briefly introduced the field of distributed computing, in which LANs and their protocols are playing a key part. We have discussed the motivations, issues and difficulties behind the development of distributed systems. Much remains to be done in this area.

Not discussed here are advances in languages, for example Milner's CCS (1980), which may ultimately ease the difficulties of programming distributed systems, and in computer architecture, which may produce distributed computing systems composed of non-von Neumann machines, with an integral communications subsystem. One of the most promising new architectures is the dataflow machine, an example of which is being developed at Manchester University (Gurd *et al.*, 1985). These two research topics are progressing in parallel (Myers, 1982), but the latest direction is for the most part language driven (Vegdahl, 1984).

Lastly, as outlined in Chapter 3, there is considerable progress in the technology of the communications subsystem itself. Very high speed networks are rapidly being developed, for both wide and local area applications. In the case of wide area networks, point-to-point links of up to 2.048 Mbits/sec are being offered. Users can choose one or more 64 Kbits/sec channels up to this capacity. These high speed WANs will be integrated with the public ISDNs which will be offering a range of digital voice and data services.

The raw data rates of baseband local networks are increasing beyond 100 Mbits/sec, and integrated services LANs such as FDDI-II are rapidly being introduced. In addition, broadband LANs with very large bandwidth potential are commercially available. As has been frequently the case in computing and communications over the years, technology is ahead, and techniques as well as applications are having to chase to catch it up. The challenges in distributed computing, in the opportunities made possible by the combination of computers and local area networks, remain undiminished.

References

ANSA Project, (1987). *ANSA reference manual*, Cambridge, UK

Birrell, A.D., Levin, R., Needham, R.M. and Schroeder, M.D., (1982). 'Grapevine: an exercise in distributed computing' *CACM*, **25**,(4), April, 260–274

Birrell, A.D. and Nelson, B.J., (1984). 'Implementing remote procedure calls' *ACM Transactions on Computer Systems*, **2**,(1), February

Blair, G.S., Hutchison, D. and Shepherd, W.D., (1982). 'MIMAS – a network operating system for Strathnet' *Proc. 3rd International Conference on Distributed Computing Systems*, Ft. Lauderdale, Florida, October

Blair, G.S., Hutchison, D. and Shepherd, W.D., (1983). 'Implementation of a local area network operating system' *Local area networks: strategy & systems*: Online Publications, 387–398

Brownbridge, D.R., Marshall, L.F. and Randell, B., (1982). 'The Newcastle Connection, or UNIXes of the world unite!' *Software Practice and Experience*, **12**,(6), 1147–1162

Ceri, S. and Pelagatti, G., (1985). *Distributed databases: principles and systems*. McGraw-Hill

Cunningham, I., (1983). 'Message-handling systems and protocols' *Proc. IEEE*, **71**,(12), December, 1425–1430

Enslow, P.H., (1978). 'What is a "distributed" data processing system?' *Computer*, January, 13–21

Gurd, J.R., Kirkham, C.C. and Watson, I., (1985). 'The Manchester prototype dataflow computer' *CACM*, **28**,(1), January, 34–52

Lindsay, B.G., Haas, L.M., Mohan, C., Wilms, P.F. and Yost, R.A., (1983). 'Computation and communication in R*: a distributed database manager' *Proc. 9th ACM Symposium on Operating Systems Principles*, Bretton Woods, USA, October

Milner, R., (1980). *A Calculus of Communicating Systems*. Springer-Verlag: New York

Mitchell, J.G. and Dion, J., (1982). 'A comparison of two network-based file servers' *CACM*, **25**,(4), April, 233–245

Muir, S.J., Hutchison, D. and Shepherd, W.D., (1985). 'Arca: a local network file server' *The Computer Journal*, **28**,(3), 243–249

Myers, G.J., (1982). *Advances in computer architecture*. Wiley, 2nd edition

Needham, R.M. and Herbert, A.J., (1982). *The Cambridge Distributed Computing System*. Addison-Wesley

Nelson, B.J., (1981). *Remote procedure call*, Ph.D. dissertation, Carnegie-Mellon University, Pittsburgh, USA. Reprinted as Technical Report CSL-81-9, Xerox PARC, Palo Alto, California

Nicol, J.R., Blair, G.S. and Shepherd, W.D., (1985). *A tailored kernel design for a distributed operating system* internal report, Department of Computing, University of Lancaster, Lancaster, UK

Page, T.W., Weinstein, M.J. and Popek, G.J., (1985). 'Genesis: a distributed database operating system' *ACM SIGMOD*, 374–387

Postel, J. (editor), (1980a). 'DoD standard internet protocol' *ACM Computer Communication Review*, **10**,(4), October, 12–51

Postel, J. (editor), (1980b). 'DoD standard transmission control protocol' *ACM Computer Communication Review*, **10**,(4), October, 52–132

Stankovic, J.A., (1984). 'A perspective on distributed computer systems' *IEEE Transactions on Computers*, **33**,(12), December, 1102–1115

Tanenbaum, A.S. and van Renesse, R., (1985). 'Distributed operating systems' *ACM Computer Surveys*, **17**,(4), December, 419–470

Tanenbaum, A.S. and Mullender, S.J., (1986). 'The design of a capability-based distributed operating system' *The Computer Journal*, **29**,(4), August, 289–299

Vegdahl, S.R., (1984). 'A survey of proposed architectures for the execution of functional languages' *IEEE Transactions on Computers*, **33**,(12), December, 1050–1071

Xerox, (1981). *Courier: the remote procedure call protocol*, Xerox System Integration Standard XSIS 038112, December

Exercises

Chapter 1

1.1 Describe what is meant by the 'architecture' of a network.

1.2 Review the reasons for the emergence of local area networks (LANs).

1.3 List and discuss the characteristics of LANs and compare them with the characteristics of long-haul or wide area networks (WANs).

1.4 Explain why standards are important in computer networking. What benefits are there for a network vendor to build products conforming to standards? Would a vendor not be better developing a proprietary network rather than conforming to a standard?

1.5 LAN-based systems occupy the middle ground between tightly coupled multiprocessor systems and loosely coupled wide area networks. To what extent is the present generation of LANs likely to become used as the basis of multiprocessor systems, in place of parallel buses? Looking ahead ten years, will the situation have changed significantly?

1.6 Compare the functionality of a PABX with that of a LAN.

1.7 Discuss the ways in which a LAN with distributed services offers a better alternative to a single, large computer system offering an equivalent set of services.

1.8 Discuss the likely impact of the LAN in office automation over the next five years.

1.9 In conjunction with standardization activities in LAN communications, how important do you think are standards for communications wiring in buildings?

1.10 Discuss the factors affecting whether voice and data networks will be separate, or integrated together, in the office environment.

Chapter 2

2.1 Summarize the structure of the ISO's OSI reference model, identifying the main purpose of each of its layers. Describe what is meant by 'peer layers', and show how information passes from layer n in the local end system to peer layer n in a remote end system.

2.2 The standardization cycle takes several years: this is regarded as essential by the ISO to ensure wide consultation before stabilizing international standards. On the other hand, vendors would prefer this time to be very much shorter to enable products to be developed and reach the market place earlier. Discuss how, or whether, this conflict could be resolved.

2.3 Review the reasons why the primitives used in the IEEE 802 LAN model are different from those defined for the OSI reference model. Illustrate your answer using time sequence diagrams.

2.4 Compare the different types of LLC service and state a likely application area for each.

2.5 Explain why layering, as in the OSI reference model, is considered useful in describing an architecture. Is it necessary to maintain this layering through to implementation of the architecture?

2.6 Distinguish between protocols and services in the OSI model, using the transport layer as an example.

2.7 Illustrate the LAN reference model, comparing its structure with that of the OSI model. List four specific LAN technologies which fit into the architecture. Briefly explain the functions of each of the LAN model layers.

2.8 Explain the terms service access point (SAP), protocol data unit (PDU) and service data unit (SDU), and distinguish clearly between the uses of PDUs and SDUs.

2.9 Explain the need for (a) error checking, and (b) flow control in networks. Summarize how sequence numbers together with the window technique can be used to implement flow control and re-send erroneous frames in HDLC.

2.10   Design and write a procedure to implement HDLC flow control and error control. Use pseudo-code or English if you wish.

Chapter 3

3.1   Summarize the various types of LAN which have been developed. Comment on the likelihood of non-standard LANs surviving in the marketplace.

3.2   Could digital PABXs, with their star topology and fixed 64 Kbits/sec channels, provide sufficient flexibility to take the place of a general purpose LAN in carrying data traffic? Discuss the capability of conventional LANs for carrying voice traffic.

3.3   What factors will affect the adoption of ISDN by corporate and domestic users?

3.4   ISDN will initially be integrated only at the customer access point: separate networks will provide for the different types of traffic. Ultimately there may be only a single, truly integrated network: discuss whether this network will be based on circuit switching or on packet switching, or on a hybrid approach.

3.5   Develop an analytical model of the operation of an ALOHA network and produce a plot of throughput against loading. At what figure of loading does the performance break down? Show the effect of a slotted ALOHA network on the plot and on the loading breakdown point.

3.6   Write a simulation of the ALOHA network and check the throughput versus loading figures against those of the analytical model. Repeat for a slotted ALOHA.

3.7   Discuss the applicability of CSMA/CD on the one hand and the token bus on the other in real-time industrial applications.

3.8   Review the factors affecting the performance of a LAN. Which of the two measures, access delay and throughput, is likely to be more important in (a) office and (b) real-time industrial applications?

3.9   State why the ratio of propagation delay to transmission time is important in determining the performance of a LAN. Does this ratio affect throughput, access delay, or both?

3.10   Discuss the likely impact of advances in LAN technology over the next ten years on applications in (a) the office, and (b) the industrial environment.

Chapter 4

4.1   State the essential features of the CSMA/CD LAN, and summarize its operation in terms of a sending station.

4.2   Write a simulation which captures the main features of CSMA/CD. At what offered load does the number of collisions cause the performance to fall off dramatically?

4.3   In the standard CSMA/CD the maximum end-to-end network length is 2.5 km, but the maximum segment length is 500 m, where segments are connected by repeaters. Work out the possible range of segment configurations, including the maximum number of segments and repeaters in series between any two stations.

4.4   Explain why there is a minimum and a maximum frame length in the standard CSMA/CD, i.e. in IS 8802/3. What would be the effect on this minimum and maximum if the data rate were to be doubled to 20 Mbits/sec?

4.5   Suggest a simple backoff algorithm suitable for use in CSMA/CD collision resolution, and analyse its effectiveness (if possible, consult the original Ethernet backoff algorithm described in Metcalfe and Boggs (1976) and compare it with your suggestion).

4.6   Review the development of protocols from the pure ALOHA through the experimental Ethernet to the standard CSMA/CD LAN (see also Chapter 3, Section 3.2.2), highlighting any improvements in performance or functionality at the various stages.

4.7   Compare the PUP, XNS and TCP/IP protocol hierarchies, identifying their similarities and differences. Compare the TCP/IP hierarchy with the OSI model architecture.

4.8   Distinguish between broadcast and multicast. Explain how these are provided in the standard CSMA/CD. Suggest LAN applications in which each may be useful.

4.9   Explain the purpose and operation of the Manchester encoding scheme. For a 10 Mbits/sec raw data rate, what clock frequency is required to implement Manchester encoding? Attempt to describe how the CSMA/CD hardware can put together the separate data and clock signals at a sending station and separate them again at a receiver.

4.10 In general terms, describe how a local area network will be interfaced to a host computer system. In particular, show how the network protocols might be interfaced to the computer's operating system.

Chapter 5

5.1 State the essential features of (a) the standard token ring, and (b) the standard token bus, and summarize their respective operations in terms of a sending station.

5.2 Write a simulation which captures the main feature of a standard token ring having up to 32 stations, and investigate the effect on throughput of varying the offered load. What changes would you have to make to simulate a standard token bus network?

5.3 Discuss the relative merits of a token ring against a token bus for use as a network supporting (a) a general purpose computing environment, and (b) an industrial environment including some real-time working. Assume that the raw data rates of both LANs are the same.

5.4 A token bus system must use successor and predecessor tables to enable a logical ring to be maintained. Outline a procedure for initializing such a system. What might be the procedure for (a) introducing a new station into the system, (b) taking out a station for maintenance?

5.5 Does the performance of a token ring deteriorate as the length of the ring becomes greater? Does its performance depend on other factors including the number of stations in the ring, the length of the token holding timer, and so on?

5.6 Compare the problem of a corrupt or lost token, and the recovery measures called for, in (a) a token ring, (b) a token bus. Design an algorithm to implement a distributed token recovery scheme in a token ring.

5.7 Discuss whether it would be possible to operate a token passing scheme using multiple tokens.

5.8   Compare the standard CSMA/CD and token bus LANs under the following headings: communications medium, topology, medium access protocol, and behaviour under (a) light, and (b) heavy network loading.

5.9   Outline the aims of MAP, and discuss whether a functional architecture based on standard OSI protocols is the best approach to meeting these aims.

5.10   Do you think that in a factory there should be a hierarchy of local networks, with MAP as the backbone? Should there be a parallel TOP network to serve the needs of the office areas in the factory? Is a PROWAY-type network suitable for use at the lowest levels of a manufacturing or process control plant?

Chapter 6

6.1   State the essential features of the Cambridge Ring LAN, and summarize its operation in terms of a sending station.

6.2   Write a simulation which captures the main features of a Cambridge Ring which has 40-bit minipackets and uses the packet protocol. Allow for up to 32 stations and 10 minipacket slots. Investigate the throughput of the network as a function of the offered load, varying the number of minipackets.

6.3   Determine, using either an analytical or a simulation model of the Cambridge Ring, whether there is an optimum number of circulating minipackets for particular numbers of attached stations.

6.4   Describe the role of the monitor station in the Cambridge Ring. Compare its role with that of the token ring monitor station.

6.5   Assume that a Cambridge Fast Ring has a raw data rate of at least 50 Mbits/sec, a data field length of 256 bits, and source/destination fields of 16 bits each. What advantages over a conventional 10 Mbits/sec Cambridge Ring result from these increased field lengths and data rate?

6.6   The Orwell ring resets the minipacket availability bit at the destination station rather than once the minipacket returns to the source. Discuss the benefits of this alteration to the conventional Cambridge Ring protocol. Might there be any disadvantages?

6.7   Write a concise specification of (a) the packet protocol, (b) the single shot protocol, and (c) the byte stream protocol used in the Cambridge Ring (you may use a combination of English text, diagrams and tables).

6.8   For each of the protocols in Exercise 6.7, give a comparative analysis of the complexity of implementing it. Using your specifications, explain how you might tackle implementing each protocol in software, including outline data structures and a sketch of the main program in each case (use pseudo-code or English if you wish).

6.9   Compare in detail the frame structure and access protocols of the Cambridge Ring and the standard token ring, identifying any possible differences in their performance.

6.10   Discuss the relative merits of bus and ring LANs.

Chapter 7

7.1   Distinguish between a bridge and a gateway in terms of their functionality and operation.

7.2   Is it feasible to attempt to introduce a truly global addressing scheme for networks, both local and wide area? How would a global directory service work? Identify any problems which you think may occur.

7.3   If all networks used 48-bit addressing, would this be a sufficient address range to implement a truly global internetwork?

7.4   Describe briefly the purpose and structure of (a) the OSI network layer, (b) the OSI transport layer, indicating the inter-relationship between the two layers.

7.5   What are the design issues involved in bridging between two Cambridge Rings? Would the issues be different for the problem of bridging between two CSMA/CD LANs?

7.6   For the Cambridge Ring explain whether it is easier to build a minipacket or a packet level bridge, giving the advantages and disadvantages associated with each approach.

7.7   Explain the notion of a lightweight virtual circuit and how it may be used in implementing a bridge between two Cambridge Rings.

7.8 Explain how the PUP internet architecture provides a network independent abstraction. Describe briefly the addressing used by the PUP and the technique for sending a PUP over a series of networks from its source to its destination.

7.9 Discuss the factors affecting whether internetworking should be based on datagram or virtual circuit techniques.

7.10 If two LANs to be linked together use the same protocols above the MAC layer, should they always be connected by a bridge or are there circumstances in which a higher-level relay should be used?

Chapter 8

8.1 Explain why it is natural to group together, on the one hand, the lowermost four layers of the OSI model and, on the other, the uppermost three layers.

8.2 What is the collective purpose of the three layers in the OSI upper layer architecture?

8.3 Summarize the functions performed by the OSI session layer, pointing out the role of tokens and synchronization points.

8.4 Summarize the need for the OSI presentation layer, giving an example of an application in which this layer is necessary.

8.5 Describe the structure of the OSI application layer, clearly identifying the role of the application entity (AE) and application service element (ASE).

8.6 Distinguish between abstract and concrete transfer syntaxes in the context of the OSI presentation layer.

8.7 Comment on the applicability or otherwise of the OSI upper layer architecture for LAN-based applications. Support your comments by giving applications examples.

8.8 The present list of SASE protocols includes VT, FTAM and JTAM. These support, respectively, logging into remote computer systems, transferring files, and sending processing jobs to remote computer systems. For each of these protocols discuss the extent to which the support of the presentation and session layer facilities will be necessary.

8.9   What new SASE protocols are emerging from the MAP work and from work in standardizing electronic mail? (See Chapters 5 and 10.)

8.10   Suggest another application area likely to produce an additional SASE protocol, and describe the possible nature of the new protocol in this area.

Chapter 9

9.1   Should management be considered as a part of the overall operation of the organization in which the network is situated?

9.2   Develop a control model of an organization which includes a corporate network that is managed.

9.3   Domains are a way of splitting up management into smaller problems: should domains be organized along geographical lines only, or are there any other ways of arranging them?

9.4   Discuss whether network management facilities should be made available to the network user, and if so to what extent?

9.5   The management information base (MIB) is a key part of a network management system. Propose a detailed design and implementation for the MIB in dealing with configuration and fault management.

9.6   Explain the distinction between network management and distributed systems management (DSM), giving an application in which each could be used.

9.7   Compare the need for management in WANs and LANs. Identify the management functions required in each class of network.

9.8   Discuss the feasibility that an expert system could provide for automated .management. What context-dependent knowledge would the expert system have to be provided with?

9.9   In Section 9.10.3 a list of distributed systems applications is given, and Figure 9.4 shows a possible mapping of these applications on to appropriate classes of management. For one application in each of the DSM, MDAP and 'limited' classes, justify its placement in that class by considering the management requirements of the application in detail.

9.10 Is accounting management likely to be a necessity in any LAN-based systems? Consider both a 'closed' LAN and one which is part of a larger (WAN-based) internetwork.

Chapter 10

10.1 Review and expand on the enabling factors leading to the feasibility of building distributed computing systems based on LANs.

10.2 What factors should be considered in deciding whether to base RPCs on a virtual circuit or datagram communications subsystem?

10.3 Illustrate the action of a RPC by means of a time sequence diagram.

10.4 The ideal semantics of a RPC correspond to 'exactly once', as in a local procedure call. Discuss whether it is possible to achieve this level of semantics in practice. Consider the cases of communications errors and failures, and both client and server crashes.

10.5 Develop an algorithm which attempts to implement 'exactly once' semantics for a RPC, for both the client and server ends of the call. (*Hint*: stable storage is required at the server to maintain information about the attempted calls. This is storage whose information survives through server failures.)

10.6 Summarize the structure and operation of an electronic mail system, paying particular attention to the addressing scheme.

10.7 Assess the likely impact of the X.400 standards on the present proliferation of commercial electronic mail systems in the USA and Europe.

10.8 It is harder to build a global operating system than a network operating system. Bearing this in mind, are the likely benefits resulting from a global operating system worth the extra effort?

10.9 Review the essential properties of an atomic transaction. Summarize the implementation problems in ensuring these properties, and indicate the solution paths being explored in current research work.

10.10 Suggest six research topics in distributed computing which deserve investigation over the next five years.

Appendix
The main standards organizations

1. ITU

The ITU, or International Telecommunication Union, is an inter-governmental organization founded in 1865 to harmonize the activities of European telegraph systems. In 1947 it became an agency of the United Nations, specializing in telecommunications. Its two standards committees are the CCITT (see below) and the CCIR (International Radio Consultative Committee). These are normally attended by national telecommunications administrations amongst others. From its European origins it has become a worldwide organization dealing with technical, political and financial issues of communication.

General Secretariat, ITU
Place des Nations
1211 GENEVA 20   *Telephone number*:
Switzerland   (22) 99 51 11

2. ISO

The ISO, or International Standards Organisation, is an independent international agency with the aim of developing and promoting standards throughout the world. It was founded in 1947. There are some 90 national standards bodies which constitute its membership. It covers standards in all fields except electrical and electronic engineering, where the International Electrotechnical Commission has responsibility. There are some 165 technical committees (TCs) operating through a hierarchy of structures to draft and finalize proposals.

Central Secretariat
1 Rue de Varembe
1211 GENEVA 20
Switzerland   (22) 34 12 40

3. CCITT

The CCITT, or International Telegraph and Telephone Consultative Committee, is part of the ITU. It was formed in 1956 to ensure cooperation between the previously separate committees dealing with telegraph, data and telephone issues respectively. Its members include national communications administrations (PTTs), major telecommunications carriers (RPOAs) and a number of other organizations, including user groups. Its functions are largely technical and its operation is complex. Criticism has been made in the past of its slowness of operation and the difficulty of locating information. It is organized into a number of study groups (SGs) which keep existing recommendations up to date and produce new recommendations when required. Every four years there is a plenary session of the CCITT to approve the work carried out in the foregoing period and to specify its work programme for the next period. The recommendations themselves are issued in the form of 'coloured books', so called because the covers used to bind its material are issued in a different colour on each occasion. The contents of the books serve an important purpose in guiding European telecommunications service providers and suppliers. There are five classes of member, and only certain of these are permitted to vote. Increasingly, CCITT cooperates with the ISO. Important study groups are as follows:

- SGI – telegraph, telex and telematic services
- SGII – telephone operation and quality of service
- SGIII – general tariff principles
- SGVII – data communication networks
- SGVIII – terminal equipment for telematic services (e.g. teletex)
- SGXV – transmission systems
- SGXVII – modems (data communication over the telephone network)
- SGXVIII – digital networks (ISDN).

Its recommendations are classified as follows:

- F: facility/feature
- S: service
- X: data networks
- V: telephone networks.

2 Rue de Varembe
1211 GENEVA 20
Switzerland   (22) 99 51 11

4. British Standards Institution

The BSI, or British Standards Institution, is the recognized UK organization for the formulation of national standards. It participates at ISO meetings through membership of the various technical subcommittees. As at ISO, participation in BSI committees is restricted to professional bodies or trade associations. BSI also operates through a hierarchy of committees and working groups. Committees of interest to the information technology industry are as follows:

- IST/-: information systems technology.
- AMT/-: advanced manufacturing technology.

  Work on LAN and related standards is carried out within IST. IST/- meets annually and approves new work items put forward by its technical committees, and ratifies standards proposals made.

Head Office
2 Park Street
LONDON W1A 2BS
UK   (44) 1-629-9000

5. ECMA

ECMA, or the European Computer Manufacturers Association, is a group set up and managed by a number of companies developing and marketing computer systems in Europe. Its purpose when it was set up in 1961 was to develop data processing standards and this has extended into the field of communications. It has successfully produced many standards and has been instrumental in assisting ISO in this field. As with other organizations, its work is carried out by technical committees which themselves set up working groups for particular tasks. Its committees may however meet more frequently than those of other organizations.

  Members include:

- AEG-Telefunken
- Burroughs
- Honeywell
- IBM Europe
- Siemens
- Olivetti

- Ferranti
- ICL
- Nixdorf
- NCR.

Rue de Rhone 114
1204 GENEVA
Switzerland   (22) 35 36 34

6. IEEE

The IEEE, or Institute of Electrical and Electronics Engineers, is a US-based professional body which was originally similar in its aims to the National Physical Laboratory (NPL) in the UK. It gained a wider scope in 1965 with its responsibilities to provide data processing guidance to the Federal Government. It has produced the standards known as FIPS (federal information processing standards) which are observed by all government agencies in their data processing work. Many of these standards are now *de facto* industry standards because of the weight of government importance behind them. It contracts to industry to produce standards as required.

345 East 47th Street
NEW YORK
NY 10017
USA

7. ANSI

ANSI, or American National Standards Institute, is the US counterpart to BSI. It also has a committee/subcommittee structure where standardization for the data transmission industry is governed by the X3 committee. Its subcommittees are very active and many of its experts take part in ISO work. In fact ANSI has the secretariat of the ISO TC97 committee. There is also an American National Bureau of Standards (NBS) which is active in standardization in the information technology area. Standards developed by both ANSI and NBS often become used in industry.

1430 Broadway
NEW YORK
NY 10018
USA

8. DIN (Deutsche Institut für Normung)

This is the West German national standards body analogous to BSI. DIN standards are well recognized in areas of everyday use.

Postfach 1107
D 1000 BERLIN 30
West Germany

9. AFNOR (Association Française de Normalisation)

This is the French national standards body. It is very active within ISO.

Tour Europe
CEDEX 7
92 PARIS La Defense
France

10. IEC

IEC, the International Electrotechnical Commission, is an independent international agency which specializes in the formulation of international standards in the area referred to by its name. It is separate from the ISO but is of equal status as far as standards making is concerned. Its membership comprises representatives of major national electrical and electronics manufacturers and consumer groups, organized into national committees. There are some 40 such committees. Its origins date from 1906. Its standards are regarded as authoritative and are used in most major countries of the world. As with ISO, its structure consists of a large number of technical committees and subcommittees, with associated working groups. A new technical committee (no. 83, information technology equipment) has been working on local area networks and related issues and in particular the relationship to PROWAY.

3 Rue de Varembe
1211 GENEVA 20
Switzerland   (22) 34 01 50

11. IFIP

IFIP, the International Federation for Information Processing, is an international federation of professional and technical groups with interests in promoting information science and technology and assisting in research development and education. The British Computer Society (BCS) is the UK member (each country is represented by one full member).

IFIP Administrative Secretary
32 Rue de l'Athenée
1206 GENEVA
Switzerland

12. CEN/CENELEC/CEPT/ITSTC

ITSTC is the Information Technology Steering Committee for the three bodies CEN, CENELEC and CEPT. CEN is the European Committee for Standardization (a European counterpart to the ISO), CENELEC is the European Committee for Electrotechnical Standardization (a European counterpart to the IEC), and CEPT is the Conference of European Post and Telecommunication Administrations. Their working groups have come together to produce a programme for development of functional standards for information technology, for the benefit of the European IT industry and its users.

CEN/CENELEC/CEPT/ITSTC
Rue Brederode 2
PO Box 5
1000 BRUSSELS
Belgium   (32) 2 5137930

13. JISC

JISC, the Japanese Industrial Standards Committee, is the Japanese standards-making body. JSA (Japanese Standards Association) promotes Japanese industry standards.

JSA
16 Chemin de la Voie-Creuse
1202 GENEVA
Switzerland

Listed below are names and addresses of a number of other organizations which participate in the formation of standards.

14. National Computing Centre Limited
Oxford Road
MANCHESTER M1 7ED
UK   (44) 61-228-6333

15. ITSU, Information Technology Standards Unit
Department of Trade and Industry
Kingsgate House
66–74 Victoria Street
LONDON SW1E 6SW
UK   (44) 1-215-2723

16. British Computer Society
13 Mansfield Street
LONDON WIM OBP
UK   (44) 1-637-0471

17. BETA, Business Equipment Trade Association
8 Southampton Place
LONDON WC1A 2EF
UK   (44) 1-405-6233

18. Electronic Industries Association (EIA)
2001 Eye Street
WASHINGTON DC 20006
USA   (202-) 457-4900

19. Institute for Computer Sciences and Technology (ICST)
(NBS Federal Information Processing Standards (FIPS) program)
Technology Building, Room B-253
National Bureau of Standards (NBS)
GAITHERSBURG, MD 20899
USA   (301-) 921-2731

Annotated bibliography

Whereas the chapter references contain details of papers and books intended to help the reader follow up specific areas of interest, this bibliography gives information on books covering the general areas within communications, computer networks and distributed computing.

Ceri, S. and Pelagatti, G., (1985). *Distributed databases: principles and systems*. McGraw-Hill. An excellent review of the mechanisms underlying the design and construction of distributed databases, together with descriptions of some prominent database systems. Separates well those issues which are in the current research domain from the techniques used in building commercial databases.

Chambers, F.B., Duce, D.A. and Jones, G.P. (eds.), (1984). *Distributed computing*. Academic Press. This book is a collection of papers contributed by participants in the British Distributed Computing Systems research programme funded by the Science and Engineering Research Council between 1977 and 1984. Five main areas are covered: dataflow, declarative languages, modelling concurrent systems, loosely coupled distribution, and finally closely coupled distribution. A well chosen and consistently interesting set of papers.

Davies, D.W., Barber, D.L.A., Price, W.L. and Solomonides, C.M., (1979). *Computer networks and their protocols*. Wiley. A very well written text. Excellent on packet switching, routing, flow control and congestion, HDLC and X.25, and authentication. Does not cover local area networks.

Filman, R.E. and Friedman, D.P., (1984). *Coordinated computing: tools and techniques for distributed software*. McGraw-Hill. An advanced treatment of how loosely coupled computing systems can be organized to work together. Communications is dealt with at an abstract level. The material is in three parts: modelling distributed systems, programming languages (including Concurrent Pascal, and Ada), and 'heuristics' (the problems of organizing distributed systems).

251

Halsall, F., (1988). *Data communications, computer networks and OSI*. Addison-Wesley (2nd edn). A detailed and very clearly illustrated introduction to the principles and techniques of data communications. Deals with networks, including local networks, mainly at the physical and data link levels.

Hammond, J.L. and O'Reilly, P.J.P., (1986). *Performance analysis of local computer networks*. Addison-Wesley. An excellent coverage of the performance of the various local area network technologies, including CSMA/CD, token bus and ring and slotted ring. Models of the various LAN types are developed, and these give considerable insight into the detailed operation of each technology.

Hutchison, D., Mariani, J.A. and Shepherd, W.D. (eds.), (1985). *Local area networks: an advanced course*. Springer-Verlag Lecture Notes in Computer Science (No. 184), Springer-Verlag. A good coverage of the up-to-date technology, techniques and research in local area networks presented in this collection of papers by authors from the USA, Europe and Britain.

Lampson, B.W., Paul M., and Siegert, H.J. (eds.), (1981). *Distributed systems – architecture and implementation: an advanced course*. Springer-Verlag Lecture Notes in Computer Science (No. 105), Springer-Verlag. An excellent coverage, in terms of both breadth and depth, of the key issues in distributed computing.

McNamara, J.E., (1982). *Technical aspects of data communication*. Digital Press (2nd edn.). A comprehensive treatment of data communications up to and including the data link level. Contains good detail on V.24/RS-232C, X.21 and SDLC and on many other topics.

Mayne, A.J., (1986). *Linked local area networks*. Wiley (2nd edn.). Despite the title, this book is not primarily about internetworking. It contains, however, a vast compendium of facts and references on research, products and applications in the field of local networks.

Meijer, A. and Peeters, P., (1982). *Computer network architectures*. Pitman. A very highly regarded coverage of the architecture of networks, presented in three sections: the OSI model and other standards including X.21, HDLC and X.25; proprietary architectures including IBM's SNA and DEC's DECNET; and public data networks.

Needham, R.M. and Herbert, A.J., (1982). *The Cambridge Distributed Computing System*. Addison-Wesley. A concise and lucid description of the structure of the distributed system based on Cambridge Rings at the Cambridge University computer laboratory. Explains clearly the various design issues and decisions in the development of the system.

Popek, G.J. and Walker, B.J. (eds.), (1985). *The LOCUS distributed system architecture*. MIT Press. A stimulating set of papers on aspects of the design and implementation of LOCUS, a distributed version of the UNIX operating system developed at the Massachusetts Institute of Technology.

Schwartz, M., (1987). *Telecommunication networks: protocols, modeling and analysis*. Addison-Wesley. Gives a very detailed presentation of the key issues involved in networks, including excellent analyses of protocols at layers 1 to 4 of the OSI model. Contains some material on local networks, and a considerable amount on circuit switched networks and PABXs.

Tanenbaum, A.S., (1981). *Computer networks*. Prentice-Hall. A first rate book on networks, treated in a layered way along the lines of the OSI model. Starts at the physical layer and works up to the application layer. Does not, however, give much information on local networks.

Glossary

ANSI The American National Standards Institute is responsible for developing standards (in all fields) in the USA, and is a voting member of the International Standards Organisation (ISO). See also IEEE, IEC and ECMA.

Application layer The uppermost layer (layer 7) of the OSI reference model, providing facilities by which applications can arrange to communicate across networks without having to know the network characteristics. In addition to the core facilities contained in the common application service element (CASE) part of this layer, several specific protocols are provided in the SASE part, including file transfer, access and management (FTAM), virtual terminal protocol (VTP), and message handling systems (MHS).

Arpanet One of the early computer networks, whose development was sponsored by ARPA, the Advanced Research Projects Agency of the US Department of Defense (DoD). The Arpanet is a wide area network connecting research establishments across much of the USA, and is now controlled by the Defense Communications Agency on behalf of ARPA and other sponsoring US government agencies.

ASN.1 Abstract Syntax Notation One, defined in ISO documents 8824 (specification) and 8825 (encoding rules), is the method adopted within OSI for defining data structures in an abstract way, independent of their implementation.

Bandwidth The information capacity of a communications line, this is measured in Hertz (Hz) and is the difference between the lowest and highest frequency which can be carried on the line.

Baseband A method of data transmission in which voltages differently representing binary 0 and 1 are directly applied to the communications line.

Bridge A data link level device connecting two like networks together, where the higher level protocols are the same on both networks.

Broadband A method of data transmission in which a number of channels of data are accommodated on a single communications line by allocating a part of the total bandwidth to each channel. Within each channel the data is modulated on a single frequency.

255

BSI The British Standards Institution is responsible for developing standards (in all fields) in the UK and is a voting member of the ISO. It has a committee structure which mirrors that of the ISO.

Bus A linear topology for communications. The most prominent LAN example is CSMA/CD (Ethernet). The two other common LAN topologies are the ring and star.

CASE Common application service elements, the core of the application layer of OSI, providing facilities for setting up, maintaining and closing down associations between users.

CCITT Comité Consultatif International Télégraphique et Téléphonique: based in Geneva, responsible for developing, amongst others, the V,X and I series standards.

Coaxial cable A widely used type of communications medium in which the central conducting core is contained within concentric layers of insulator, braided earth wire and finally a tough outer plastic coating. Has good electrical noise immunity.

CRC Cyclic redundancy check: a method used to detect transmission errors in frames of data (at the data link level), for example in HDLC.

CSMA/CD Carrier sense multiple access with collision detection, the well known local network medium access protocol which originated with Ethernet.

DARPA The US body responsible for running the Arpanet.

Data link Layer 2 of the OSI reference model, responsible for framing bits and ensuring the detection of transmission errors.

Datagram An individually addressed unit of data sent over a network, rather like a letter or package sent by mail (also referred to as the connectionless mode of operation). Contrast virtual circuit.

DCE CCITT terminology for the access point to a network, for example a X.25 network – short for data circuit-terminating equipment. Connects to a DTE.

DoD The US Department of Defense.

DOS Distributed operating system.

DSM Distributed systems management.

DTE CCITT terminology for a terminal, or computer, attached to a network – short for data terminating equipment. Connects to a DCE.

DTI The UK Department of Trade and Industry.

ECMA The European Computer Manufacturers Association, based in Geneva.

FCS Frame check sequence, an extended form of CRC, used in local networks.

Fibre optic An increasingly popular type of communications medium in which light travelling within very fine fibres carries information: offers very high bandwidth, and is immune to electromagnetic noise.

Flow control   Name given to techniques for throttling back fast transmitters in a network, to allow a slower receiver to process data.

Frame   A grouping of bits transmitted at layer 2 of the OSI model, containing user data, source and destination addresses, and a CRC.

FTAM   File transfer, access and management, one of the specific layer 7 protocols in OSI.

FTP   File transfer protocol, a generic name for file transfer.

Gateway   A device interconnecting two networks. It is connected to each network as a host, but is normally transparent to the user. The gateway must in general perform protocol translation as the two networks will use different protocols.

HDLC   High level data link control: an ISO protocol which forms the basis for level 2 of the X.25 packet network access protocol (IS 3309,4335,7809).

Host   An end user computer connected to a network.

IEC   The International Electrotechnical Commission, responsible for standardization in the area of electrical engineering.

IEEE   The Institute of Electrical and Electronics Engineers: the US professional institute also involved in developing and recommending standards.

Intercept strategy   The UK initiative in recommending an OSI migration strategy to developers during the formative years of OSI standards.

Internet   The name for the interconnected research networks in the USA, of which the Arpanet is the most prominent.

IP   The Internet protocol developed for the US Arpanet.

IPSS   International Packet Switched Service, operated by British Telecom. IPSS connects the UK public data network PSS to networks in other countries.

ISO   The International Standards Organisation, based in Geneva.

ITSU   The Information Technology Standards Unit located in the UK DTI.

JANET   The UK Joint Academic Network, the packet switched network managed by the Joint Network Team for the academic community in the UK.

JTMP   The job transfer and manipulation protocol, one of the specific layer 7 protocols in OSI (IS 8831,8832).

LAN   Local area network.

LLC   Logical link control, a sublayer of the IEEE/ISO LAN reference model.

MAC   Medium access control, also a sublayer of the LAN reference model. Together with the higher LLC, corresponds to the OSI data link layer.

Manchester encoding   A signal encoding scheme in which each bit cell has a level transition in the middle. Thus this is a self-clocking system.

MHS   Message handling systems (basically, electronic mail), a specific layer 7 protocol in OSI. Actually, there are several documents covering different aspects of MHS. Originated as the CCITT X.400 series of standards.

MMS   Manufacturing message service (IS 9506), one of the specific layer 7 OSI protocols, an application layer protocol developed by the MAP community for factory networking.

Network   In this context, short for a computer network.

Network layer   Layer 3 of OSI, dealing with internetworking, addressing and subnetworking (IS 8648,8348,8473). Related standards include X.25 (8208), networking service over X.25 (8878), networking service over LANs (8880) and X.25 on LANs (8881).

Network management   The monitoring and control of resources in a network so as to ensure its smooth running.

Node   In a local network, the combination of host and network access equipment. In a packet switched network, usually a switch within the communications subnetwork.

OSI   Open systems interconnection, the name for the 7-layer reference model of networks standardized by the ISO.

Packet   A block of information, generally at the OSI network layer or equivalent.

PAD   Packet assembler/disassembler, the interface between a user's terminal and a packet switched network for assembling the user's input characters into packets for network transmission, and disassembling packets into their individual characters for output on the terminal.

PDN   Public data network.

Physical layer   Layer 1 of the OSI reference model, dealing with the electrical and mechanical characteristics of the communications medium.

Preamble   Precedes the operational part of a frame and is used for receiver synchronization.

Presentation layer   Layer 6 of the OSI reference model, used for ensuring the representation of user data in a form understood by each communicating partner.

Protocol   The rules by which communicating entities conduct their dialogue.

PSS   British Telecom's Packet SwitchStream service, based on X.25 access.

PSTN   The public switched telephone network, for countrywide voice communication.

PTT   Post, telegraph and telephone authority, of which there is one in most European countries and also in Japan.

PUP   PARC universal packet, one of the early datagram internetwork packets on which the DARPA Internet IP packet is based.

Relay   A generic title equivalent to gateway, but sometimes applied to internetworking at the network layer.

Ring   One of the three common LAN topologies, the others being the bus and star.

SASE   Specific application service elements, part of the OSI application layer containing specific protocols of considerable usefulness, including FTAM, JTMP, VTP, MHS and MMS.

Session layer   Layer 5 of the OSI reference model, responsible for organizing user dialogues into 'sessions' which may optionally contain synchronization points, and for ensuring duplex or half duplex operation as required (IS 8326,8327).

Sliding window   A method of implementing flow and error control in which sender and receiver maintain a (small) window of frames sent/received but not yet acknowledged to be correct.

Slotted ring   A type of LAN technology in which the access is governed by a continuously circulating minipacket or slot into which (when empty) data is placed and conveyed to its intended destination. The best known example is the Cambridge Ring (IS 8802/7).

Star   One of the three common LAN topologies, the others being the bus and ring.

Station   In local networking, means the end user equipment attached to the network, including the network interface. Each station has a network-unique address.

Synchronous   A term meaning there is a fixed time relationship between successive units of transmission, so that sender and receiver must have synchronized clocks.

TCP   Transmission control protocol, the host-to-host protocol which all Internet hosts use to communicate.

Telnet   The terminal control protocol used in the Arpanet and its Internet.

Token passing   The name of a class of access protocol used in local area networks, in which a circulating token gives each station in sequence the right to transmit over the network (bus=IS 8802/4, ring=8802/5).

Transport layer   Layer 4 in the OSI reference model, is responsible for ensuring a reliable end-to-end service, dealing with end user addressing and providing the required quality of service. In addition to the connection-oriented (CO) facilities there is now a connectionless (CL) transport layer definition (CO=IS 8072,8073, CL=8602).

Triple-X   Means the combination of X.3/X.28/X.29, the protocol standards documents defining the operation of a PAD, and hence terminal control, in an X.25 network.

Twisted pair   A type of communications medium in which the two conductors are twisted around each other to provide better noise immunity. Basically this is ordinary local loop telephone wire.

UNIX   A well known computer operating system which was developed at AT&T Bell Laboratories in the USA. Version 4.2 BSD was the first to incorporate the TCP/IP protocol suite. Various local networking developments have been included with recent UNIX releases by Sun Microsystems.

Virtual circuit   The method of data communications in which a connection is established between both parties before any data is transferred. The connection is normally broken immediately following the completion of the data transfer.

VTP   Virtual terminal protocol, an application level protocol in OSI terms which permits a local user to login and use a remote computer over a network (IS 9040,9041).

X.25   The well known CCITT access protocol for packet switching networks used in many European wide area networks. It covers layers 1–3 of the OSI reference model.

X.400   The CCITT overview document for the series of standards on message handling systems (see also MHS).

Index